ROOTS OF CONFLICT

Roots

BRITISH ARMED FORCES

of

AND COLONIAL AMERICANS,

Conflict

1677–1763

DOUGLAS EDWARD LEACH

THE UNIVERSITY OF NORTH CAROLINA PRESS

CHAPEL HILL AND LONDON

Manufactured in the United States of America

Library of Congress Cataloging-in-Publication Data

Leach, Douglas Edward, 1920–

  Roots of conflict.

  Bibliography: p.

  Includes index.

1. United States—History, Military—To 1900.

2. Great Britain—Armed Forces—History—17th Century.

3. Great Britain—Armed Forces—History—18th century.

4. United States—History—Revolution, 1775–1783—

Causes. I. Title.

E181.L438   1986   973.2   85-24492

ISBN 0-8078-4258-3 (pbk.)

93 92 91   6 5 4 3

This book is dedicated to the memory of
three stimulating and wise historians,
each of whom has helped in the shaping
of my work.

SAMUEL ELIOT MORISON

RAY ALLEN BILLINGTON

LOUIS MORTON

CONTENTS

PREFACE

HIS book has been many years in the making. As early as the 1960s, while doing the research for my *Arms for Empire: A Military History of the British Colonies in North America, 1607–1763*, I became increasingly aware of the tensions arising in the colonies as a by-product of the British professional military-naval presence. My preliminary perception of this potentially significant condition was presented in the form of a paper read to the American Historical Association convened at Boston in 1970. Simultaneously, other historians were exploring various aspects of the same phenomenon. As a consequence, we are now gaining a much deeper understanding of the causal relationship between Anglo-American military friction prior to 1763 and the very rapid growth of intense and eventually decisive antagonism after that date.

John Shy pioneered with his highly suggestive *Toward Lexington: The Role of the British Army in the Coming of the American Revolution*, which, although focused mainly on the period 1760–1775, begins with a review of earlier conditions. Next, Alan Rogers took a more intensive look into the period dominated by the last of the great colonial wars with his *Empire and Liberty: American Resistance to British Authority, 1755–1763*. Stephen S. Webb then began drawing attention to the inherently military character of British colonial administration, first in "Army and Empire: English Garrison Government in Britain and America, 1569 to 1763," published in 1977 in the *William and Mary Quarterly*, and subsequently in his provocative book *The Governors-General: The English Army and the Definition of the Empire, 1569–1681*, with more to follow. William Pencak and Fred Anderson, with equal imagination and skill, have focused on the key colony of Massachusetts Bay. I stand indebted to these and a host of other scholars, all of whom are listed in my bibliography, but in the main I have relied upon my own research in primary sources, both published and unpublished. My major conclusion, and the thesis of this book, is that Anglo-American friction caused by the presence of British regular forces prior to 1763 was indeed an important contributing factor in the coming of the American Revolution, especially in the form of intergroup attitudes and perceptions hardening into stereotypes and traditions.

In retrospect, my experience of research for this book seems like a long, long trail a-winding, with many pleasant stopping points along the way. To be somewhat more specific, that trail led from Vanderbilt University to the University of Leeds, and then to the Institute of Historical Research in London, where William Kellaway made me welcome. Next it was on to the Public Record Office; the British Library; the Bodleian Library at Oxford; Lambeth Palace Library; the National Maritime Museum at Greenwich; and the Pepysian Library at Magdalene College, Cambridge, where R. C. Latham most kindly locked me in and out. Continuing along the trail, I profited by periods of research at the Henry E. Huntington Library in San Marino; the William L. Clements Library in Ann Arbor, where Howard H. Peckham and John C. Dann gave me a cordial welcome; the New York Public Library; the New-York Historical Society; the Historical Society of Pennsylvania; the Library of Congress; the Massachusetts Historical Society, where I was warmly greeted by Stephen T. Riley and Malcolm Freiberg; the New England Historic Genealogical Society; the libraries of Harvard University; the Massachusetts State Archives; the Boston Public Library; the American Antiquarian Society; the Connecticut State Library; the Connecticut Historical Society; the South Carolina State Archives; the South Carolina Historical Society; and the Charleston Library Society. Eventually the trail even led, most pleasantly, to the University of Hawaii (Oahu) and the University of Auckland, New Zealand. At the latter institution I was kindly aided by Nicholas Tarling, head of the Department of History, who provided me with office space and access to the library. At all these many and varied institutions of learning the professional staff assisted me with commendable competence. The work they do is absolutely essential in research, and we who benefit by it must be forever grateful.

Among others to whom I am indebted for interest and assistance are John M. Hemphill of the Colonial Williamsburg Foundation, James C. Kelly of the Tennessee State Museum, Paul E. Kopperman of Oregon State University, Jessica Kross of the University of South Carolina, Thomas L. Purvis of the University of Georgia, and Wilcomb E. Washburn of the Smithsonian Institution. The National Endowment for the Humanities provided a generous fellowship, making possible most of the extensive travel and research described above. My own university, Vanderbilt, granted me much-needed academic leave in 1975–76 and again in 1984. In addition, the university's Graduate Research Council allotted a timely supplementary grant. Expert typing and other clerical assistance has been cheerfully rendered by the office staff of my department, especially

Anna B. Luton, Sally C. Miller, and Kiddy Moore. In the later stages of production I have benefited greatly from the systematic and highly professional assistance rendered by the staff of the University of North Carolina Press, especially editor-in-chief Iris Tillman Hill, managing editor Gwen Duffey, and copyeditor Nancy H. Margolis. No author could wish for a better team.

During the period of research for this book I gave much of my attention to documentary sources of the seventeenth and eighteenth centuries, which proved to be extremely revealing. As a consequence, I have quoted them frequently, and here wish to express my gratitude for permission to do so. In particular, the quotations from the Crown-copyright documents in the Public Record Office appear by gracious permission of the Controller of Her Majesty's Stationery Office. Documents in the great collections of the British Library, the National Maritime Museum, the William L. Clements Library, the Henry E. Huntington Library, and the New-York Historical Society, also have been quoted by courtesy of those institutions. In quoting, I have tried to remain scrupulously faithful to the original, except for a few routine concessions in the interest of clarity, consistency, and simplicity. These include the substitution of "and" for the ampersand, and "th" for the early English thorn; the lowering of superior letters to the line; the supplying of omitted letters represented by an apostrophe; and the spelling out of some obvious abbreviations. Readers may be confident that the meaning of the original text has in no way been altered. In dealing with dates prior to the adoption of the Gregorian Calendar in 1752, I have retained the old rendering of the days and months, while making the appropriate annual adjustment for the transitional period between 1 January and 25 March.

My special and very personal thanks go to those exemplary Kiwis, Murray and Nessie Sweetman of Auckland, for incomparable hospitality including a quiet place in which to revise the manuscript when I was sojourning in New Zealand. Indeed, it has been a long, long trail, and on such a venture there is nothing so cherished as a good companion. My dear wife Brenda has been that good companion, sharing it all with quiet cheerfulness and unwavering faith. The finished product, which you now hold, belongs to her also.

Douglas Edward Leach
Nashville, Tennessee
August 1985

ROOTS OF CONFLICT

INTRODUCTION

NGLISH colonists living along the eastern seaboard of North America during the first half of the seventeenth century, being fully occupied with the problem of immediate survival, apparently gave little thought to the nature, condition, and role of the mother country's armed forces. They saw no regular soldiers; the occasional visit paid by an English man-of-war for the purpose of delivering a new governor or replenishing supplies was a rarity. At most, such occasional contacts with the professional armed forces constituted a tangible link with a faraway homeland to which these early colonists felt a continuing sense of attachment. England still was "home."

The decade of the 1640s, however, brought to the motherland a terribly divisive civil war, the killing of the king, and the rule of a stern Puritan dictator who was master of a dedicated, hard-driving army called the New Model. English folk of widely differing views learned to fear the ruthless power of that military machine until finally, with the Restoration in 1660, the army was disbanded. A year later the new monarch Charles II, citing the need for greater royal security, established several regiments of foot guards and troops of horse, all under his direct control. These plus a number of independent (unregimented) companies of royal soldiery in widely scattered garrison towns constituted England's first legitimate standing army, a powerful force constantly available to crush any challenge to the royal prerogative. This professional army, together with the longer-established navy, owed allegiance not to the people of England but to the monarch.[1]

Anyone cognizant of current affairs in the European states beyond the Channel realized only too well that a powerful standing army was, at least potentially, a vital ingredient for despotic government. Almost as though to mark the point, twice during the ensuing twenty-five years the English monarch ordered his royal troops concentrated in such a place and manner as to pose an immediate threat against political opposition—first at Blackheath in 1673 and then at Hounslow Heath in 1686. On the latter occasion the despotic James II assembled as many as 13,000 redcoats near the present site of Heathrow International Airport, barely fifteen miles from the heart of London, ready to strike decisively at any budding insurrection.

Adding to the popular distaste for such an armed force was the generally bad impression constantly being given by the personnel of the army itself. The commissioned officers were either from the upper class and thus bred to arrogance and self-indulgence, or else they were hard-climbing sons of somewhat lesser breeds who had managed to gain rank by a combination of successful violence and political favoritism. In any case, they stood forth as unquestioning upholders of the royal will. Stephen S. Webb has explained it well: "For the officer, devotion to the prerogative was more than reflection of political opinion, it was an in-bred, nonpartisan manifestation of his military experience."[2] The king's word was the officer's law. As for the common soldiers, most of them were a sorry lot, enlisted with little or no hope of release except by desertion, disability, or death. Some of them, hopeless debtors or even felons, had ducked into the army as a way of escape from something even worse. Others were merely hapless, gullible lads who, in a moment of blinding weakness disguised as patriotism, had permitted themselves to be persuaded to "take the king's shilling," an act they almost invariably learned to regret. Still others, perhaps, had deliberately "gone for a soldier" because a regiment was the only ordered and reasonably stable community to which they could gain admittance. So it should not be surprising that ordinary English folk were prone to view the redcoats with a combination of contempt and fear; whenever the soldiers were in the neighborhood, the neighbors prudently looked to their purses, poultry, and progeny (especially daughters).

Latent opposition to the royal military establishment persisted throughout the remainder of the seventeenth century and beyond, inspired by a profound fear of renewed despotism. "No standing army!" proved to be a popular and effective political slogan, heard all over England; shrewd politicians soon discovered that one sure way to weaken an opponent was to smear him as an advocate of the standing army. Let the navy defend us against invasion, they said, and the militia help preserve domestic tranquillity, if necessary, but the army threatens our very liberties. The issue was a highly emotional one, born of long and sometimes terrifying experience with the naked sword of tyranny in a land that gradually, over an extensive span of time, was developing a strong tradition of justice and personal rights within a well-founded system of civil law.[3]

The salty-sea crossing from the British Isles to the eastern coast of North America, despite its notorious hardships, was never long enough or wet enough to wash away an Englishman's basic attitude or outlook derived from homeland tradition and experience, not excepting his abiding distaste for the professional army. Nor is it at all surprising that in every colony begun prior to 1680 the leaders were quick to organize some form of militia composed of adult male colonists required to serve on a part-time basis. That was the preferred type of security force for confronting either foreign foes or domestic incendiaries.

As circumstances began to change, the Crown finally was moved to send some regular troops into the colonies, with results that were not always happy. Furthermore, as Webb has demonstrated, the very concept of British imperial administration was fundamentally military. The majority of royal governors in the colonies were or had been professional military or naval officers. Accustomed to rendering unqualified obedience to the Crown while requiring unquestioning obedience from subordinates, these imperial officials sought to create an authoritative regime overlaid with a veneer of representative government and undergirded with the actual or at least potential presence of British military-naval power. The nature of the developing relationship between the American colonists and the British regulars stationed in the various provinces is the object of our study here.

As we were reminded some years ago, "group images, that is, the typical mental pictures that the members have of themselves and others and that serve as basic frames of reference in terms of which they define their relations to one another, play an important part in determining the nature of intergroup contacts."[4] Civilian populations and armed forces, in their mutual relationship under a great range of circumstances, certainly are no exception. Therefore, it is my intention to devote particular attention to the attitudes and perceptions of colonists and regulars, especially in times of stress. There is a possible psychological reason for such mutual hostility which may be used as a working hypothesis. The colonist was a person who had left his homeland in order to make a fresh start in a new environment. In effect, he had stepped quite deliberately across a significant line dividing old from new, traditional from innovative, an action that seemed to imply a prior dissatisfaction with the homeland or at least a preference for the outland. Once counted among those who had crossed that line, the colonist felt a strong need to justify his action by making obvious his willing identification with and preference for the colony. In similar fashion the homelander, now enrolled in His Majesty's forces serving in America, felt compelled to justify his continuing attachment to Old England by flaunting the superiority of its people and way of life. How easy and natural it was for the colonist to view with a certain disdain those who appeared to be willing adherents of that which he himself had abandoned, how easy and natural for the true Briton in uniform to scorn the colonist as one who, having failed to measure up at home, had opted out for a crude existence in the wilderness. I would not suggest that such attitudes were always coherently entertained or displayed by the people involved, but it does seem likely that they were often present and influential in shaping overt actions and responses.

Today, thanks to extremely favorable circumstances, the American people in general do not view their country's armed forces as a threatening instrument of internal repression. Yet in the past, on occasion and possibly more often than we now readily remember, the government has employed troops to suppress opposition. Whether this use of armed force was seen as legitimate or otherwise depended upon the particular viewpoint and interests of the observer. During the era of Reconstruction following the Civil War, to cite one notable example, most Southern whites saw the federal forces as oppressors, but newly freed blacks, in contrast, viewed them as protectors. A more recent example was President Eisenhower's use of federal troops to enforce a court order that was being defied by local authority. On numerous occasions, too, state governments have called out the militia or national guard to control dangerous internal situations beyond the capacity of the civil police. Generally, however, such use of the military has been measured and restrained, being considered an extraordinary response to an extraordinary crisis. In most such instances, the military has been withdrawn as soon as feasible.

Even more important, in our system of constitutional government, based, as it truly is, upon British precedent and tradition, the armed forces remain always under the control of civil authority. Their commander in chief, the president, is a civilian without military rank. All funds enabling the armed forces to remain in being are appropriated by the Congress, which represents the people. Another factor that helps sustain the good relationship existing between the military and the American public is the fact that the armed forces of the United States actually are of the people. All their personnel, including the commissioned officers, are recruited from among the general population, and indeed, to a remarkably large degree they continue to interact with the civilian community.

Such favorable conditions did not prevail in the American colonies prior to Independence. As a consequence, the colonists rarely identified with British professional military personnel, often came to dislike them heartily as individuals or a group, and clearly perceived them as a potential instrument of oppression. Not surprisingly, this antipathetic attitude, the product of many decades of tension-breeding contact, was reciprocated; eventually the opposing sides came close to despising each other. When in 1768 the turbulent Boston mob threatened British civil authority, the Crown dispatched a man-of-war and several regiments of regular troops to uphold that authority. Then, after about two years of very unpleasant friction between the local populace and the redcoats, there was a sudden, shattering volley of army musketry in a Boston street and blood on the snow. Five years after the "Boston Massacre" the insistent clanging of church bells across the Massachusetts countryside summoned the minutemen to Lexington Green and a fateful encounter marking the start of the War for Independence.

How explain the rapidity with which such military hostility flared? The answer is to be found, at least in part, in the long, slow development of the mutual antipathy already mentioned. When, after 1760, really serious political differences did begin to arise between Great Britain and the continental colonies, the smoldering resentment found a ready vent as the regular armed forces assumed an obviously repressive role. Thus the army and the navy, trying to perform their duty, found themselves an obvious butt for American anger. At the same time, even as the colonists felt some sense of elation in settling old scores with the redcoats, the latter were taking satisfaction in their attempt to humble the upstart provincials. Such mutual venting of latent hostility was highly inflammatory in a time of intensifying political quarreling, which helps explain why rebellion rather than accommodation finally prevailed in 1775.

CHAPTER I.

EARLY TIMES OF TROUBLE

VIRGINIA, MASSACHUSETTS,

NEW YORK

 RITISH regular forces in significant strength began to be stationed in some of the North American colonies during the last quarter of the seventeenth century. As a result, antagonism between them and colonists began its long, ominous development, highlighted by three major episodes. In the first of these, occurring in Virginia, serious overt hostility is not evident, but there is good reason to conclude that some real tension did develop. The second, in Massachusetts, produced a few tense hours of direct confrontation, fortunately without serious bloodshed. During the third, which happened in New York, there was some actual fighting between armed colonists and the redcoats, with resulting casualties. Included among the consequences of these three episodes was a sharpened awareness by many of the colonists that the British regular forces in their midst did represent authoritarian if distant government, an unpleasant reminder of power and repression.

Bacon's Rebellion, which erupted in Virginia in 1675, was the first major insurrection in British North America; as such, it has commanded much interest ever since, if only by the coincidence of having occurred exactly a century before the outbreak of America's War for Independence. Actually, it is unlikely that Nathaniel Bacon and his well-armed followers had any serious intention of renouncing allegiance to England. In reality, what began as an angry protest against the rigidly authoritarian and self-serving policies of the aged royal governor, Sir William

Berkeley, and his inner circle of political cronies quickly developed into a small but devastating civil war pitting Virginians against Virginians. At the time there was no garrison of regulars in the colony, so it was a fight to the finish between Berkeley's supporters and Bacon's followers. Much of the colony except for the eastern peninsula came under rebel control, but eventually Berkeley gained enough strength to return to his devastated capital, stamp on the last embers of the dying insurrection, and restore royal authority. Bacon had already died, leaving his disheartened followers to face the consequences.

At one point in the rebellion, when Bacon was riding the crest of military success while the fortunes of Governor Berkeley were at low ebb, the rebel leader, in a burst of confident enthusiasm, had sworn to "oppose what Forces shall be sent out of England by his Majesty against Me, till such time as I have acquainted the King with the state of this Country, and have had his Answer."[1] This would appear to indicate that although the rebels did continue to profess allegiance to the Crown, they were of a mind to do battle with any royal force sent from England to overwhelm them. In sum, there can be no doubt that Bacon's Rebellion did represent a serious challenge to established royal government, and therefore an intolerable threat in an empire of scattered colonies.

When Charles II and his councilors in London finally received definite word of the uprising in distant Virginia, they found themselves confronted with a complex problem. If the political consequences were potentially disastrous, so were the possible economic results, for the Crown might lose the large annual revenue derived from the tobacco trade. Also to be noted is the fact that for some time now the king had been growing increasingly dissatisfied with Berkeley's performance as royal governor, and therefore was inclined to attribute the uprising, at least in part, to the governor's own waning competence. Here, then, was an unprecedented crisis in the new American empire, requiring a decisive response. In England itself during the preceding decades of the turbulent seventeenth century there had been numerous episodes of local resistance and rebellion. Typically, the government had acted decisively, dispatching overwhelming numbers of heavily armed troops to crush all opposition and punish the guilty. The standard policy was to guarantee legitimate authority by the extreme severity of the repression. In carrying out such a policy the standing army had gained intensive experience.

So it was that the royal government now set in motion the ponderous machinery for assembling a large military-naval expedition, including the necessary transport vessels, naval escorts, and well over 1,000 regular troops. Of the latter, some 500 were drafted from the several guards regiments and possibly some of the garrison companies, and about an equal number were brought in as newly enlisted volunteers. All these were organized in five companies of 200 men each, constituting a regiment. In addition, there was a train of royal artillery supporting the foot. As the population of Virginia at that time was only about 35,000, this force was the equivalent of more than 150,000 soldiers poured into the state of Virginia in 1980 for the purpose of suppressing civil disorder![2]

The king appointed three special commissioners to accompany the expedition and supervise the restoration of royal authority in the rebellious colony. One was Colonel Francis Moryson, a former lieutenant governor of Virginia, who had some knowledge of the colony's people and problems. Another was a naval officer, Sir John Berry, assigned to command the fleet of ships. The third, and chief among the three, was a career army officer, Captain Herbert Jeffreys, now promoted to the rank of lieutenant colonel and designated commander of the expedition. From the king's perspective, Jeffreys was the very man for the job. An experienced professional soldier totally loyal to the Crown, he could be counted on to use his regiment effectively in upholding the prerogative. Previously he had demonstrated his mettle by his vigorous repression of civil upheavals in a number of English towns—Portsmouth, York, Leeds, and London. A modern scholar has labeled Jeffreys "the most active and expert Guardsman in the political police function of the courtier army," and "the Crown's chief troubleshooter."[3] Now Jeffreys's assignment was first to do whatever was necessary to crush any opposition to royal authority, and then to function as chief executive in the colony while the unfortunate Berkeley returned home to explain his failure. Although Jeffreys wore the mailed glove comfortably, he was not an unreasonable man.

By the time the first ships of the expeditionary force had dropped anchor in Virginia waters at the end of January 1677, Bacon was dead, his followers were in desperate disarray, and the grim old governor was busy visiting his vengeance upon the surviving rebels and their families. If there was any urgent need for the army, it was not to fight rebels but to protect the colonists from Berkeley's ruthless retaliation.

Jeffreys's sea-weary redcoats yearned for solid ground under their feet, some decent food, and a warm, dry place in which to bed down. That was a difficult order to fill, for Virginia had been ravaged and wrecked. The colonists had no surplus of provisions to share with the army, nor any spare rooms for quarters. Except for Jamestown, itself only a very small community that now lay in ruins, Virginia was a colony of scattered farms. So it was that many of the soldiers had to remain unhappily quartered on board their fetid ships for a further period of time, until the army could establish a base camp at Middle Plantation (now Williamsburg). Men sickened and many died. By early June, England had word that over half of the troops were dead. Although that almost certainly was an exaggeration, the rate of mortality was undoubtedly high, undermining the morale of the survivors, who must have resented the seemingly frigid reception given them by the disheartened colonists. At best it was an uncomfortable, cheerless situation for nearly all involved.[4]

The Virginians, especially those who could be identified as former Baconians, naturally had assumed at the outset that the king's troops had been sent there to wreak vengeance. As soon as the fleet began arriving, many of the colonists seemed "ready to desert their Plantations, and retreat to other Parts," hoping to escape retribution.[5] Fortunately for them, however, Jeffreys and his two colleagues had come to Virginia with a low regard for Berkeley, and, finding the rebellion already extinguished, were inclined to question the governor's vengeful policy. They inaugurated a much more just and reasonable policy, actually seeking for the grievances that gave rise to armed insurrection. This, in turn, offended the Berkeleyites, who had expected free rein in the aftermath of their victory over the rebels. The army's role thus attracted some support and, at the same time, created some resentment on the part of both factions of colonists. After Jeffreys formally took charge of the provincial government, a deeply disgruntled Berkeley belatedly bowed to the royal command and sailed for England, never to return.[6]

Jeffreys served as acting governor of Virginia until his death in November 1678. By that time the greater part of his regiment of redcoats had either succumbed to disease or been relieved of their tedious assignment as peacekeepers in a slowly recovering colony. Some of the soldiers were released from the army and allowed to remain in Virginia as settlers; others were shipped back to the British Isles. A regular garrison of about 200 men, organized in two companies, was retained in the colony as a constant reminder of royal authority. Their continuing presence prolonged a tension with the local inhabitants that was not soon forgotten. Lacking barracks, many of those soldiers had to be quartered in civilian dwellings or outbuildings as unwelcome guests. Although compensation was promised to the owners, it was often tardy, which caused much grumbling.[7] The troops themselves suffered appreciably not only from the hostility or indifference of the colonists but perhaps even more from neglect on the part of a distant parsimonious government. London was dilatory in the matter of wages, and there was no practical way to raise sufficient funds in Virginia, not in the colony's unhappy condition and mood. This simply meant that the soldiers were frequently in real distress. They began to take on the semblance of hungry scarecrows-in-arms, shivering in their tattered uniforms. As their commander himself reported, "the soldiers and officers are now farr in arreare [as to pay] and the soldiers cloathing of all sorts quite worne out, soe that if they be not provided for against winter they will inevitably perish."[8] Tempers grew shorter. There was a rumor that some of the men were preparing to seize army supplies and join forces with a renewed rebellion.[9] In such a state of tension, neither the soldiers nor their reluctant hosts were able to view each other with any degree of favor. The army had overstayed its welcome, if welcome there had ever been.

Eventually, on 7 June 1682, the two companies of ragged redcoats were disbanded. It is believed that most of them remained in America, quickly disappearing into the general population.[10] This marked the conclusion of a trying episode in the history of colonial Virginia, when colonists first were shown the reach and power of the royal arm, and first experienced the disadvantages of being forced to play host to a garrison of redcoats, while the army itself began to learn something about the stubborn hostility of the American colonial populace.

Two years after the last of the British regulars were withdrawn from Virginia, the independent-minded Puritan state of Massachusetts Bay lost the protection of its cherished charter. For that colony the next seven years would be a time of wrenching change until the new royal charter of 1691 imposed a form of government that was to last until the American Revolution. Before his death in 1685 Charles II, a great admirer of French absolutism, became convinced that English control of the several distinct and diverse New England colonies would never be fully effective until they all were consolidated as a royal dominion under a single government. It remained for his successor brother, the despotic James II, to put this concept into actual play in 1686, at which time New Hampshire, Massachusetts, Plymouth Colony, and Rhode Island were deprived of their separate governments and consolidated as the Dominion of New England. Subsequently Connecticut, New York, and New Jersey were tacked on, further complicating an already difficult administrative problem. It was a fateful experiment in political engineering, without benefit of adequate information or insight, to say nothing of the consent of those to be governed.

The king sent as royal governor-general of this large and variegated dominion a professional army officer, Sir Edmund Andros, a man who had gained extensive previous experience as proprietary governor of New York, in which post he had managed to earn the deep distrust of many New Englanders. Hence the appointment was anything but auspicious.[11] Andros was accompanied by a retinue that included the mercantilistic bureaucrat Edward Randolph, already well known for his deep animus against the Massachusetts Puritans. That too was inauspicious. As tangible backing for these new authorities the Crown provided a garrison force of about a hundred redcoats under the command of Colonel Francis Nicholson, and a frigate, HMS *Rose*, under the command of Captain John George. For the first time in its history, Puritan Boston was being required to serve as host, on a regular basis, to a royal governor and the armed forces of a Roman Catholic monarch.

As a soldier-governor, Andros intended to preside over the dominion with both authority and efficiency, for the advantage of his royal master who expected no less. Well aware of the enormous latent hostility to his rule, and realizing that his authoritarian policies might intensify the opposition, he made the kind of preparations that one would expect of a military commander. HMS *Rose* was kept on call, in case of sudden need, ready to direct her guns against any insurgency. Several miles below Boston, standing guard over the sea channel, stood a fort on Castle Island, too remote to be of any use against a popular uprising in town, so Andros hastened to improve a defensive site within the town itself, a place known as Fort Hill. There, near the water's edge so as to command the adjacent waterfront, he had a battery of cannon emplaced. Farther back, at a higher elevation, he had other guns sited within a fortification commanding the nearby streets. Andros ordered his garrison troops to man both Castle Island and Fort Hill.[12]

At first, many of Boston's enterprising merchants who had long chafed under moralistic Puritan economic restraints were inclined to feel liberated by the new anti-Puritan regime. Before long, however, as the intentions of the imperious governor were actually put into practice and the energetic Randolph hounded all violators of the Navigation Acts, the merchants began having second thoughts. The old-line Puritans and the bulk of the people already saw tyranny in their path; now the merchants were joining them in opposition, and support for Andros dwindled. Government without free town meetings and an elected representative general court seemed intolerable, and would not long have been tolerated except for the ominous presence of HMS *Rose* and the garrison of redcoats.

That enmity arose between the people of Boston and the king's men is readily apparent, more so than in the earlier case of Virginia. For one thing, the soldiers and sailors were markedly un-Puritan in outlook and behavior, being openly contemptuous of the narrow-minded, self-righteous Puritan community. One indignant Puritan told of sailors from the *Rose* "playing Reakes on shoar to the great Offence and Disturbance of the Inhabitants," which probably meant roaring intoxication and affronts to modest young women. A constable complained that he "was stabbed as soon as he came out of his dores and another Constable had his stuffe taken out of his house, and had a pass made at him, and was fourced to fly for his life, and that by men belonging to the Ships that was the Kings." The redcoats, too, were widely criticized and denounced. "*Standing Forces*," snorted Increase Mather, a leading spokesman, "A word not so very grateful to the pallate of English Parliaments. *Standing Forces*! . . . Do they mean those that were brought a thousand Leagues to keep the Country in awe? A crew that began to teach *New-England* to Drab, Drink, Blaspheme, Curse and Damm. A crew that were every foot moving Tumults and Committing Insufferable Riots amongst a quiet and peacible people, and that without Redress upon frequent Complaints. These were the *Standing Forces*."[13] Allowing for the fact that much of this recorded criticism served the purpose of justifying rebellion, it leaves no doubt that the regular armed forces were indeed highly offensive to a Puritan community that not only had been long accustomed to having its own way but considered that way ordained by God. To make matters even worse, Andros himself was inclined to pass off such complaints as trivial if not obstructionist. Every governor-general in every garrison town had heard plenty of the like, though generally not of such a moralistic tone.

Affairs began to move toward a crisis in the late autumn of 1688, when Indians in Maine were threatening the security of the northern frontier. Andros, soldier that he was, called for a punitive expedition under his own command, in strange defiance of the approaching winter. The core of that expedition consisted of the regular troops of the Boston garrison, leaving behind in the castle and fort only a skeleton defensive force. That Andros dared not leave Boston without at least a few redcoats on guard, despite his immediate need for all the trained soldiers he could muster, is surely significant. Yet the regulars he dared take with him were far too few to chastise the troublesome Indians, and so he had hundreds of Massachusetts men drafted out of the militia as a reinforcement. For everyone involved it proved to be a grueling ordeal, tramping through the frozen northern wilderness in the depth of winter, on short rations. When not on the move, the troops were dispersed into isolated outposts where they huddled in misery and tried to survive. The regular officers found the New Englanders stubbornly averse to any command they thought discriminatory or unreasonable; when the officers tried to overcome the problem with harsh discipline, the provincials quickly marked it down as bestial cruelty. Each side became contemptuous and hostile toward the other.

Exactly what, if anything, was accomplished by Andros's winter foray remains as unclear as a New England February. Andros thought that he was doing a creditable job of forestalling an Indian uprising, but many Massachusetts families, hearing the doleful reports that were filtering down from the northern frontier and fearing for the well-being of their sons in arms, saw things rather differently. It was whispered about that for some mysterious reason the governor was proving to be unaccountably easy on the Indians and hard on his New England troops. What could that possibly mean? The Stuart king on England's throne was known to be both a papist and an admirer of the divine-right monarch Louis XIV, the most powerful champion of a resurgent Roman Catholicism in Europe. Could it be that James and Louis together were secretly plotting to destroy Puritanism in New England, using French Canada and the hostile Indians as their hammer? This disturbing thought was reinforced by widespread suspicion that among the garrison force, including the commissioned officers, were a not inconsiderable number of closet Catholics. Even Andros himself, some New Englanders were prepared to believe, although ostensibly an Anglican, had cast his lot with Rome. Such nightmarish speculations combined with all the bitter resentment of Andros's domestic policies and practices came to a head in March of 1689, as New England began hearing vague reports of an invasion of England by the Dutch Protestant champion William of Orange.

Anticipating trouble in Boston, Andros left his unhappy army in Maine and returned to the capital. There was grumbling on board the *Rose*. Some members of the crew, possibly impressed Americans or disgruntled Britons, had heard that Captain George intended to set sail for home, presumably to join in support of the threatened James II. Whether or not that really was George's plan, and it seems unlikely, enough of his crew opposed it to prevent him from proceeding.[14] Also in or around Boston at the time were numbers of disaffected provincial soldiers who, having deserted from the northern expedition, were stirring up trouble by telling how badly they and their comrades had been abused by the regulars.[15] Boston by this time was seething with reports and rumors, mostly unfavorable to the regime. To maintain his authority Andros now had only the moored frigate together with the handful of redcoats on guard at Castle Island and Fort Hill.

The flash point was reached on 18 April 1689. What happened on that memorable day could not have been entirely spontaneous; local leaders must have conferred a short time earlier with a view to shaping the course of the impending explosion. Those people who decided to act probably were emboldened by their expectation, still not fully substantiated, that the mother country now had a new king, a Protestant monarch who would not condemn the overthrow of a tyrannical governor who was the servant of the deposed James II. When the day dawned in Boston, momentous events began occurring in rapid sequence, to the bewilderment and outrage of Andros, Randolph, and the regulars.

Early that morning Captain George, ashore on business or pleasure, suddenly was confronted in the street by a gang of men led by his own ship's carpenter. Quickly they disarmed the startled captain, making him their prisoner. News of this event spread rapidly through the excited town, drums began to beat insistently, and men were seen running, guns in hand. The armed men soon converged on the town house, seat of local government, and began forming into military companies. On board the *Rose* the lieutenant in command, alarmed, prepared his ship for action. Elsewhere, prominent members of the Andros administration were unsure what to think or do. Some quickly fell into the hands of armed parties of Bostonians and, like George, were made prisoners of the people. Others, including Andros himself, managed to gain refuge in the fort on the hill. The garrison, of course, was by now on the alert, muskets in hand. By noontime, hundreds of aroused colonists were under arms at the town house, where the popularly recognized leaders of the community had gathered. One of these respected men read to the multitude a prepared declaration. Then someone gave the order to proceed to Fort Hill.

As the insurgents swarmed along the waterfront they saw a boat being frantically rowed from the *Rose* toward the battery just below the fort. At the same time, Andros and some of his officials started down from the fort toward the approaching boat—an attempt to escape. The armed colonists got there first, forcing the thwarted governor and his party to reverse their course and scramble back to the shelter of the fort. Jubilant, the colonists manhandled the cannons of the waterfront battery around so that they bore on the fort itself. Next, two designated emissaries advanced up the hill toward the entrance of the fort intending to demand its surrender. Red-coated sentries guarding the portal raised their muskets; shouts from the surging crowd warned that if they fired and killed, it would cost them their lives; the soldiers lowered their muskets and disappeared inside. After a parley, a flushed Andros and his official party emerged to be conducted through the streets to the town house, where they were made prisoners. The troops in the fort surrendered to the insurgents. Thus, by the time the sun had gone down on that momentous day, a royal governor was safely in custody, and Boston had been restored to local control. Remarkably, no lives had been taken by either side; it was a bloodless coup.

The next day the small garrison on Castle Island also surrendered, "with cursing," as it was said.[16] And what of HMS *Rose*? If she managed to get underway from her moorings, she could set Boston afire with her guns and blockade the town. To prevent these calamities, the insurgents boarded the frigate, fortunately without resistance from her crew, and confiscated all the sails, which was like depriving a policeman of his trousers.[17] That was a humiliation the Royal Navy could not soon forget.

When news of what had happened in Boston reached the army in Maine the effect was to dissolve the glue of military authority. Provincial soldiers simply disarmed the regular officers who had commanded them, and sent them down to Boston under guard. The regular enlisted men of the expedition presumably were allowed to wander off where inclination directed, and the triumphant provincials simply trudged homeward. Thus a royal army fell apart.[18]

Later, the Massachusetts soldiers had opportunity to lodge detailed complaints concerning their treatment at the hands of the regulars, and undoubtedly were encouraged to do so as a part of the colony's case against the Andros regime. Such recorded complaints obviously should not be considered unbiased. Nevertheless, taken as a whole they do reveal a pattern of callous, abusive behavior on the part of at least some of the regular officers, the effect of which was to fix in the provincial mind a most unfavorable image of those men who carried the king's commission. Once fixed, the image was not to be readily dissolved. Summary examples of the testimony given by provincial soldiers show why. Samuel Wright and six others stated that on "the long march" Andros had ordered a sergeant "to kill them Souldiers that were not able, or unwilling to tr[avel]." Two men remembered what they described as the English officers' "unhumaine destroying of souldiers that were here Imprest." Isaac Prince charged that Captain George Locker was "the cause of the death of two of his souldiers by inhumaine usage." Peter Plympton could not forget "Sir Edmunds Cruelty to three sick Souldiers in presence of Lt. Coll: Magregory and Capt. Locker." David Folton, Joseph Breden, and Zachariah Mash testified that Lieutenant Colonel Patrick Magregory

> did keep back from them the allowance the Governour allowed them, and that he would not lett them have no more in seven dayes then they might eat in four dayes, and that he kept away their rum, pease, and flower, and in stead thereof gave them Indian corne which was a great wrong to them; and that he fourced them to march when they were not able both in Respect of victualls and Shooes, some haveing neither bread nor meat nor shooes, and it was in his power to give releife in all, and yet marched them from tuesday to fryday night, and that some of them had Sterved if they had not found some Indian corne most part rotton, and a drowned Deere. . . .

Some of the most damning charges were directed against Lieutenant John Jourdan, who was said to have disciplined a soldier by having him suspended "by the hand with a cod line clear from the ground only bearing one foote upon a sharp stake a long time, and afterwards tied neck and heels, and after that tyed up by the other hand as before, with his other hand and foote tyed cross behind him, and after that bound down with his back upon a sharp rayle or stake, saying that he would so punnish him that he should not be able to earn his liveing if he lived but begg from Dore to Dore."[19]

We can only guess why the regular officers dealt so harshly with the provincials. Certainly under the difficult and dangerous conditions of wilderness campaigning, strict discipline was essential. Regular officers required instant, unquestioning obedience from their own men, and presumably expected the same from the colonial troops. The latter, however, were accustomed to the much looser discipline of the militia, maintained by officers with whom they were personally acquainted. To these provincial soldiers, the red-coated officers were strangers who had no interest in their welfare. As morale declined during the long winter campaign, the

Massachusetts men probably became increasingly and stubbornly insubordinate, while the regular officers lost whatever tolerance they might have had, and resorted to extreme measures that were not only cruel but unwise. This, in turn, raised undying hostility in the minds of the provincials. On both sides, significant attitudes were being formed and hardened.

Although Andros himself eventually was officially exonerated from a charge of maladministration as governor of the Dominion of New England, he never did satisfactorily refute the accusation that his military officers had alienated the provincial troops by unnecessarily callous and even cruel behavior. Ever after that unforgettable winter expedition, New Englanders were certain in their own minds that they preferred to serve under local officers whom they knew and respected, their own neighbors who, despite discrepancy of rank, had a decent regard for them as fellow colonists. Thus, in the future, New Englanders would have a strong aversion to placing themselves under the control of regular officers. The latter, in turn, were becoming convinced that provincials made unbelievably bad soldiers. In any event, the new royal charter granted to Massachusetts by William and Mary in 1691 included no guarantee that the redcoats would not return to the Bay Colony in the future.

When New York and New Jersey were attached to the Dominion of New England in 1688, Governor Andros needed a deputy governor to administer the newly incorporated region. The man he sent to New York for that purpose was the commander of the Boston garrison, a career army officer, Colonel Francis Nicholson. Already in New York were two small garrisons of regulars, the first stationed in Fort James at the southern tip of Manhattan Island and the second nearly 150 miles upriver at Albany.

New York was markedly different from Massachusetts Bay. Having been founded originally by the Dutch and subsequently conquered by the English, the province contained a population that was diverse in both ethnic identity and religious affiliation. Most of the inhabitants belonged to one or another of the Protestant churches. The two major, and competing, ethnic groups were the Dutch and the English. Actually, the Dutch majority as well as the English and other groups had been prospering reasonably well under English rule, but the old Dutch elite, formerly dominant, were now becoming increasingly jealous and dissatisfied as they watched the newer English elite rising above them in economic and political power. Below these competing elites were the common folk struggling to survive in the strong crosscurrents of such a diverse community. The imposition of dominion government under an English colonel who in turn was responsible to an English governor-general in Boston capped this unhappy melange. Nicholson had his hands more than full.[20]

By 26 April 1689 the people of Manhattan had learned of the sudden toppling of the Andros regime in Boston. That, in turn, immediately raised doubts concerning the legitimacy of Nicholson's rule, doubts that were sharpened by a widespread suspicion that he was a closet Catholic. Nicholson, sensing that the most reasonable course was to stand fast until he received definite instructions from higher authority, sought to bolster the effective strength of his feeble garrison by arranging to have his regulars in Fort James reinforced with rotating groups of local militia. This proved a dubious benefit, for the scheme brought armed New Yorkers inside the only bastion of royal authority in the town. Moreover, the militiamen who did serve in the fort were more than a little annoyed by the obvious mistrust evinced by the regular officers of the garrison, the former being strictly confined to certain open areas and specifically excluded from the magazine where gunpowder was stored. Under such conditions, naturally, the relations between the redcoats and militiamen underwent considerable strain during the next few weeks while the whole town sifted every rumor and nervously awaited further developments.[21]

One of the captains of the New York militia was Jacob Leisler, a prosperous and influential merchant of German background who shared the anti-English resentment so strongly felt by most of the Dutch. A staunch Calvinist, Leisler had become convinced that the integrity and perhaps the very life of the province were threatened by a secret Roman Catholic conspiracy involving Nicholson himself. Although the deputy governor ostensibly was an Anglican, Leisler doubted the fact and likewise suspected what was indeed the case, that some of the regular officers and soldiers of the garrison were Catholic.[22]

Matters came to a head toward the end of May. First, about a half-dozen Irish (and probably Catholic) regulars from the disbanded garrison in Massachusetts arrived at New York and were welcomed by Nicholson, which immediately increased popular suspicion.[23] Next occurred an unfortunate dispute between regulars and militia in the fort. It began when a militia officer, Lieutenant Henry Cuyler, ordered his corporal to station a sentry at a certain point. When the corporal tried to carry out this order he was prevented by a regular corporal because the order had not come from Nicholson. Later, when Cuyler tried to explain the matter to Nicholson, the deputy governor flew into a rage, brandished a pistol, and threatened to have the whole troublesome town set ablaze. Nicholson, it must be said, was ill served by his notoriously violent temper; in his defense we may well surmise that the outburst was the result of prolonged strain under conditions that were becoming increasingly unstable and threatening. In any case, word of his imprudent tirade spread quickly, losing nothing in the telling.[24]

On the next day, which was 31 May, the local militia, aroused, assembled in arms under their own leaders, took over control of Fort James, and proceeded to disarm the regular garrison. Leisler then raised from the militia a new company, which, under his quickly rising leadership, assumed the responsibility of manning the king's fort. Thus deprived of employment, the company of redcoats dissolved, leaving the individual soldiers free to shift for themselves. Subsequently, the garrison at Albany also was cast adrift. As for the deeply humiliated deputy governor, he prudently boarded ship for England, leaving Leisler and a patchwork revolutionary administration in control.[25]

So far as the evidence shows, the Leislerian regime that so suddenly assumed power never for a moment intended to renounce English sovereignty, and in fact did not do so. On the contrary, Leisler and his supporters presented themselves as enthusiastically loyal subjects of the new sovereigns William and Mary, ready to obey the royal commands whenever received. Although undoubtedly well intentioned, Leisler was something of an extremist with an unfortunate tendency to bully and browbeat his opponents. As time went on and no official royal instructions arrived from England, Leisler too began showing signs of tension. During this long period of waiting he managed to alienate more and more of the colonists, especially those not of Dutch heritage.

As it happened, the new English sovereigns were not favorably impressed by the reports they received from or about Leisler. In due course, therefore, they ordered Colonel Henry Sloughter, an officer of the regular army, to proceed to New York, assume the governorship of that royal province, and restore legitimate government. Assigned to accompany Sloughter were two companies of redcoats under the command of Major Richard Ingoldsby. The small size of this force, as compared with the earlier expedition to Virginia at the time of Bacon's Rebellion, indicated confidence that Leisler would not dispute the new authority.

Sloughter sailed in a separate vessel that was long delayed; as a consequence, Ingoldesby and his troops arrived at New York first, near the end of January 1691. The major immediately informed Leisler of his intention to garrison the fort, and was promptly refused permission to do so. Knowing that a newly appointed royal governor was en route, the suspicious Leisler felt that he had no right to yield the king's fort to any person lacking clear authorization. It was a fine point of propriety, and Leisler insisted on sticking to it, despite the fact that Ingoldesby undoubtedly was the senior military officer present. The major, of course, was outraged at this apparent defiance.[26]

After some negotiation, it was agreed that the two companies of regulars would take temporary quarters in the town hall. Accordingly, on 6 February the redcoats stepped ashore, as their commander reported, "with as much caution as if we had made a descent into an Enemies' Country."[27] Thereupon the vexed major and his men proceeded to establish their headquarters in the designated building, within cannon range of the fort where Leisler's troops stood guard. Ingoldesby assumed that he now was officially occupying the town, an assumption that soon produced more serious trouble. Areas patrolled by Leisler's troops and Ingoldesby's redcoats overlapped, causing vitriolic disputes over who had the right to be where. Especially annoying to Leisler was the insistent and repeated marching of redcoat patrols close to the walls of the fort itself, a practice that probably should be viewed as simply a tactic in a war of nerves. After this had continued for some time, Leisler's patience was approaching its limit. On 4 March one of the redcoat patrols refused to halt when challenged by a Leislerian sentry, whereupon Leisler had the surprised sergeant and his three men arrested and confined as a warning. Releasing the king's soldiers the following day, Leisler angrily denounced Ingoldesby's presumptuous behavior and called for reinforcements from the militia. The major was furious.[28]

While awaiting the impending arrival of Governor Sloughter, both sides were vying for the support of the confused and divided local populace. Several hundred armed colonists responded to Ingoldesby's call for men, adding considerable strength to his position in the area of the town hall; others, of a different mind, hastened to join Leisler and his militiamen in the fort. Both sides had access to artillery. If the royal governor did not soon arrive to take command in the name of the king, anything might happen.

Finally, on 17 March Leisler formally demanded that Ingoldesby get rid of his armed colonial supporters, which the major, naturally enough, refused to do. Thereupon the guns began to speak, colonists firing upon regulars positioned in the vicinity of the town hall, regulars upon colonists at the fort. To discover which side fired the first shot verges on the impossible, just as at Lexington Green in 1775, because the evidence is sharply contradictory and incomplete. Probably the elusive fact really is much less important than the undeniable one that here for the first time in North America an armed, organized force of provincials was in actual combat with the standing army of the Crown. The angry exchange of fire may have been fairly intense for a time, but the relative lightness of casualties and other damage suggests that it did not long persist, except for occasional random shots. On Ingoldesby's side two persons were killed and a number wounded; among the latter was one of the regular soldiers.[29]

Fortunately, there was little time left for Leisler and Ingoldesby to glare at each other across a few hundred yards of lower Manhattan. Sloughter's ship now was approaching, bringing a stern commander already unfavorably disposed toward the militia captain who had been lording it over a king's province for nearly two years. It was on 19 March 1691 that the long-awaited vessel finally arrived. Sloughter hurried ashore, where he soon was listening to Ingoldesby's damning revelation of Leisler's stubborn resistance. Thus informed, a very grim governor proceeded to publish his royal commission and demand the surrender of the fort.[30] Most unwisely, Leisler still procrastinated, which only worsened his case. An old soldier like Sloughter was not accustomed to being toyed with by his inferiors. So he ordered the major to march his redcoats up to the gates of the fort and demand admittance. Stubborn to the end, Leisler permitted only Ingoldesby himself to enter, but that was sufficient. When the red-coated major, standing all alone inside the king's fort, loudly called out to Leisler's men to lay down their arms they obeyed, gratefully accepting a proffered pardon. As for Leisler, he was quickly seized, dragged before the stern royal governor, and thrown into a cell to await trial. On 17 May 1691, after a trial before a biased court, the insurrectionist was hanged.[31]

Bacon's Rebellion and the uprisings of 1689 in Massachusetts and New York were the result of diverse and complex grievances—political, economic, social, and religious—felt by colonists under royal rule. It would be a gross exaggeration to imply that these early explosions of discontent were sparked primarily by American hostility toward the regular armed forces, and indeed no such claim is made here. In the case of Virginia the regulars were not even present when the upheaval began. In the later cases of Boston and New York the regulars were indeed present from the outset, and certainly some mutual hostility had already arisen between them and the community, but it cannot be said to have been the impelling or even a major cause of insurrection. Rather, the armed forces became involved in every instance because of the repressive role they were required to play; in playing that role they managed to intensify the feelings of hostility.

It must be remembered that in the American colonies, as in Restoration England, the royal armed forces served as a form of internal police, upholding constituted authority. Virginia, Massachusetts, and New York all saw the standing army actually functioning in that role and, in the end, prevailing. Any colonists who stood in opposition to a royal governor, especially any who were repressed by the regulars while attempting to resist the regime, deeply resented the military power that blocked their way and threatened them with dire punishment. So it was easy to perceive the standing army as a repressive instrument of tyranny, a constant threat to civil liberties. As for the officers and men of the armed forces, they knew exactly why they had been thrust upon such a diverse and turbulent people in distant America, and stood ready to do their job regardless. Having little cause to like the general run of colonist and much cause to see themselves as a target for colonial enmity, these often miserable and resentful men existed on the edge of a basically hostile society.

By the end of the seventeenth century the North American colonies were being drawn fully into the mainstream of a rapidly developing mercantile-imperial system whose center of control was in London. The colonists, sharing the strong English distaste for a royal standing army, and having had considerable experience with the regular armed forces on station in their midst, had also had occasion to see the king's men in their role as a police power. Consequently, mistrustful and even antagonistic attitudes, on both sides, were already forming and beginning to harden. During the first half of the new century, the century of the American Revolution, those attitudes were to be shaped and intensified by further experience.

CHAPTER 2.

BOSTON AND THE ILL-FATED

CANADA EXPEDITION, 1711

OLLOWING the overthrow of the Dominion of New England in 1689, the new sovereigns William and Mary, with the support of a willing Parliament, proceeded to make new imperial arrangements conducive to more effective royal government in the colonies. The largely self-governing colonies of Connecticut and Rhode Island stand out as exceptions to this trend, and even they were subject to the Acts of Trade and Navigation. New Hampshire remained a royal colony, as did New York. By the terms of a royal charter issued in 1691, Massachusetts Bay and Plymouth Colony, along with the line of coastal settlements in Maine, became a single colony with a royally appointed governor and an elected legislature. Some inhabitants groaned at this new arrangement, and others rejoiced, but all had to accept and obey. The era of Puritan self-determination was ended.

During this same period, from 1689 to 1697, England and her colonies were engaged in war against France and her colonies, the first in a series of four international imperial conflicts that finally drew to a close in 1763. By and large, in the first of these wars at least, England expected her North American colonies to look after their own security. Some ships of the Royal Navy were based in colonial seaports, being welcomed as protectors. But when these same ships resorted to the practice of impressing local seamen to fill their empty berths, they generally aroused the resentment of the affected community. Popular resistance to such impressment in the 1690s did much to build Boston's notoriety among professional naval officers as a stubbornly hostile town where obstructionism was practiced like a religion.

A small garrison of regular troops was stationed in the province of New York, but the condition of these soldiers rapidly deteriorated, largely as a result of serious neglect on the part of the authorities in faraway London. In the spring of 1696, during the later stages of King William's War, Governor Benjamin Fletcher sought to reinforce these debilitated redcoats with a small contingent of provincial soldiers drawn from neighboring Connecticut over whose militia he supposedly exercised authority as royally designated commander in chief. What Fletcher proposed to the government of Connecticut was that sixty men from the militia be sent to serve with the regulars at Albany for a period of one year, as a means of strengthening the exposed frontier. "It will be a great advantage to the youth of Connecticut to be taught the use of arms after the modern way of the King's army," he remarked by way of further explanation to Connecticut's Governor Treat, thereby signalling his intention that the raw provincial troops be brought under the immediate command of his regular officers. Treat and his council, however, knew better than Fletcher the temper of the Connecticut mind. So instead they decided to send their own militia officers with the contingent, at the same time placing a much closer terminal date on the period of service, while retaining the right to recall their contingent at any time should Connecticut herself be invaded. A quick reply from New York made clear that Fletcher insisted on his right to assign command, whereupon Treat and his council drafted a response that stands as unmistakable early evidence of the strong American reluctance to become integrated with British regular forces: "It seemed most for the King's interest that our soldiers should have officers from among ourselves, for we hope we have men fitted to command against such enemies as infest our frontiers in these parts, and if our soldiers have officers whom they know and love they will be more free to attend the service and more forward and courageous against the enemy." Concluded this frank message, "If you do not concede this to us you will find our soldiers very unwilling to march to Albany."[1]

Correspondence from Fletcher's successor as governor, the Earl of Bellomont, confirms the low state of the New York garrison by 1700. "I have a parcel of the swearingest and drunkenest souldiers . . . that ever were known in the world," Bellomont complained. Two of the officers, contrary to the Articles of War, were in business as tavern keepers. A third was, as the governor put it, "a most sad, drunken sott, and under no good character for manhood." Shortly after this some fresh recruits arrived from Ireland. Bellomont sized them up as "a parcel of the vilest fellows that ever wore the King's livery, the very scum of the army in Ireland." Once ashore, these redcoats began brawling in the town, causing injury to several of the inhabitants. Their bad example helped under-mine the discipline of the unhappy garrison, spreading the infection of disorder. Soon the men were shouting for their long overdue pay and some new clothing to replace their rags. Bellomont, by arming the out-raged local burghers, finally was able to bring his mutinous troops under control. A court martial then condemned four to be shot, two of whom were spared only seconds before the fatal volley. Such behavior by royal soldiers did nothing to increase colonial respect for the regulars, serving only to intensify popular distaste for the military establishment.[2]

During the second of the colonial wars, Queen Anne's, lasting from 1702 to 1713, Britain was involved in widespread hostilities against the combined strength of France and Spain. Her major effort was concen-trated on the continent of Europe, where the great Marlborough led the queen's armies. In the mind of the Whig ministry, Europe had clear priority; any campaigning that might take place in America was of rela-tively minor importance. New England had a quite different perspective on the war. French Canada and Acadia (Nova Scotia) seemed a constant and very immediate menace. On the western coast of the Acadian penin-sula, northeast of Boston, stood Port Royal, a base and haven for French privateers preying upon New England shipping. Even more menacing to colonial expansion and security was New France, whose center of popu-lation, trade, and government was the elongated valley of the St. Law-rence River, with major strength concentrated at the two settlements of Montreal and Quebec. The enterprising French seemed a growing threat to the English colonies because they were unshakably Roman Catholic, were actively pursuing the highly competitive and profitable fur trade of the interior, and had powerful Indian allies who, in wartime, could be a terrifying menace to the lengthy and exposed frontier. If only New En-gland could find a way to conquer Acadia and New France, thereby erasing French power in that whole vast region, the future growth and prosperity of England's northern colonies would be guaranteed.

On one occasion in 1690 New England itself, on its own initiative and with only its own limited resources of ships, manpower, and equipment, had sent an expedition by sea to capture Quebec. The humiliating failure of that hopeful enterprise had convinced many of New England's leaders that no such attempt should again be made without the active participa-tion of British regular forces. In this way, the very region that had shown such distaste for the king's fighting men in 1689 was brought to desire their reappearance and help after 1702. The scheme that was formulated to effect the conquest of Canada seemed simple and practical. One army of provincial troops would be assembled at Albany, another army and fleet at Boston. Then the Albany force, serving as one arm of a giant pincer, would advance northward along 150 miles of wilderness waterways to seize Montreal, while the Boston force, serving as the other arm of the pincer, would sail around Acadia and up the St. Lawrence River to capture Quebec. With adequate military and naval support from the mother country, especially for the Boston force, victory seemed virtually guaranteed, for New France had a very small population and limited defenses. An enterprising merchant named Samuel Vetch carried the plan to England, gained the attention of the Board of Trade, and eventually obtained royal assent. Britain and her northern colonies, in a great cooperative military enterprise, would conquer Canada and eliminate for all time the French menace in North America.[3]

Official acceptance of the scheme meant that a powerful squadron of the Royal Navy together with a large fleet of transport vessels carrying thousands of redcoats would appear at Boston, the very town that so gleefully had humiliated the king's regular forces in 1689. But now the circumstances were drastically different, for the regulars would be coming to aid the colonists in an enterprise of great mutual advantage. It would be wrong to assume, however, that all colonists who contemplated the prospect were of one mind. The royal governor of Massachusetts, Joseph Dudley, was himself intensely disliked by many who could not forget that he had been one of Andros's colleagues in Dominion days. Moreover, he was now thought to be hand-in-glove with a coterie of favored Boston merchants some of whom, including Vetch, were suspected of profiting by trading secretly with the enemy. To the common folk of Massachusetts, struggling daily to survive in the difficult circumstances of war, Dudley and his wealthy cronies seemed distant, arrogant, and self-serving. Thus New England, especially Massachusetts, stood divided by internal resentments and suspicions, a condition that cannot have been totally unknown to the ministry in London.[4]

The queen's ministers viewed the enterprise as a venture involving all the northern colonies from New Hampshire to Pennsylvania, all being expected to contribute as required. Contingents of provincial troops raised in Connecticut, New York, New Jersey, and Pennsylvania would comprise the Albany army. Other provincial troops raised in New Hampshire, Massachusetts, and Rhode Island would assemble at Boston preparatory to sailing with the British regulars for Quebec. In addition to troops, the colonies were expected to gather and make available adequate quantities of provisions, specially constructed landing craft, and auxiliary shipping. Orders for all these preparations were sent from England to the colonies well in advance so that once the regular forces had arrived the whole operation could begin no later than May 1709.

When officially notified of the requirements, the various colonies moved with unwonted promptness and vigor to complete their respective assignments. The lure of Canadian conquest with ample British aid seemed to have an almost magical effect, apparently overcoming all former lethargy and intercolonial jealousy, except in Quaker Pennsylvania where preparations for combat always were routinely deplored. Assemblies from New Hampshire to New Jersey began making the necessary appropriations, levying extra taxes in order to raise their assigned quotas of troops and materiel. Once organized, the soldiers began moving off along the roads or coastal waterways leading to the main assembly areas at Albany and Boston. Colonial authorities imposed an embargo upon ordinary shipping at the various ports, so as to make enough merchant ships and seamen available for the expedition, and also to prevent news of these extensive preparations from reaching the French.[5]

With every passing day the costs of these measures mounted, but enthusiasm and optimism also seemed high, as all involved eagerly awaited the first appearance of the powerful fleet from England. By the end of May the expected armada had not yet been sighted. June passed, and so did July, with the hundreds of troops at Albany and Boston still standing at arms and expecting their pay. In the meantime Vetch, Dudley, and the other colonial sponsors were becoming more and more edgy and, understandably, baffled. August went the way of July, and September the way of August. One discouraged New England taxpayer labelled September "a costly month by reason of an idle armie," which was no exaggeration.[6]

Where was the promised fleet with its thousands of professional sailors and soldiers, its supplies and heavy guns? Where was the promised professional commander who would lead them in the conquest of Canada? The answer to these burning questions finally was given on 11 October 1709 when a ship from England reached Boston with official notification that the great enterprise had been cancelled. Why? Why? The dispatch from the ministry failed to provide a candid explanation. What now seems closest to the truth is that peace feelers from the French court, advanced as early as the fall of 1708, had made the British government chary of an expensive attempt to seize French territory that, by the terms of a subsequent treaty of peace, might have to be relinquished. Canada fell within that possibility, and besides, affairs in faraway North

America, when measured against the great campaigns being waged in Europe, seemed to the Whig ministry fairly inconsequential. Whatever the reason, the queen's government in London had changed its mind.

Britain's failure to carry through with its promise, viewed against the backdrop of the costly preparations actually made by the colonies in accordance with specific instructions from British authority, left Americans feeling deeply resentful. It was hard for them to bury the very live suspicion that, all things considered, they did occupy a low rung on the ladder of ministerial concerns. They would have been even more resentful had they known that the ministry had reached its decision to cancel the Canadian venture as early as the end of May! With what in retrospect can only be called incredible indifference, the men in Whitehall then had delayed until July the drafting of the required letters to the colonial governments, and it was not until August that those dispatches actually were on their way across the ocean. Even at that, the vessel carrying them was dilatory in its voyage, which is why the news did not arrive at Boston until almost mid-October. A ministry that really felt some concern for American interests could have spared the colonies enormous worry and expense by seeing that a fast ship was sent off promptly so as to reach Boston before the end of July.[7]

As it was, London did sugar the bad news with a positive suggestion— that the provincial troops already mobilized proceed to capture Port Royal. For even that limited endeavor, however, some assistance from the Royal Navy was needed. Colonial leaders, hoping to salvage some victory for the year's expenditures, promptly solicited the aid of the several naval vessels then present in New England waters, only to receive polite but positive refusals from all but one of the captains, on the grounds of prior orders and responsibilities.[8] This topping rejection killed the new project, to the further disgruntlement of the colonial leaders. For the provincial soldiers themselves, perhaps, it was just as well. Those who had survived not only boredom but disease in camp during the futile weeks of waiting all through the summer and well into the fall were more than ready to head for home. So the year 1709 ended in frustration and futility, with the rapid demobilization of the provincial forces, and higher taxes for no apparent gain.

Some colonial leaders, including Vetch and Dudley, were eager to try again, which indicates if nothing else how important the conquest of Acadia and Canada seemed to such ambitious men.[9] In 1710 Whitehall again became cooperative, at least to the extent of sending a few ships and one regiment of royal marines to join with provincial forces in an operation against Port Royal. This time the forces from England actually did arrive. The colonies involved, despite their deep disappointment of the previous year, also proved cooperative by augmenting the professional forces with supplies, vessels, and some troops. As a way of raising the level of discipline and proficiency in the provincial units, a regular officer was attached to every company, an arrangement that may have reminded some New Englanders of unhappy days with the Andros expedition.[10] The attempt against Port Royal proved successful, with the French garrison yielding to the Anglo-American force on 1 October 1710, after which the place was renamed Annapolis Royal in honor of the queen. A combined garrison of regulars and provincial volunteers under Vetch was left to hold the new acquisition, with results that might have been predicted. By mid-June 1711 Vetch had lost over a hundred of his men by death and desertion. Those remaining, he reported, "fall verry often into disputes about command precedency and other nicietys, which creates a great many heats amongst both officers and souldiers."[11] It was another early indication of the almost inevitable tensions inherent in the combining of regular and provincial forces.

Pleased with the possession of Annapolis Royal, New England leaders still yearned for the conquest of Canada, and continued to urge the project upon the government in London. Toward the end of 1710 their pleas fell upon more receptive ears, for in recent months there had occurred some significant changes in high places. The Duchess of Marlborough, consort of the great continental campaigner, had been supplanted as the queen's close personal confidante by Abigail Masham. More important, the Whig ministry had been replaced with a Tory ministry eager for some great military success overseas to help solidify their hold on war-weary England. Canada seemed the perfect prospect. So it was that for the third time Whitehall began drawing up plans and making the requisite preparations for a great Anglo-American campaign.[12]

By this time, perhaps understandably, the mood of the northern colonies also had undergone some change, not drastic but nonetheless important. Officially still eager for the conquest of Canada, the colonies now were more cautious in their attitude toward Britain's requirements, for they had received such instructions twice before, and the resulting preparations had cost them dearly. What is more, some of the colonies believed that their own particular efforts and sacrifices on previous occasions had surpassed those of their neighbors, a situation they preferred not to have repeated. Rhode Island, for example, took a look at its assigned quota of troops for the 1711 campaign, proclaimed the figure too high, and simply decided for itself how many men the colony would provide. In addition, the governor of that small but independent-minded colony was so bold as to spurn an offer of British regular officers for the Rhode Island contingent. But despite some hesitancy and grumbling, the governors and legislatures of the various northern colonies did issue the necessary orders, and once again the costly preparations were begun, this time in anticipation of an actual, not just a promised campaign.[13]

The authorities in France and Canada had ample sources of information, and knew what was afoot. During that busy spring of preparation there arrived in Boston a French emissary, the Sieur de la Ronde Denis, ostensibly to negotiate an exchange of prisoners. His secret instructions, however, were to sow among the people of Boston the frightening idea that the powerful fleet and army expected from England to lead in the conquest of Canada really were being sent for the purpose of imposing upon the Bay Colony a more strictly authoritarian form of royal government, possibly like that of the defunct Dominion. Incredibly, the authorities at Boston permitted La Ronde to perambulate more or less at will, which gave him ample opportunity to drop his seeds of suspicion and discord among the people. Just how effective La Ronde was cannot be measured, but he may have been able to turn the minds of at least some fairly influential Bostonians against the British force whose arrival was impending.[14]

Pitching and rolling as they cut their way across the Atlantic Ocean were a dozen men-of-war and forty transports carrying seven regiments of redcoats and a battalion of marines. Altogether the troops totalled about 4,300, the seamen perhaps another 4,000.[15] It was the largest armada that had ever approached the New England coast. Commanding the fleet was Admiral Sir Hovenden Walker, a career naval officer of many years' experience but no real distinction. He had visited Boston once before, aboard HMS *Dartmouth* in 1686, but seems to have acquired precious little practical knowlege of the colonies. Surely, though, as a professional naval officer he cannot have been totally unaware of Boston's reputation as a seaport where "the press-masters are knocked down at broad noon" and captains of the Royal Navy were likely to be more despised than respected.[16] Commanding the army was Brigadier General John Hill, whose elevation almost certainly may be attributed to the fact that he was none other than Abigail Masham's brother. Hill seems to have known even less than Walker about New England, yet he was to command in the campaign against Canada not only the disciplined regulars but also the provincial troops coming from New Hampshire, Massachusetts, and Rhode Island, with authority to establish rules and punish offenders, a power which, if exercised without discretion, would be certain to arouse resentment.[17]

In the hope of deceiving French agents anxious to ascertain the fleet's destination, the quantity of provisions supplied to the ships prior to their departure from England had been more in keeping with a southern European than an American destination, a clever ruse perhaps, but one that would require the acquisition of large quantities of additional foodstuffs in New England. As the British government unfortunately had neglected to provide Walker with an adequate supply of sterling, substantial credit would have to be arranged at Boston in order to make the necessary purchases. What the admiral did not know, apparently, was that Boston itself was experiencing a shortage of food, being forced to feed its own people by seeking provisions elsewhere in the colonies. On the other hand, Walker did realize that his fleet would have to be augmented by numbers of local vessels manned by New England seamen, in order to transport the additional supplies as well as the provincial troops. Finally, Walker knew that he would have to obtain pilots from among the few New England mariners who had some familiarity with the varying depths, treacherous currents, and blinding fogs of the St. Lawrence River, which constituted Quebec's most immediate and awesome natural defense. Captain Cyprian Southack, a Bostonian of considerable maritime reputation, already had been selected by the ministry to serve as chief pilot for the fleet.[18]

During the last week of June the fleet arrived at Nantasket Road, the sheltered anchorage near the seaward end of the channel leading to Boston. By that time colonial preparations were far advanced, with hundreds of provincial soldiers encamped near the village of Roxbury just to the south of the capital, and a number of merchant vessels already taken into government service. Boston's ten thousand inhabitants received the news of the fleet's arrival with understandable excitement mixed with some degree of apprehension and latent hostility as a result of past experience and La Ronde's subtle influence.

At the earliest opportunity Walker and Hill started for Boston by boat to meet with Governor Dudley and other local dignitaries and specify their requirements. It is interesting to imagine the thoughts of the two professional officers as they sat in that boat proceeding slowly toward the Puritan capital, contemplating the passing scene. We may wonder what, if anything, they knew of previous occurrences at particular places along the way. Probably the ship's boat passed within gun range of Castle Island in whose fort the deposed Governor Andros had been incarcerated by the Boston insurrectionists twenty-two years earlier. In 1702 the guns of Castle Island had actually fired on one of the queen's ships, HMS *Swift*, to prevent her from leaving port with impressed seamen on board.[19] Approaching now the Boston waterfront, Walker and Hill might have reflected on a certain day in 1693 when, at one of the prominent wharves, a mercurial New England–born governor, William Phips, had come to blows with Captain Richard Short of HMS *Nonesuch*, badly battering the naval officer before the astonished eyes of a rapidly gathering waterfront crowd.[20] Possibly, too, they could recall the unhappy experience of Admiral Sir Francis Wheeler after arriving at Boston in 1693 with a fleet from the West Indies. The admiral had designs upon Quebec, but the colonial authorities, unprepared for such a venture, had rejected his request for provincial troops, thereby causing Wheeler to abandon the plan and return to England with nothing to show for such a long cruise.[21] Clearly, where the regular forces were involved, Boston could not be called the most openhearted of towns, and now the pair of professional officers preparing to disembark may well have wondered just how cheerfully their own legitimate demands would be met.

Governor Dudley, a vulnerable placeman, was eager to cooperate. His council, elected from among the leading men of the colony, could be readily convened, but the assembly, the more popular branch of the bicameral legislature, was not scheduled to meet until 18 July. Many things needed to be accomplished as speedily as possible, starting immediately. On the afternoon of 27 June, Walker's transport vessels, a-swarm with sea-wrung but curious redcoats, carefully processed up the channel while equally curious throngs along the waterfront stared and perhaps ventured a cheer.[22] For reasons of health and military efficiency the troops needed to get ashore, but attempting to quarter such a large number of soldiers in the town itself, or even having them encamp in open country outside the town, where desertion would have been a constant temptation, seemed close to folly. Therefore, the men were ferried to nearby Noddles Island, opposite the town. There, on available land, a regular military camp quickly arose, while the ships dropped back down to Nantasket. It must have been obvious to all observers that the British arrangement—troops on an island, seamen aboard ships anchored offshore—reflected official concern about possible large-scale desertion in an area so attractive as Boston.

Extant documents, in particular the journals and correspondence of Walker, Hill, and lesser officers, focus on the next four or five weeks at

Boston in a way that throws a clear shaft of light upon the problem of Anglo-American friction.[23] The basic facts to remember are two: that the New England colonies twice already had made heavy sacrifices with little consideration from London, and that in 1711 the arrival of the Walker expedition plus provincial troops from various parts of New England just about doubled the number of hungry mouths in Boston. If a letter from a British general thirty-five years after the event may be credited, so scarce were provisions during the early summer of 1711 that the inhabitants slaughtered most of their breeding stock for food, and eventually had to be resupplied from Ireland.[24] Be that as it may, Walker and Hill very soon became aware that the local business community, almost to a man, as well as many minor political figures and the working population in general, seemed strangely cool toward the newly arrived British.

Walker made known to the local authorities his pressing need for both credit and supplies. There was an almost Pavlovian reaction. Every Bostonian possessing a little of either began to calculate, Yankee fashion, how to gain the most profit from the admiral's need. Local merchants and tradesmen were not interested in promises from the army and navy; they wanted cash. Butchers refused to slaughter animals without first seeing cash on the counter. The shortage of meat was accompanied by a shortage of bread, yet despite the most urgent demands of the British, bakers in Puritan Boston refused to violate the Sabbath by remaining at their ovens. Those merchants who were capable of extending the needed credit showed no readiness to do so. To Walker and his fellow officers, this negative attitude on the part of the New Englanders seemed "a very great Mystery." At last Dudley, with Walker, Hill, and several other high-ranking officers present and looking deeply concerned, was able to persuade the council itself to provide for a preliminary loan to the British forces.[25]

As sterling was not readily available in any case, once Walker's credit had been established he had to deal in provincial paper at a rate of exchange acceptable to both sides. Here the leading merchants of Boston apparently conspired to establish a rate of exchange distinctly advantageous to themselves. The previous year £100 sterling would buy £155 in Massachusetts paper. As recently as March 1711, the same amount would buy £140. But now at the end of June the local merchants insisted on a differential of only 20 percent, which meant that £100 sterling could command no more than £120 of colonial currency. This conveyed to the admiral and officers the distinct impression that the merchants were deliberately undervaluing sterling so as to maximize their profits in the sale of provisions and services to the forces. Walker became so furious that he even threatened to take his ships and men elsewhere, but actually he was helpless, for there was no better place to go, and any such move would have meant further delay of the operation.[26] So it was decided to refer the problem to the general court which, as we have noted, was not scheduled to meet until 18 July, meaning further delay. When the legislature finally did convene, it saw the light and quite promptly set the differential at 40 percent, which was reasonable under the circumstances. Also it made available to Walker additional colony bills of credit, at first £40,000 and later £10,000 more, thereby making possible the readier purchase of services and supplies.[27]

Unfortunately, the problem still was complicated by the actual shortage of provisions in Boston. With local inhabitants and British commissary officers vying in the markets for whatever was available, prices rose alarmingly, further convincing Walker that the colonists were engaged in unconscionable profiteering. "The Demands upon Exchange, and the Prices for Provisions, and other Necessaries for the Fleet and Army in *New England*," he bitterly complained to the admiralty, "were very exorbitant and excessive; but . . . we were obliged to comply with them, they being resolved to make an Advantage of our Necessities."[28]

Realizing what was happening, the general court tried to freeze prices. In addition, the legislature went so far as to authorize actual impressment of provisions, ordering various towns to send livestock, root vegetables, greens, and fruit regularly to Noddles Island where, under the supervision of appointed referees, they were to be sold to the military at "Moderate Customary Rates and prices."[29] Some of the local residents, possibly including wholesale and retail distributors, began hoarding provisions, either for their own consumption or for later sale at higher prices. Governor Dudley dealt with this new development by having designated persons search systematically for concealed provisions, with authorization to break down doors if necessary.[30] The actions of the governor and general court clearly show a desire to assist the expedition, but it is equally true that many lesser officials, and the colonists in general, were keeping their eyes fixed on the main chance, with very little concern for the actual well-being of their British visitors. Such profiteers were made even more antagonistic by any official pressure exerted against them.

Even while struggling with complex problems of finance and supply, Walker and Hill were made to realize that their fears about desertion were indeed well justified. Noddles Island was separated from Boston and the mainland shore only by narrow stretches of relatively calm water. To British soldiers and sailors alike, the busy streets and shops of Boston, and the fresh, green countryside beyond the town, must have been almost irresistibly inviting, all the more so when word began spreading through the ranks that some of the local people were eager to hire workers and willing to conceal deserters. Local shipmasters and other employers, hampered by a shortage of labor, could pay wages that, when compared with the meager pay provided by the queen, were highly attractive. So it should not have been surprising that desertion from the ships of the fleet and the regiments ashore became almost a daily occurrence.

After two or three weeks of steady drain by desertion, the anger of the regular officers was intense. Colonels "began to complain that the people of the country have deboached severall of their soldiers and favoured their desertion"; Hill growled that his troops "continued to desert by the help of the people of the country"; Walker reported with some restraint that "amongst other Inconveniences which we met with, the continual Desertion of the Seamen, Marines, and Soldiers, was not the least." The admiral went on to speak of "many Consultations, and published Advertisements, promising great Rewards" for the capture of deserters. Beyond that, Walker even pondered a measure that surely, if adopted, would have proved incendiary: it was proposed, he said, "to have a Proclamation published for pardoning all Deserters that should surrender themselves by a certain Day; and in order to incite the Inhabitants to exert themselves in taking them up, declaring that when we should leave this Place, the Number of Deserters should be made up out of such as were Natives and Inhabitants of the Province." That would have been impressment with a vengeance, possibly causing a riot that might have been joined by the provincial troops themselves. Certain it is that the British officers, angrily contemplating the continuing desertion, tended to blame the local populace almost as much as their own unreliable men.[31]

Walker and Hill carried their complaint to Dudley, who in turn took the drastic step of ordering certain companies of the Massachusetts militia to maintain a watch at harbors and along roads, questioning travelers and arresting any suspected as deserters. Monetary rewards were promised for persons who succeeded in returning deserters to their officers. But as Walker soon had to admit, "Notwithstanding all that had hitherto been done Men still desert, and several Houses and People are said to harbour them." Although he conceded that "the government here at the general and admiral's desire have fallen into such measures in appearance as would prevent the people from concealing or enticeing away our men," Colonel Richard King, commander of the artillery, complained that more than 250 men had been lost by desertion during the first four weeks at Boston.[32]

Precious days were slipping by while preparations for the coming campaign continued amidst frequent wrangling. The general stubbornness of the New Englanders, an almost mulish refusal to be pushed any faster than they wanted to go, coupled with a tenacious reluctance to subordinate self-interest to the immediate needs of the British military, convinced the regulars that, incredible as it seemed, at least some of the colonists did not want the expedition to succeed. Colonel King could not imagine "what their designs could be by all these delays if they were not to detain us here till the advanced season of the year will probably defeat us." And just how would such failure benefit Massachusetts? "It's certain," continued the frustrated colonel, "that those who rule and proffitt by their present dissorderly government now see how reasonable it is to change it; that the conquest of Canada will naturaly lead the Queen into it, and shew her how absolutely necessary it is to put all this northern continent of America under one form of government for the real good of the present coloneys, for the establishing of others, for their mutual support, and the vast advantages that will thereby accrue to Great Britain."[33] This same officer, writing to the secretary of state in London, spiced his words with cayenne pepper in denouncing the "ill nature and sowerness of these people [of Massachusetts], whose government, doctrine, and manners, whose hypocrisy and canting are insupportable," and went on to predict that "till they are all settled under one government . . . they will grow every day more stiff and disobedient, more burthensume than advantageous to Great Britain."[34] So there it was again—the old royalist remedy of a unified, authoritarian government for unruly New England, a concept that remained alive in the minds of colonists as well as British imperialists, linking 1711 with 1689.[35]

Added to problems of finance, supply, and desertion was the matter of pilots for the dangerous voyage up the St. Lawrence River. Walker considered this extremely important, even going so far as to establish his residence in the home of Captain Cyprian Southack so that he might readily consult that knowledgeable mariner and be in close touch with the effort to recruit others of the fraternity. It soon became obvious, however, that Southack himself preferred not to serve, and, with striking unanimity, others also were hanging back. In addition to Southack at least thirteen experienced mariners had been identified as potential pilots, none of whom reported to the designated ships at the appointed time. Angrily Walker notified the governor, who then issued warrants for the apprehension of the truants. Several days later, as a result, a few pilots did report for duty, but the disgruntled admiral readily perceived "a very great Unwillingness in all the Pilots, for going in that Station abord the Men of War, alledging in general, their Incapacity for such a Charge, and the long time since many of them had been up that River. Others complained of the Hardship of compelling them against their Wills . . .; and several of them named others that would do better in their steads."[36] These were the excuses of sullen, coerced men. Almost certainly the real reason for their reluctance was fear. Knowing how hazardous was navigation in the St. Lawrence River, and lacking adequate experience there with large ships such as Walker's, the New England pilots dreaded the heavy blame that would cascade upon their heads if they should make a fatal error.

Walker and Hill knew that as the time drew near when the entire expeditionary force finally might get underway, the rate of desertion almost certainly would rise even more. To forestall this, they ordered the regiments back on board the transports, starting on 20 July. Four days later the provincial troops also were embarked. Gradually the entire fleet of warships, transports, and auxiliary vessels, about seventy sail carrying some 12,000 men, assembled in Nantasket Road. At about the same time, the more than 2,000 troops of the Albany force under the command of Colonel Francis Nicholson, former deputy governor of New York under Andros, were making their final preparations for the interior thrust against Montreal. At long last, on 30 July Walker's powerful fleet set sail and proceeded majestically out into the open sea on course for the gaping mouth of the St. Lawrence. The lateness of this start had been caused, Walker firmly believed, by the unaccountable perversity of the New Englanders; thus, if the expedition should fail for lack of time he was more than ready to cast the blame on them. Above all, the admiral dreaded the possibility of being trapped at Quebec by rapidly forming autumn ice, which could mean mass starvation for his men.[37]

After entering the great river, the ships soon found themselves enveloped in dread fog, while unfamiliar currents began leading them astray. As they groped their way upstream, driven by a fresh wind, their actual position in the narrowing river diverged more and more from the theoretical position reckoned by the navigators. No wonder the New England pilots had been reluctant. Finally, during the dark night of 23–24 August, there was a sudden alarm as breakers were sighted dead ahead. One after another, eight leading ships of the fleet ground onto the rocks of the north shore, foundering with a loss of life totaling nearly 900, mostly British redcoats and seamen. The remaining ships, fortunately, including those carrying the provincial troops, managed to escape destruction.[38]

In theory, Walker and Hill even yet had a force large enough to carry on and make the attempt against Quebec, but by now the badly shaken admiral had no stomach left for the venture. A council of war held on board one of the ships endorsed his opinion that the risk of proceeding was too great, and so the operation was cancelled. The surviving regulars were returned to Britain, and the provincial troops were sent home, disillusioned by their experience but thankful to be alive. Walker's failure made it necessary for Nicholson's army to halt its laborious advance through the northern wilderness and return to Albany, where the provincial troops were dismissed. So ended a once-hopeful and very costly adventure.[39]

On the return voyage, Walker, Hill, and the other professional officers had ample time to share their perceptions of American governments and colonists, with little of favor or credit to say. Once the bad news of Walker's failure was known in London, the Tory ministry, becoming the butt of strong criticism from its political opponents, grasped for extenuating excuses. Here Walker and Hill were able to be of some assistance by laying stress upon the tangle of difficulties they had experienced at Boston. So potentially damaging were their charges against New England that Jeremiah Dummer, agent for Massachusetts in England, hastened to publish a rebuttal specifically denying that "a few smuggling Traders," fearing that the conquest of Canada would destroy their profitable trade with the enemy, had deliberately sabotaged the Walker expedition.[40] But the damage had been done. Britons who remembered something of New England's origin and history quite readily embraced the current wisdom that the colonists of that region cared only for independence and material gain, even at the expense of national honor.

In retrospect it seems clear that the events of 1709 to 1711 in the northern continental colonies, capped by the monstrous failure of the Walker expedition, further soured the Anglo-American relationship, reinforcing unfavorable impressions cherished by both sides ever since the late seventeenth century. Firmly established by this time, especially, was Boston's growing reputation among the officers of Britain's regular forces as a center of colonial obstinacy, perversity, and hostility. Nothing good was to be expected from the Puritan capital. On the other hand,

New Englanders who had experienced the apparent careless indifference of the British government, or the overbearing manner of indignant British officers, found their prejudices similarly reinforced. Such hardening perceptions on both sides were ominous for the future of Anglo-American relations in an era of colonial wars.[41]

CHAPTER 3.

FLORIDA, THE CARIBBEAN,

AND GEORGIA, 1739–1748

ITH the Peace of Utrecht in 1713, the North American colonies began a twenty-six-year period of freedom from international warfare, a period finally ended in 1739 by the outbreak of war between Britain and Spain. Early in that interval of relative peace the British government began to feel growing concern over the apparent weakness and vulnerability of American flank colonies such as Carolina, and in 1721 sent an independent company of regular troops for the defense of the southern frontier. Eleven years later the Crown granted a charter for the establishment of a new colony, Georgia, to provide a defensive buffer between South Carolina and Spanish Florida. Georgia's first organized settlers founded Savannah in 1733, under the leadership of a well-known member of Parliament and former subaltern in the British army, James Oglethorpe. Then, in 1737, with the Spanish threat increasing, Britain provided a newly raised regiment of regulars for the new colony, using the old independent company of South Carolina as a nucleus, a regiment soon to be known as the Forty-second Foot. Command of this regiment was given to Oglethorpe, with the rank of brigadier general, even though he had been a civilian for more than twenty years. In addition, Oglethorpe was designated commander in chief of all British forces in both Georgia and Carolina, with primary responsibility for defending the area against the Spaniards.[1]

Britain's declaration of war against Spain in October 1739 gave Oglethorpe a desired opportunity to mount an offensive against Florida, with the objective of capturing St. Augustine, the principal Spanish base on the east coast 150 miles below Savannah. In reality, St. Augustine was little more than a sleepy garrison town located on a harbor having a northern entrance and a southern entrance thirteen miles apart, providing excellent shelter for Spanish shipping. The town itself, located almost directly opposite the northern entrance, was guarded by an impressive fortification called the Castillo de San Marcos, which had proved its mettle in 1702 when an expedition from South Carolina had tried and failed to take it. But now General Oglethorpe was convinced that he had the resources to deprive the Spaniards of their base at St. Augustine, and early in 1740 began making preparations for a full-scale military-naval expedition. Available land forces consisted of the Forty-second Foot, a regiment of South Carolina provincial troops commanded by Colonel Alexander Vander Dussen, a contingent of Georgia provincials, and some friendly Indians—truly a mixed lot. Also essential for success was a small squadron of the Royal Navy that happened to be on the coast of Carolina, under the command of Commodore Vincent Pearce. The principal service to be performed by this squadron was to patrol off the entrances to the harbor in order to intercept any Spanish ships bringing reinforcements and supplies from the Spanish base at Havana.[2]

South Carolina was happy at the prospect of ravaging Florida, but before agreeing to participate in the venture the legislature at Charleston proposed to Oglethorpe certain conditions. The South Carolina troops, provincials to the last man, were to remain a distinct contingent subject to the orders of their own colony. Any plunder taken at St. Augustine was to be divided and distributed among the troops as specified by a council of war in which South Carolina officers, as well as Oglethorpe's regular officers, were to be included. Indeed, in all councils of war during the operation, South Carolina officers were to have equal votes with regular officers of the same rank, while yielding "Place and Precedence to General Oglethorpe's Officers of the same Rank." Of particular importance in the successful raising of the South Carolina regiment was the legislature's insistence that "all offences committed by any of the Troops from this Government shall be finally determined and punished, by the officers of their own regiment only."[3] Such provisions clearly reflect the provincials' profound reluctance to come under the full authority and control of the regular forces, a reluctance arising from long tradition and experience. Oglethorpe, responding to these proposals, promised that the provincial troops would be subject to trial by their own regimental officers, reserving to himself only the right either to approve or suspend any penalties imposed. In addition, he specified that all plunder would be divided in accordance with a system regularly used in the navy, thereby avoiding the unseemly wrangling that might occur over such an issue in a mixed council of war. Finally, too, the general promised that the Carolinians would be free to return home after four months of service. That Oglethorpe was not willing to leave the training and disciplining of the raw provincials entirely to their own officers, however, is indicated by the fact that he temporarily detached Lieutenants Cadogan and Maxwell from the Forty-second Foot in order to assist in preparing the South Carolina regiment for active duty.[4]

In April, Pearce's naval squadron began patrolling off the Florida coast. A month later the land force, consisting of the regulars and provincials from Georgia and South Carolina, advanced southward from the mouth of the St. Johns River overland toward St. Augustine. Relations among the three major components of the British forces—Pearce's squadron, Oglethorpe's regiment of redcoats, and Vander Dussen's provincials—both during and after the operation, are of particular interest. The surviving evidence, some of it markedly partisan and very bitter, is clouded with controversy. Throughout we can gain clear glimpses of both intercolonial and interservice friction, some of it apparently trivial, but all contributing to an atmosphere of mutual antipathy.

Almost from the outset, it seems, Oglethorpe did not get along well with the Carolinians, who later charged that the general had confiscated for his own purposes Florida horses, which they had rounded up to carry their baggage, but would not permit the soldiers to slaughter Florida cattle for meat without compensating the owners. Possibly the conscientious Oglethorpe simply was intent upon protecting the property of Spanish ranchers in order to gain their good will, but such a policy seemed outrageous to the plunder-seeking provincials. As the army advanced close to St. Augustine, Colonel John Palmer of the South Carolina volunteers, an experienced frontier fighter, became convinced that the town could be taken by a sudden swift attack before the Spaniards had time to complete their preparations. Going to Oglethorpe, he volunteered to lead 200 of his fellow colonists in such an attack, but the general rejected the proposal out-of-hand as too risky. Perhaps it was, but Palmer was not convinced. Shortly thereafter, when Lieutenant Jonathan Bryan and several rangers crept very close to the fringes of the Spanish town they detected signs of confusion within. They too thought that a quick, determined assault would succeed, but again the general refused to give his consent. His unwavering opposition only infuriated the South Carolinians, who felt that a good opportunity for a speedy victory and plenty of plunder had been tossed aside.[5]

One outpost overrun early by the British was Fort Moosa, two miles north of St. Augustine, but in taking the place they had destroyed the gates and made breaches in the walls, thereby rendering it virtually indefensible. Left standing within the walls, however, was a substantial structure capable of sheltering a considerable number of troops. Here Oglethorpe and his staff established temporary headquarters, posting a sentinel at the door. When a sudden downpour of rain occurred, a small horde of Carolinians, among them Colonel Palmer and other provincial officers, pushed into the building to escape a drenching. This unexpected and disorderly intrusion greatly annoyed the general, who sharply rebuked his sentry for not blocking the entrance, and then actually ordered Palmer and his companions back outside.[6] The episode was symptomatic and perhaps symbolic of the animosity that was steadily rising between the Georgians and Carolinians, the regulars and provincials. When it came to making military decisions, Oglethorpe conferred mostly with his own regular officers, occasionally with his naval colleagues, who also were professionals, but seldom in any formal way with the provincial officers from South Carolina, a neglect that was bitterly resented. The Carolinians, weakened by sickness, disillusioned with Oglethorpe's inability to force a surrender, and grievously disappointed in their expectation of plunder, saw themselves being dealt with like mere pawns. This they deeply resented, remembering well the promises their own legislature had extracted from the general. Finally, they embodied their frustrations in a written complaint dated 17 June 1740 and signed by the lieutenant colonel, the major, and every captain and lieutenant of the provincial regiment.[7]

A quick trip back to ruined Fort Moosa reveals yet more. Oglethorpe had thrown together a provisional company of about 140 men to patrol the vicinity of that outpost. The composition of the company was unusual, for it included a dozen regulars of the Forty-second Foot, nine Carolina rangers, some Georgia provincials, and a number of Indians. Commanding this variegated outfit was Colonel Palmer of South Carolina, assisted by Captains Hugh Mackay and John McIntosh of the regulars. Unlike the two captains, the colonel had no royal commission, a lack that apparently raised in the minds of Mackay and McIntosh serious doubts concerning Palmer's ability to command and their obligation to obey. Once the company had established itself at the remains of Fort Moosa the trouble began, with Mackay and McIntosh opposing the decisions and policies of Colonel Palmer. There was a dispute over the placement of sentries, with the consequence that arrangements to prevent surprise were inadequate. There was a quarrel about whether it was preferable to remain overnight within the dubious protection of the breached walls or bivouac in concealment outside, with the result that some of the troops did one thing and some the other. Palmer, as an old Indian fighter, knew that dawn was the most likely time for an enemy attack and so, early every morning, he would order all hands up and under arms for a dawn alert. The regulars, enjoying their best sleep at that time, were most uncooperative. As was said later, "none knew who had the chief Command really." One morning at early light a Spanish raiding party made a daring surprise attack upon Fort Moosa, killing about half of the garrison. Ironically, Mackay was among the half who survived, Palmer among the dead.[8]

Nor was the navy always cooperative. Some time before Oglethorpe's army had arrived at St. Augustine and begun the siege, the Spaniards had managed to slip six galleys and a couple of supply vessels from Cuba into the harbor to bolster the defenses. The galleys, shallow-draft vessels armed with long brass nine-pounders, could be positioned so as to prevent any British approach in force across the harbor to the fort and town. Consequently, the very success or failure of Oglethorpe's endeavor now appeared to hinge upon the elimination of those galleys. For once, Oglethorpe and Vander Dussen were in agreement—the galleys must be attacked and destroyed. Accordingly, the militia colonel from South Carolina offered to lead some of his provincials in a surprise night attack with that objective, if the navy would provide him with a sufficient number of pinnaces and longboats manned by seamen from Pearce's squadron. When Vander Dussen proposed his scheme to naval officers on shore, they seemed favorably impressed, but Commodore Pearce had serious doubts about the feasibility of such an attempt, and vacillated. Consulting his own officers he finally came out with a flat refusal, which meant that the galleys remained secure, while discouragement among the officers and men of the besieging army continued to grow.[9]

Further aggravating the situation was Commodore Pearce's warning that his squadron could remain on the Florida coast no later than 5 July. With the navy gone, Oglethorpe's divided, dwindling, and constantly bickering army would have no choice but to begin a humiliating and hazardous withdrawal. Toward the end of June, as fate would have it, the wind swung into the east and picked up force, presaging a nasty storm capable of driving the ships ashore. So imminent was the danger that Pearce now ordered his squadron to make for the relative security of the open sea until the storm should subside, when they would return for the few remaining days. One of the ships, leaving its station off the southern entrance to the harbor preparatory to joining Pearce, sighted sails approaching, but instead of taking the initiative and investigating, obeyed orders and continued on its course. As a result, Spanish supply vessels from Cuba were able to gain the southern entrance without interference and deliver their much-needed cargoes. To the army ashore, regulars and provincials alike, it seemed that the navy was neither efficient nor enthusiastic in its support of the siege; Pearce and his officers seem to have had equivalent respect for the behavior of the land force. Captain Peter Warren of HMS *Squirrel* probably was expressing the general opinion held by his colleagues when he referred with scorn to "the ill-concerted and worse conducted attack on St. Augustine. I hope," Warren fervently concluded,"I shall never have any part in such an expedition again."[10] After the storm had subsided, Pearce did return, but he held adamantly to his deadline for final departure, which now was very close. Both Oglethorpe and Vander Dussen begged him to leave behind a couple of his ships to guard the approaches, and to let a number of his seamen remain with the besieging army, but all in vain. On 5 July the greater part of the squadron set sail and soon disappeared beyond the horizon, while the morale of the troops on shore sank to new depths.

Oglethorpe, weakened by fever, now was convinced that any further attempt against St. Augustine would be futile if not positively disastrous, and ordered a general withdrawal. Vander Dussen, on the other hand, was loath to quit, and tried to convince the general that the Spanish galleys still could be checkmated and the town taken. His enthusiasm was not contagious. Rather, a sense of defeat prevailed, and so the siege, which had lasted more than five weeks, was abandoned. Not unexpectedly, the army's withdrawal to Georgia and South Carolina was less than a model of order and discipline, with Oglethorpe's already limited authority rapidly disintegrating amid further quarreling between regulars and provincials. Indeed, the Spanish commander at St. Augustine was left in some wonderment at the haste and waste of the British departure.[11]

This account of mistrust and dissension would not be complete without a brief review of the intercolonial, interservice controversy that erupted in the wake of the inglorious St. Augustine operation. As early as mid-July, long before the troops had returned, the people of Charleston were agonizing over reports of failure, and beginning to lay blame upon Pearce and, especially, Oglethorpe.[12] The South Carolina legislature established a joint committee charged with the responsibility of conducting a thorough investigation. Shortly thereafter, when Vander Dussen and his weary, disgusted soldiers put in their appearance at Charleston having suffered much and gained nothing, the colonists heard more concerning military and naval mismanagement. Soon the bitter recriminations were spreading fast, with Oglethorpe placing the blame for failure "wholly upon the Sea Officers, They upon him, and Col. Vanderdussen upon both of 'em," as Charles Pinckney reported.[13] A most unpleasant *post mortem* was getting underway, with regulars and provincials in bitter contention.

As could have been predicted, the legislative committee's extensive, heavily documented report, which was published at Charleston in 1742, endorsed the conduct of the Carolinians, and criticized both Pearce and Oglethorpe.[14] The main points of the indictment were summarized in the *South Carolina Gazette* of 5–12 July 1742. This, in turn, inspired Oglethorpe and his principal defenders to draft and sign a certificate specifically denying the charge that at the conclusion of the siege the navy and the Forty-second Foot had left the South Carolina regiment to fend for itself. On the contrary, Oglethorpe insisted, during the subsequent withdrawal Vander Dussen and his provincials had advanced to the rear with unsoldierlike haste and disorder. One officer of the Forty-second Foot, Lieutenant Colonel Alexander Heron, in a letter from the regiment's base at Frederica, Georgia, laid blame on Vander Dussen, Palmer, and the Carolinians in general, while defending Oglethorpe at every point.[15]

The argument spread extensively through the press. Widely disseminated was a pamphlet published in London in 1742 under the title *An Impartial Account of the Late Expedition Against St. Augustine Under General Oglethorpe*, authored by one James Kilpatrick in defense of South Carolina's role. Here Oglethorpe was depicted as a fumbling commander who declined to accept good advice from his subordinates. Pearce, too, came under censure for his opposition to Vander Dussen's proposal for eliminating the Spanish galleys and for his squadron's failure to prevent critically needed supplies from reaching the Spanish garrison. Kilpatrick's partisan pamphlet was answered the following year by Lieutenant George Cadogan of the Forty-second Foot in a pamphlet titled *The Spanish Hireling Detected*, also published in London. Calling Kilpatrick's work "a Compendium of Malice, Scandal, and Falshood," Cadogan charged the South Carolina provincials with a lack of spirit, and especially condemned their officers for wanting to reach military decisions by counting votes, a practice far from common in the regular army.[16] Kilpatrick responded with *A Full Reply to Lieut. Cadogan's Spanish Hireling &c.*, a detailed refutation supported by numerous excerpts from pertinent documents, which was distributed by South Carolina's unwearying advocates to a considerable number of high public officials in London, including the members of the Board of Trade.[17] A subsequent blow for Oglethorpe was struck by an adulating Edward Kimber who made public his opinion that the Georgia general had been "betrayed and neglected by the mean Carolina Regiment, and many of the Men of War."[18]

By 1744 Oglethorpe himself was in England. Learning that his old antagonist Vander Dussen was applying for a regular commission, the controversial general composed a letter to the secretary at war, calling the application impudent, and stating that if Vander Dussen had been a regular officer instead of a provincial officer in the expedition of 1740 his behavior would have cost him his commission. That certainly was not the last word in the controversy, but it does stand out as one clear indication of a British regular officer's opinion of a provincial commander.[19]

While Oglethorpe had been fumbling and failing in Florida, a much greater military operation elsewhere, initiated by the ministry in London, was getting underway. It was to be a massive British effort to strike a decisive blow against Spanish wealth and power in the Caribbean. In due course a mighty expeditionary force consisting of a large fleet and many regiments of regular troops would be assembled and dispatched across the Atlantic to the British colony of Jamaica. Supreme naval command rested with Vice Admiral Edward Vernon; command of the army devolved upon Brigadier General Thomas Wentworth. At some point in the early planning somebody in Whitehall had the bright idea that it would be helpful to get the North American colonies in on the action, at least to the extent of contributing a large contingent of provincial troops. That idea, gaining official approval, was quickly built into the plan, thereby opening the way for another experiment in Anglo-American military relations.[20]

Soon the question was being asked: Will the American contingent come directly under the authority of the British high command in the Caribbean, being subject to the latter's orders and discipline just like the regulars? To this inquiry the ministry replied rather stiffly, "We can see no Reason for distinguishing the American Troops, by particular Instructions, from the Rest of His Majesty's Forces . . . in point of Subjection and Discipline, if they are subject thereto by the Laws now in being."[21] As far as Whitehall was concerned, that appeared to be the end of the issue. Alexander Spotswood, former lieutenant governor of Virginia, already had cautioned against too great a reliance on the provincials. It was essential, he felt, to have a substantial body of regulars present with colonial troops in any West Indian operation in order to "sustain and support such a loose force, and to serve upon all occasions where Order and Discipline is chiefly required and even . . . to oblige those Voluntiers to submit to Rule and Command."[22] Spotswood's view was in perfect accord with the opinion prevalent among British officials, including the officers of the professional armed forces, who considered provincial troops slackly disciplined and unreliable.

At the outset, command of the American contingent for the operation in the Caribbean was given by the Crown to Spotswood. When Spotswood died unexpectedly before the contingent was actually raised, the command passed to the lieutenant governor of Virginia, William Gooch, a conscientious and energetic administrator who, as a young man, had served under Marlborough. Eleven colonies, from New England to North Carolina, were to supply the troops, each colony raising a number of companies to be combined into a very large regiment totaling, it was hoped, something over three thousand men.

In the spring of 1740, while Oglethorpe was busy preparing for his attempt against St. Augustine, the Crown sent to the colonies a regular officer, Colonel William Blakeney, to assist in raising, organizing, and preparing Gooch's regiment. Blakeney carried with him royal instructions for the various provincial governors involved, instructions that reveal much about the ministry's intentions. All staff and field officers of the regiment were to be appointed by the Crown, company officers by the respective governors, with the regular army providing an experienced lieutenant and a sergeant for each of the companies as a means of elevating the level of training and discipline. For the governor's use, Blakeney was able to supply a limited number of blank commissions, presumably carefully differentiated from regular commissions so that the recipients, although clearly being made subject to the authority of the British high command, would not subsequently be eligible to retire upon half pay.[23]

The king agreed to furnish Gooch's American Foot, as the regiment came to be known, with uniforms, tents, weapons, and ammunition. In addition, "the Troops to be raised in pursuance of these Our Instructions, as well Officers, as Soldiers, shall enter into Our Pay, and enjoy the same Rank and Pay with the rest of Our British Troops, so long as they shall continue in Our Service." Once arrived at Jamaica, "they shall be provided for in every other respect as Our British Troops."[24] These were generous terms, deliberately made so in hope of arousing a willing response on the part of colonial legislatures, which were being asked to appropriate funds for subsisting the troops until they joined the main British forces and transporting them from their respective colonies to the Caribbean rendezvous. That the ministry entertained some doubt as to the assemblies' willingness to make even that minimal provision of funds is shown by the drafting of secret instructions to the governors, authorizing any one of them with a balky assembly to draw upon credit to be provided by the commissioners of the navy. Finally, too, Americans who did enlist in any of the companies were promised that when the operation was concluded they would be free to return home, with transportation provided at royal expense.[25]

As in the case of St. Augustine, recruiting thrived mainly on the glittering prospect of plunder. Commanders would get the most, of course, but every man involved down to the lowliest recruit expected a share, according to rank, as was customary in the armed forces at that time, and as the ministry had promised.[26] With this in view, numerous militia officers in the various colonies each set about trying to enlist enough men to form a company. The great majority of potential recruits preferred to serve only under an officer whom they knew, at least by reputation, and few if any who enlisted for the expedition thought they were making any commitment to the British army as such. Certainly all took very seriously the king's official promise to return them home at the end of the venture. In general, the recruiting seems to have gone remarkably well, even in New England, which during Queen Anne's War some thirty-eight years earlier had sent soldiers to the Caribbean with disillusioning results.[27] Blakeney reported from New York "a strong Disposition in the People of these Provinces to engage in the Expedition." Lieutenant Governor Clarke quickly identified the reason—"the expectation of growing rich by the Booty, and by gifts of lands and houses."[28] An observant woman in the same colony remarked that "our City is Very Lively with all these Officeiers and beating Up for Soldiers," but added the prophetic warning that if the recruits should be disappointed in their expectations, the British would not again find the Americans "soe Readily Disposed to fallow the beat of a drum."[29] Blakeney, who was learning fast, agreed. "From the highest to the lowest," he observed, "the Inhabitants of these Provinces seem to set a great Value on themselves, and think a Regard is due to them, especially in the Assistance they are able to give the Mother Country on such Occasions; and, as they are a growing Power, should they be disappointed in what is promised them and which they expect, future Occasions of the like Nature may suffer for it."³⁰ In sum, it was considered important that the provincial troops not undergo any systematic or serious mistreatment while serving with the British.

There is little evidence to suggest that the infusion of British regular lieutenants and sergeants caused any great difficulty, and every reason to believe that it actually did help the raw American troops develop an appearance that might be described as military. Benjamin Franklin reported in August, through the pages of his *Pennsylvania Gazette*, that four of his colony's companies, "by the Care and Diligence of the British Lieutenants wherewith they are furnished, have made considerable Progress in the new Exercise."³¹ This is not to say that the British had no difficulty with recruiting in Quaker Pennsylvania, a colony with an unequalled record of noncooperation in military ventures. To the usual reluctance of the pacifists was added a grievance that undoubtedly was experienced to some extent in all the colonies—the enlisting of indentured servants. Many a bored or lazy or abused or moonstruck male servant, eager to become both free and rich, took the opportunity to escape his legal obligation by sauntering up to the recruiting table and taking the king's shilling. Masters, thus deprived of needed labor for which they had already contracted and paid, were furious, and appealed to the assembly for rectification, preferably the forced release and return of the servants. This situation, in Pennsylvania, provided the Quaker-dominated assembly with a justification for withholding needed funds from the proprietary governor until he had dealt properly with the complaint. The assembly demanded the return of all enlisted servants, which the governor refused, but he did manage to effect the release of some, and advised any master who still felt aggrieved to initiate legal action against the enlisting officer. This aggravating controversy did not prevent Pennsylvania from eventually contributing eight companies to Gooch's American Foot, but it had the effect of engendering some sense of dissatisfaction in nearly everyone affected—governor, assemblymen, recruiting officers, masters, and even the servants. British regular officers may have had previous experience with the master-servant problem when recruiting in England; what was startlingly new to them in America was the aggressive stance of an elected provincial assembly in opposition to an appointed governor and officers bearing the king's commission.³²

In many respects Gooch's American Foot was an unusual regiment. Much larger than the normal British regiment, it was subdivided for administrative purposes into four battalions. The thirty-six companies came from eleven different colonies. Each company clung to its own provincial identity, with the common soldiers exclusively loyal to their own provincial officers, most of whom were from the large middle class, ambitious men on the make. Marching in the ranks were men and boys of diverse backgrounds, the great majority ordinary colonists together with some Indians and probably a few blacks. Some, undoubtedly, were from the outermost fringes of American colonial society, and not all volunteers. A modern study of the personnel in two of the Massachusetts companies has revealed that only 17 percent were immigrants. Less than 20 percent described themselves as laborers; nearly a third claimed to be artisans; the remainder, close to one-half of the total, were farmers. In all likelihood, a large proportion had been impelled to enlist by some form of economic hardship of the kind often experienced by the young in colonial society, including shortage of land and temporary unemployment with consequent debts.[33] During the fall of 1740, when reasonably ready, the various companies were embarked in chartered merchant vessels at various colonial seaports and carried to Jamaica where, at Kingston and Port Royal, the great British expeditionary force was assembling.

So then, off they went, some 3,500 of them altogether, hot for adventure and, especially, plunder. Arriving at Jamaica, a lush tropical island such as few of them had ever seen before, what did they find? A British military bureaucracy almost totally unprepared to receive them and integrate them smoothly into the team. Lacking tents (contrary to promise), the newcomers were forced to remain quartered on board the crowded transports, subsisting on a meager and monotonous diet scraped from rapidly dwindling shipboard stores, without the fresh vegetables needed for the maintenance of health. Their officers, venturing ashore in hope of purchasing fresh provisions for the men with whatever small supplies of cash they might have in pocket, were confronted in the markets with avaricious Jamaican hucksters demanding grossly inflated prices. One officer, obviously with something other than vegetables in mind, complained that "You cannot open your Mouth at an Ordinary under 4 or 5s. Sterling a Man."[34] Whenever groups of the Americans were given shore leave they rambled, gawking, through unfamiliar streets, and almost invariably found their way to the taverns, where they proceeded to take on a full cargo. Hearing of this, and rightly concerned for both health and discipline, Admiral Vernon sent a reproving letter to Gooch, recommending that the transports be shifted to an anchorage more remote from the center of vice.[35]

Inevitably, under such conditions, the Americans began to sicken, and some died. A Massachusetts company that had made a smart appearance before leaving Boston was now "quite dishearted." According to another account, the men "lay dying like rotten Sheep," a simile that spoke vividly to farmers back home. By early January, one-tenth of the provincials were on the sick list. Gooch reported that nine of his officers and approximately a hundred of his men had been buried in Jamaica since their arrival. Grumbling against those deemed responsible—the British high command—became epidemic.[36]

Much of the immediate deprivation suffered by Gooch's men might have been remedied if the American regiment had had ready access to adequate funds. As it was, however, not only was it difficult to purchase needed supplies, but there was little or no money available for the men's wages. Adequate funding clearly was the responsibility of the British government. Who, then, was to blame for the shortage? There is no simple answer. We do know that two Jamaican merchants, Edward Manning and John Meriwether, had been designated by the ministry in London to serve as agents for transmitting funds to the army. When Blakeney, who had arrived with Gooch's American Foot, applied to these agents for funds with which to pay the provincial soldiers, they coolly replied that as yet they had not received from London any authorization concerning the Americans, and accordingly declined. Manning did manage to come up with £2,000 in borrowed money, an amount grossly inadequate for such a large regiment. Later John Colebrooke, a British disbursing officer who investigated the problem, made serious allegations of unscrupulous financial manipulation and profiteering against Manning, Meriwether, and others, but the charges were not proved. All that the frustrated American officers knew was that somehow they were unable to collect from any responsible official the money so desperately needed.[37]

Turning to the other side of the coin, we quickly discover that the British professional officers were somewhat less than favorably impressed with the general appearance of the American troops. After having inspected one of Gooch's battalions, General Wentworth reported that "there are amongst 'em very good men, and some exceeding bad; they are very little acquainted with discipline, but if they prove, what they appear to be, men accustomed to fatigue, I am in hopes that they may do good service."[38] Wentworth's comment, read carefully, reveals the high command's intention to use the Americans not as combat troops but as laborers, carrying burdens, clearing ground, and building earthworks for the regular regiments assaulting Spanish positions. Captain Charles Knowles of the navy was even less complimentary. "From the first review of the American Troops they were despised," he wrote, adding that the colonial officers were of contemptibly low origin, having been "Blacksmiths, Taylors, Barbers, Shoemakers, and all the Bandity them Colonies affords: insomuch that the other part of the Army [the regulars] held them at Scorn."[39] Gooch was not even accorded the courtesy of membership in the council of war, despite the size of his command.[40] In short, before the Americans had been in Jamaica two months, they were soured against the British, and the British against them, with a joint military operation yet to be launched.

And that wasn't all. The fleet that had come out from England was not fully manned, and sickness among the sailors after arrival had further diminished the crews. Facing such a problem, the high command knew the remedy, as specified in standard royal instructions that had remained virtually unchanged over many years. Wentworth was authorized "to order, That the Soldiers, under your Command, shall mann the Ships, where there shall be Occasion for Them."[41] Vernon certainly needed more deckhands, and who more available than the unsoldierly Americans! Accordingly, the necessary orders were given, and soon groups of dismayed and angry provincial soldiers, who had enlisted to serve under certain colonial officers, were being separated from their units, conveyed under guard, and dumped on board various ships of war for an introduction to life in the Royal Navy. If Gooch and his officers protested, they did so in vain. It is certain that a very large proportion of Gooch's American Foot was forced to serve on board ships of the Royal Navy at one time or another, often performing heavy labor under the supervision of hard-bitten officers accustomed to driving their subordinates like slaves. Surviving records indicate that on 31 March 1741 as many as 2,479 enlisted men of the American regiment actually were serving in the fleet. This kind of duty certainly was not what the Americans had anticipated when they enlisted to fight for king and country, glory and plunder![42]

In the meantime, the high command had agreed upon Cartagena, a heavily fortified seaport on the coast of the Spanish main. Generally believed to be a storehouse of wealth, its capture would not only undermine Spanish prestige throughout the Western Hemisphere, but also greatly enrich the victors. When all was in readiness, the great British armada, including the now-scattered American contingent, took its departure from Jamaica and set course for Cartagena 550 miles to the south, arriving nearby on 4 March 1741. From this time, under the joint leadership of Vernon and Wentworth, whose relationship already was deteriorating, the campaign proceeded with remarkable ineptitude, ponderosity, and pervasive futility. After considerable delay the regulars were landed, and some of the American troops together with numbers of black laborers were set to work ashore clearing ground for a camp. The site was flanked by two Spanish batteries that could have proved extremely troublesome, so an assault party consisting of about three hundred Virginians and some sailors was sent ashore to deal with the menace, and did so with commendable thoroughness. It was also reported that while the leaders of the army were discussing the best way of capturing a certain convent perched atop a strategically located hill, a party of roving Americans, no doubt in search of plunder, made their way up to the convent and soon sent down word that they were in control of the place! Such exploits may have enhanced the Americans' reputation temporarily, but the glory was not to last.[43]

On 30 March the council of war decided that Wentworth should be reinforced by landing "all such of the American Forces, as he should judge proper to be trusted on shore." The reservation is significant, especially as the general himself remarked that from Gooch's American Foot "much can not be expected." Nevertheless, about a week later (which was fairly good time for this misnamed "expedition") about 1,000 of the Americans were landed in time to participate in the attack on a Spanish strongpoint blocking the approach to Cartagena.[44] As expected, the Americans were given an auxiliary assignment as burden bearers. One group lugged bags of grenades. Another carried scaling ladders, and yet others bore wool packs, shovels, and mattocks. The approach was made in darkness, adding to the inevitable confusion. For a number of reasons the attack failed miserably; often mentioned later by the professionals as a contributing factor was the unsoldierlike performance of Gooch's men. When Wentworth described to the ministry the unsuccessful attempt he did not forget to mention "the wretched Behaviour of the Americans, who had the Charge of the Scaling Ladders, working Tools, etc., which they threw down on the first Approach of Danger, and thereby occasioned the loss of the greatest part of 'em." A junior officer who had participated in the attack also condemned "the Americans in whom nobody had any Confidence," and who "run away as was expected." "It must be allowed," he said in exculpation of his own countrymen, "that hardly anybody, except the Americans who were without Arms, ever shewed the least Disposition to turn their Backs till they had Orders for it."[45]

Thereafter, the problems of camp and ship were more destructive than the enemy. Water was in short supply, and diminishing. Epidemic disease intensified. Graves proliferated. At last the British high command, beset by internal controversy, recognized the futility of further effort and ordered the regiments to abandon their miserable camp and reembark, which was accomplished on the night of 16–17 April. Among the last to be taken off was a rear guard of whom the majority were Americans.[46]

On board the ships during the ensuing days when Vernon lingered off the coast, and later during the return voyage to Jamaica, conditions were appalling. Wrote one Briton to his brother in faraway London, "We are in a Mesirable condition for want of fresh provision, our meet is salt as brine, our bread as it lays on the table swarms with Maggots, and the water here fluxes us all. . . . We are well one day and Dead the next."[47] By the time the fleet had dropped anchor again in the familiar waters off Port Royal, Wentworth's army, including the bedraggled American regiment, was greatly reduced, as were the crews of Vernon's ships. It was reported in the *Boston Weekly News-Letter* for 30 July–6 August 1741 that in the Massachusetts company commanded by Captain John Winslow twenty-three of the men had perished before the return from Cartagena and twenty-five plus an ensign since, a casualty rate of approximately 50 percent.

Then a field-grade vacancy occurred in the American regiment. Instead of promoting one of the meritorious provincial captains, Wentworth gave the promotion to a non-American officer with less seniority. "Whatever Reasons the General may have for not Promoting any of the American Captains I am a stranger to them," Gooch commented in a letter to the secretary of state. "I could not prevail with him to Advance any of my Own."[48]

In the meantime, the provincial soldiers considered the operation over, and were ready to head for home. So, what about that promised return? Once again the admiral began drafting soldiers from Gooch's regiment to help fill out the depleted crews of the fleet. Such duty, the reluctant Americans realized, would lessen the possibility of an early discharge and might even involve a long voyage to another part of the world, but when Vernon demanded men and Wentworth acquiesced there was no practical way for Gooch or any other officer to block the transfer. By the end of May, according to one report, most of the chartered vessels that had brought Gooch's companies from the various North American colonies had been granted clearance for the return voyage but, unhappily, the majority of the surviving provincial troops who yearned to sail with them were dispersed among the ships of the Royal Navy.[49]

Thirteen American soldiers in particular had reason to feel victimized. They were enjoying themselves ashore, not in proper uniform, when one of Vernon's press gangs pounced upon them and, despite vociferous protests, hauled them away for naval service. Later, when word of what had happened reached the officers of the American regiment, an attempt was made to have those men returned to their proper units, without success. In this case, even Wentworth was helpless. Eventually, the affair was brought to the attention of the ministry, which caused the following order, dated 16 October 1741, to be transmitted to Vernon:

> It appearing by a Return (transmitted by Major General Wentworth, and laid before The Lords Justices) of the State of the American Regiment, under his Command, That several private Soldiers belonging to the said Regiment have been impressed by Mistake on board His Majesty's Ships of War, and detained, notwithstanding Application had been made for Their being restored to their proper Officers; And Their excellencies considering, That, should These Men be treated contrary to the Promises made them at Their inlisting as Soldiers, It might discourage His Majesty's Subjects, in America, from entring into His Service, They have commanded me to signify to You Their Directions, That You should order the Soldiers abovementioned, and all others of the American Regiment, that may have been impressed on board any of His Majesty's Ships, to be immediately discharged and sent back to Their Regiment.[50]

This case underlines the fact that, unlike the thirteen soldiers out of uniform, American troops routinely transferred to duty in Vernon's ships were not impressed into the Royal Navy. Rather, they were given a temporary assignment involving naval duty, while officially remaining members of Gooch's American Foot. In practice, however, the distinction meant little, so long as they were retained on board ship.

On 12 December Wentworth informed the ministry that he actually did not know how many of the Americans were on temporary naval duty, but was painfully aware that most of them were in poor physical condition and that many had succumbed to disease. He feared that the continuing effort to gain more recruits in the North American colonies would be undermined by "the reports of the ill usage their people have received which must have been on board the Fleet, and would have been prevented had it been in my power." A few days later the general, smarting under rebuffs from Vernon, reverted to the same topic. The Americans who served in the army, he said, "have in all respects been treated in the same manner with the other troops, nor have they been employed on any service not consistent with the conditions on which they were inlisted; but it has not been in my power to prevent some of them being sent to Europe [with the navy]; tho' Brigadier Blakeny waited upon Mr. Vernon with his Majesty's instructions to the Northern Colonys, but without effect."[51]

There is strong evidence to suggest that the American troops serving in ships of the fleet were subjected to harsh treatment that extended, in some cases, to systematic abuse. Why this was so is not clear, but one may surmise that naval personnel with varying degrees of authority had remarkably low tolerance for Americans, especially those so audacious as to assert their rights. Notable cases of abuse are described in a memorial dated Kingston, 3 February 1742, addressed to Wentworth by the field officers of Gooch's regiment.[52] According to this document, drafts of American soldiers had been distributed among various ships, often unaccompanied by their own officers, which made it impossible for company commanders to submit accurate returns of their men. When HMS *Dunkirk*, for example, departed for England she had on board fifty-two Americans from sixteen different companies. Wentworth himself verified this complaint when he asserted that Vernon did not hesitate to move soldiers from ship to ship, as needed, "by which means, there are frequently, men without officers and officers without men."[53]

The American officers believed that their men were being put to the most gruelling tasks. "Many," they said, "have been obliged to Submit to the most slavish part of heaving down men of War in order to be cleaned, a work which does not properly belong to them, besides doing the duty of their own Ships at the Pump." Indeed, some had even been "removd from Ship to Ship to pump."[54] Under these circumstances, there had been cases of men denied a regular place to sleep.

In those days, sailors commonly were subject to occasional blows from impatient or brutal superiors, and from this, too, the provincial troops were not exempt. Protests by any American officers present were of little avail. Captain Park Pepper of the first battalion testified that "he was several months on board the Rippon man of War on duty, with a Detachment of Sixty five Americans, that he had frequent Complaints made by his men of the ill treatment they received on board, but was never able to relieve them, tho' frequently represented to the Officers of the Ship." In particular he cited "the cruel usage Samuel Wilson of Capt Bushrods Company received from one Slaughter a midshipman . . . by beating and kicking said Wilson in so barbarous a manner 'twas supposed he would have died." Wilson subsequently did expire. One of Pepper's own men was "kept working at the Chain pump five Glasses Successively on board the Prince Frederick, tho' it was customary to relieve every hour, and in the running of the five glasses was so unmercifully beaten by Lieut Hughes of said Ship . . . whilst naked at his Work that he was cutt into the side the mark whereof is very visible." Some of the American soldiers said that they "had rather die than undergo such usage any longer."[55]

Wentworth, to his credit, took the memorial seriously and sent it along to the ministry with his own comment, charging that navy commanders refused to let army officers publish the Articles of War to the soldiers, or even discipline their own men. "Indeed," he wrote, "the Gentlemen of the Sea, especially the Warrant Officers, do not spare to exert their Authority."[56] Even the dead were sometimes victimized. Vernon would not release prize money credited to the deceased soldiers until the heirs had gone through a legal process that might cost more than the amount due. And the abuses went on, month after month, while the list of American dead, at sea and on shore, grew ever longer. Survivors wondered impatiently when, if ever, the British high command would honor the promise under which they had enlisted.[57]

At long last, on 5 August 1742, approximately sixteen months after the futile attempt against Cartagena, the ministry ordered Vernon and Wentworth to dissolve the expedition, send home Gooch's American Foot, and return to England.[58] It is not difficult to detect in these orders a tone of serious misgiving about the way the Americans had been treated by the professional forces, with especial regard to its potentially harmful effect whenever Britain again found need to call for colonial recruits. That this apprehension was quite realistic was clearly indicated almost four years later when Britain was attempting to raise an American expedition against Canada. The evidence is found in a letter of 13 June 1746 written to the Duke of Newcastle by one of the disgruntled survivors of the Cartagena expedition, none other than Lieutenant Governor William Gooch. In his letter to the eminent secretary of state, Gooch expressed his belief that it might not be easy to persuade American colonists to enlist for the new venture, "especially, if, as I am told, we are not to expect any of those men, who were on the last Expedition, they not having digested the hard Usage of being Broke in Jamaica, and sent Home without a farthing in their Pockets."[59]

Gooch's American Foot was officially disbanded on 24 October 1742, leaving considerable numbers of its men in hospital at Jamaica, or in garrison elsewhere, or scattered among the fleet. How many of the approximately 3,500 who originally went down to the Caribbean actually survived to reach home is difficult to determine, but the number cannot have been more than a pathetic fraction of the total.[60]

Those who did return seem to have slipped quietly back into the populace of the eleven colonies from which they had come, having brought home no glory and no riches—only a pocketful of bitter memories. They had not been very effective soldiers—or very good sailors, for that matter. Their motives for joining the expedition had been less patriotic than mercenary. So they came back badly disillusioned, to spread among their people their vivid recollections of British callousness, interservice quarreling, confusion and inefficiency at all levels, and a general atmosphere of incompetence and failure. At the same time, British professional military and naval personnel who had served with the Americans in the Caribbean were bringing back to their colleagues in both services, and their countrymen in general, further support for the hardening impression in England that provincial troops were stubbornly averse to discipline and cowardly in battle. Britons and colonists alike, it seems, were beginning to sense more clearly than ever the emergence of significant differences between the two peoples, in their attitudes, their responses, their perceptions of themselves and others. So it was that the great Cartagena expedition of 1740–42 contributed heavily not only to the mutually antagonistic views of British regulars and American provincials, which had been developing for many years, but also to the emergence of a self-conscious Americanism with almost incalculable import for the future of the British Empire.[61]

From 1743 to the end of the war in 1748, the garrison town of Frederica, Georgia, home base of Oglethorpe's Forty-second Foot, provides an interesting as well as instructive case of civil-military relations. Oglethorpe himself had returned to England, leaving the regiment under the command of a grenadier captain, William Horton, a professional officer whose expansive concept of the army's jurisdiction in the community invited serious conflict with civil authority. If the bailiff and the recorder of Frederica were not exaggerating, Horton and a number of the other officers of the regiment took advantage of their position to exercise domineering authority over civilians, thwarting the normal process of civil government, harassing local townsfolk including some officials, and abusing the women of the community. Contributing heavily to the prevailing animosity was a long, divisive legal quarrel over fees owed for the salvage of a French ship.[62]

Horton, apparently, considered himself the chief magistrate of Frederica *ex officio*, for he insisted on retaining custody of the town seal. Recorder John Terry complained to the Trustees of Georgia that Horton "appropriates to him self here the Authority of a Prince (Nay Even that of Lewis the 14th) Absolutely Commanding and threatning the Magistrate and Recorder As his vassalls, or Laquais and Reprimands our Counstables for Daring to Execute the Duty of their Office, . . . he has Deprived this place of a Civill Goverment."[63] According to Bailiff John Calwell, "Horton . . . takes upon him to order and command both Civill and Military Insulting Magestrate and Recorder. not suffering us to Act or proceed even against housbrakers or Fellons but ordering all Crymes to be tryed by Reigmentell Court Martials . . . the Freeholders and strangers that come here not suffered to go about their buisiness without procuring passes from the military."[64] These detailed complaints from enraged and probably biased civil officials do provide strong evidence that the military in Frederica was indeed overstepping the bounds. Horton, presumably, was acting on the assumption that all of Frederica was a military post under his command, but if that were indeed the case, why had Oglethorpe earlier allowed the civil administration to be established? Whatever the answer, the Anglo-American tension at Frederica certainly was extreme.

Not unexpectedly, we find in the midst of this same roiling quarrel substantial evidence of the more commonplace kinds of friction between civilians and military personnel, familiar to most garrison towns of that era. Officers and soldiers were accused of insulting, beating, robbing, and raping some of the inhabitants. The victims, it was charged, often found it impossible to obtain redress or justice because of military intervention. Recorder Terry summed up the situation in a terse comment: "There is No Justice in Frederica—Nor Never will be so Long as Magistrates will have places or offices In or Under the Military."[65] After Lieutenant Colonel Alexander Heron assumed acting command of the Forty-second Foot in 1747, the tension continued, with further evidence that the military power in Frederica was taking maximum advantage of its dominant position in a small community far out on a remote frontier.[66] In Georgia as well as Virginia, New York, and New England, by the middle of the eighteenth century a man wearing the red coat was seldom viewed as a friend.

Anglo-American friction in the southern colonies and the Caribbean during the 1740s is especially significant, for it reveals that northern colonists were not the only Americans proving troublesome for British administrators and military commanders. At St. Augustine in 1740, Carolinians and Georgians feuded with each other, while both groups found cause to resent the attitude and behavior of the Royal Navy. In the Caribbean in 1740–42, provincial troops from many colonies shared hardships in a botched campaign that made virtually everyone look bad. If New Englanders groused and shirked, so did Pennsylvanians and Virginians, and the British regulars damned them all. Possibly most important is the fact that the men of the various colonial contingents were sometimes intermingled, with ample opportunity to become acquainted, discuss their condition, and share their bitterness. Nor were the disease-ravaged soldiers and sailors the only Americans to suffer during those difficult times. Wartime controls imposed by royal governors and commanders affected nearly all aspects of colonial trade and shipping, oftentimes to the detriment of the very people who normally might have been most supportive of imperial authority. More than ever, there was temptation for southerners as well as other Americans to question British benevolence, fairness, and probity. Undoubtedly, most Americans wanted to be loyal subjects, but the enormous strains of war were having their inevitable effect from one end of the colonies to the other.

CHAPTER 4.

LOUISBOURG, 1745–1746

HE grim lesson of the Caribbean was not soon forgotten by the people of the North American colonies, including those who inhabited New England. If anything, New Englanders more than most others had developed a well-grounded aversion to any close relationship with the British regular forces, an aversion based upon long, unhappy experience. What these colonists were coming to understand was that a professional army or navy was both a privileged and a closed society, utterly dependent upon and loyal to the national monarchy and government, and almost instinctively contemptuous of the disorderly civilian community over which it was expected to keep a watchful eye. In time of war, when nonprofessional military units such as hastily raised provincial regiments were joined with the regulars, the game always had to be played by the latter's rules, with the regulars maintaining dominant control. Whatever the circumstances, the nonprofessionals were required to conform; yet try as they would, they could never quite earn the genuine respect of the regulars.[1]

When in 1744 France entered the War of the 1740s as an ally of Spain, New Englanders once more found danger at their own threshold. French and Indian raiding parties again threatened the exposed northern frontier, while French privateers prowled off the coast looking for New England fishing vessels and merchantmen. The lair for such privateers, because Acadia no longer was available, was the excellent harbor at Louisbourg on Cape Breton Island, 600 miles northeast of Boston. Louisbourg had long been a base for French fishermen working on the Grand Banks. Gradually, too, an enterprising community of artisans, merchants, and traders had grown up at Louisbourg, turning the place into a small but thriving seaport where English as well as French vessels came to exchange wares. The French government, moreover, following the loss of Acadia to the British in 1713, had selected this same excellent harbor as the site for a new naval base to serve any French warships guarding the broad entrance to the St. Lawrence River. So it was that the

French had proceeded at great expense to fortify Louisbourg, constructing around the perimeter of the mercantile town a massive stone-faced rampart and dry moat after the style of Vauban, together with outlying fortifications, all carefully designed to render Louisbourg as nearly impregnable as possible. A garrison of regular troops backed by local militia stood ready to repel any intruder. New England's foremost leaders, in this time of renewed warfare, considered heavily fortified Louisbourg a distinct menace.

The idea of trying to capture Louisbourg was originated by some English captives who, as prisoners inside Louisbourg, had become aware of certain material weaknesses of the fortification itself and disaffection among the rather small garrison. After being released, these men carried the idea to Massachusetts, where it germinated in high places, eventually gaining the support of Governor William Shirley and a majority of the general court. It became a home-grown, thriving, New England project for 1745, with the promise of great material gain in the form of plunder, land, and trade. As no redcoats were to be involved in the venture, many ambitious New Englanders were glad to participate.

So it was that on 24 March a fleet of fifty-two New England vessels carrying about 2,800 Massachusetts volunteer troops set sail at Nantasket Road for Canso and ultimately Louisbourg. Other units coming from New Hampshire and Connecticut would raise this all–New England army to a strength of well over 3,000 men, all under the command of a well-respected entrepreneur and politician from Maine, William Pepperrell. Although the colonial leaders had planned this audacious operation without benefit of professional advice from London, they had been prudent enough to solicit some aid from the Royal Navy, which for obvious reasons was much needed. At first their appeal had been rebuffed by the senior naval commander in the West Indies, on the grounds that he lacked enabling orders from home. Later, however, after the expedition had sailed, Governor Shirley received the welcome news that a squadron under Commodore Peter Warren was en route from the Caribbean to participate in the operation, which certainly increased the chance for success.

Technically, Warren's royal commission gave him the right to supreme command, for Pepperrell's commission as general of the army was derived only from Governor Shirley. Recognizing the delicacy of the situation, the Massachusetts royal governor wrote urging Pepperrell to avoid any quarrel with his naval counterpart. Warren, too, was wise enough to tread lightly, and throughout the long, difficult siege at Louisbourg,

Pepperrell's New Englanders understood that he was in full charge of all activity on land, while Warren commanded the blockading ships at sea, including the armed vessels contributed by several of the New England colonies. Any attempt by the commodore to exercise direct command over the provincial army would have aroused fury among the troops and deep resentment in Massachusetts. Tensions did develop between Pepperrell and Warren as the latter became increasingly impatient with the slow progress being made by the army, but always the anger of both men was kept within manageable bounds, and in the end they sealed their professional relationship with harmony and mutual respect.[2]

Our principal concern here is not with any high-level tension, important as that may have been, but rather with the relationships between the inferior officers and enlisted men of the New England army on the one hand and the inferior officers and seamen of the Royal Navy on the other. Here is where old animosities might have been resurrected in a particularly significant way under circumstances in which the Americans had some advantage.[3]

British officers who had opportunity to observe the New England troops on an untidy battleground were not favorably impressed. Captain James McDonald of the royal marines made himself quite unwelcome in the American camp by declaring, as one vexed provincial soldier recalled, that "our encampment was not regular, or that the soldiers did not march as hansome as old regular troops, their toes were not turned enough out," and so forth. This kind of gratuitous criticism during a high-risk operation in which the amateur troops were feeling considerable pride in their gains was, to say the least, annoying. Pepperrell himself was not immune, later remarking with some degree of petulance that he thought the American army had "encampt as regular as the hills and valeys would admit of."[4]

On at least one occasion sailors from the fleet came ashore while the siege was in progress, bearing arms in case of any encounter with the enemy. Arriving within the American lines, they found that the New Englanders had ample supplies of rum that they were willing to share—for a price. Business may have been brisk, but inevitably trouble did develop, as anyone could have predicted. Surviving records fail to provide a clear picture, but apparently at some time during the sailors' visit, some of the Yankees, perhaps by trickery, managed to appropriate the jack-tars' weapons, which were king's arms. As a consequence, the rueful and rum-full seamen returned on board bare-handed and shamefaced to confront the wrath of their officers. The commodore suspected, no doubt correctly, that if missing arms were to be found anywhere it would be in the American camp. Then came a further surprise. Some New England weapons were discovered on board the British men-of-war, which suggests that the sailors were able to take as well as give. Warren dutifully returned the stolen property with an explanatory note to Pepperrell saying, "I send you some arms belonging to your troops that my rascals brought of[f], and have lost a great many of ours."[5] The records do not reveal whether any of the navy's missing weapons were ever recovered; chances are that they were well concealed, eventually sold for profit, and perhaps taken to Boston.

Victory at Louisbourg was envisioned as the result of a massive combined assault by land and sea. A day or two before that decisive attack was to occur, Pepperrell sent out to the ships about 600 of his men to assist the navy in its part of the assault, a purely temporary assignment for the soldiers involved, but one that surely resurrected unpleasant tales of the Caribbean in 1741 and naval impressment in general. At about the same time, Warren made a visit to the army ashore, addressed the troops drawn up for the occasion, told them his ships were going to force the harbor, and urged them to fight their way into the fortress on the land side. The New Englanders, possibly excited by the commodore's oratory, responded with three cheers, which proved to be very nearly the last true echo of goodwill he was to hear from that source. As it happened, the grand assault by land and by sea never was made, for only a short time before it was to commence the French capitulated.[6]

Preceding the actual surrender were certain negotiations the full details of which may never be known. It does appear that Warren sent a personal emissary into Louisbourg with advice to the French that they had better surrender to the Royal Navy rather than the army in order to avoid the uncontrolled pillaging that would be the consequence, it was said, of a surrender to the New Englanders.[7] If such a suggestion was indeed officially made by the navy it was premature, and when the French did come to the point of terms they addressed themselves to both commanders. Then began a strange race between the army and the navy to be first into the fortress. Pepperrell proposed to the French commander a time when the first units of the army would enter, but before that time arrived, Warren, it seems, had himself rowed to the town, where he conferred with the French commander and learned of Pepperrell's proposal. Thereupon the commodore addressed to his New England colleague yet another letter, somewhat more frigid in tone. "It is not regular, you will please to observe," lectured Warren, "to do it till the articles are ratified on both sides, which I will hasten to get done." He continued, "*I am sorry to find by your letter a kind of jealousy, which I thought you would never conceive of me* . . . ; and give me leave to tell you, I do not want at this time to acquire reputation, as I flatter myself mine has long before I came here been pretty well established." A French inhabitant of Louisbourg who was in a position to view these peculiar maneuvers on the part of the English and the Americans later remarked that "one could never have told that these troops belonged to the same nation and obeyed the same prince."[8] It hardly seems necessary to remind the reader that only thirty-one years later they did not.

So long as the siege continued, Anglo-American friction was kept to a moderate level, but once the articles of capitulation had been signed, the tensions began to increase. In fact, the months following the surrender, when Warren's ships rode at anchor in the littered harbor and Pepperrell's men garrisoned the battered town, constitute a most instructive period for the student of Anglo-American relations. During that time the officers and men of both services walked the streets of Louisbourg and doubtless sometimes found themselves sheltering under the same roofs. Inevitably there were interservice arguments as to whether the army or the navy contributed more to the victory, which must have afforded the rueful French inhabitants a modicum of amusement. Captain Philip Durell of the Royal Navy was quick to advance the claim of his own service. The French, he said, "delivered the Keys of the Town to Mr. *Warren*, agreeable to Articles specified in the Capitulation, saying, That if it had not been for the Ships, the Land Forces would never have been in Possession of the Place." Furthermore, according to this same officer, the governor of Louisbourg had "insisted that our Forces [the navy] should enter the Town, and not the *Americans*, whom they do not like." Another correspondent on board one of Warren's ships testified that Louisbourg "Surrendered to the Fleet Upon Condittions, and We took Poss[ess]ion of the town and all their fortifications." Just as vehemently the Americans insisted that the French had capitulated not out of fear of a naval attack but because of the immense destruction wrought by the army's artillery. Wrote one New Englander,

> There is No Harmony between the Marine officers and N E ones. I take it to be because one stands on what they have Done and the others on what they are[—]men with the Kings Commision. One of them Has been Pleased to tell the French Officers that He was the first man that went into the Grand Battrey which was absolutely

false for not one man was ashore from the ships till 4 days after. Another of them told them that He had Lay'd 17 Nights in the trenches which was as false for he never was there but twice and both times staid not above ½ an hour in the Whole.[9]

The question of which commander formally received the keys of Louisbourg became a matter of some concern in Boston, as did the even more trivial but nonetheless sensitive question of why Warren's name preceded Pepperrell's in the articles of capitulation.

Bickering such as this, not at all good-natured in tone, must have gone on for days in the damp and fog-shrouded town whenever New Englanders and navy men found themselves together. At the very least this was annoying, but there was a much more serious aspect. New England officers, and colonial leaders back in Massachusetts as well, suspected an even deeper thrust on the part of the navy, a thrust that might well deprive Pepperrell, his army, and all New England of the ultimate advantages they believed they merited by their victory. Shortly after the capitulation Warren had dispatched a personal emissary to carry the good news to the British ministry. Pepperrell apparently had not thought it necessary to match this move with an emissary of his own, and this gave rise to fears that the navy's version, spoken first, would give all the glory to Warren and the navy, with the probable result that the royal gratitude would fall in that direction.[10]

On paper, at least, both Pepperrell and Warren tried to be generous with praise. The latter's communication to the Duke of Newcastle, dated the day after the surrender, included the interesting observation that the American colonists "have the highest notions of the Rights, and Libertys, of Englishmen, and indeed are almost Levellers, they must know when, where, how, and what service they are going upon, and be Treated in a manner that few Military Bred Gentlemen would condecend to, but if they do the work in which they are Engaged, every other Ceremony should in my opinion be winked at." A day later Pepperrell informed the duke that "Nothing could have contributed more to the Success of his Majesty's Arms, than the Command of the Squadron being given to a Gentleman of Commodore Warren's distinguished Character: he is of such a Disposition as makes him greatly beloved by the people in New England, and in the Colonies, in General."[11] So much for polite persiflage.

The army's extreme sensitivity regarding all special claims by the navy was to no small degree owing to one of the terms included in the articles of capitulation. All portable private property belonging to the French inhabitants was to remain in their possession and, insofar as practicable, go with them when they were evacuated. As Pepperrell must have known of this provision and accepted it, he should not have been surprised at his soldiers' reaction. During the siege the New England troops had found opportunity to scrape the environs fairly clean without gaining any great wealth, and so they had looked forward all the more to getting their hands upon the French goods within Louisbourg itself. Now, after the surrender, they found this booty strictly denied them, with sentries stationed throughout the town to prevent unauthorized plundering. The New Englanders saw their dreams of personal gain rapidly dissolving, much as similar dreams had gone glimmering at Cartagena, and they were furious. When Pepperrell wrote to the Duke of Newcastle that his men had "generously acquiessed in the Loss of the Plunder they Expected from the Riches of the City," he was ignoring the truth in order to plaster over a very ugly situation. Closer to the mark was an anonymous diarist at Louisbourg who had heard "hot Talk about a mobbs Risin and they Say that they Did Rise So as to git what they wanted."[12] Some of the bitterly disappointed troops began stealing and concealing. Under these circumstances, legitimate gains proved slender indeed. The army did lay claim to a number of French craft found sunk in the harbor or stranded along its edges, and some vendable material was salvaged, but it made a poor show beside the lands, houses, and goods for which the soldiers had thirsted so avidly all during the siege. One Massachusetts soldier wrote in his journal what may be taken to represent the common experience: "Received part of plunder, 9 small tooth combs."[13]

All this was especially devastating to morale because of what the navy was managing to accomplish at the same time. Here let it be said that Commodore Warren was not the man to neglect his own fortune. While stationed in the West Indies prior to becoming involved in the Louisbourg operation, he had profited greatly by the system in which the proceeds from the sale of enemy prizes were distributed to all participating personnel, with a very large chunk reserved for the successful commander. At Louisbourg, after the capitulation, Warren saw to it that the French flag was left jauntily flying over the town. As a result, during the course of the summer several French merchantmen returning from the South Seas and the East Indies, richly laden, dropped in unaware and were handily seized by Warren's alert and eager men-of-war. It was a perfect trap. Warren stood to gain immensely, his subordinates in the naval service would get their share, but the troops ashore, whether offi-

cers or enlisted men, had no access to any part of the prize money. Wrote
Warren gleefully, "The Success which has attended mee in this Conquest
has been a great Addition to my fortune."[14] Stories of the navy's great
gain soon reached Boston, where they simply intensified the current un-
rest over the apparent slighting of the army. The *Boston Evening-Post* for
23 September 1745 carried a report that Warren had pulled in nearly
£500,000 sterling, adding gloomily that "what Share the poor Men in
the Garrison are to have of this mighty Treasure (which seemed all to
be intended for *them*, as a Reward for their signal Service) is not yet
certainly know[n]." The answer, of course, was none, and that really
rankled.

Toward the end of July the New Englanders' resentment approached
the boiling point. By that time the provincial troops had had more than
five weeks of contact with naval personnel in and around Louisbourg,
involving considerable guying back and forth, boasts and threats, envy
and contempt, and somewhere just below the surface, recollections of
Cartagena and impressment, all of which helped inflate the ugly mood.
On the warm and pleasant morning of 29 July the army, now including
some replacements that had arrived from New England since the surrender, was drawn up to be addressed by the general and the commodore.
Most armies that have had to endure difficult circumstances are acquainted with such addresses from on high, which may be called "incen-
tive raisers" or "morale boosters." If the dispirited New Englanders
cheered Warren at the end of his declaration, as they had done on a
previous occasion during the siege, it was because he took this opportunity to present them with three butts of wine, enough for every man to
enjoy a pint. That very same day HMS *Chester* and HMS *Mermaid*
proudly escorted into the harbor the crestfallen French merchantman
Heron, bulging with a valuable cargo. Sometime between the last speech
and the arrival of the *Heron*, or possibly even later in the day, some of
the New England troops got into a free-swinging brawl with some sailors of the Royal Navy. In all probability, the affray was intimately linked
with the two events just mentioned—the sudden availability of alcohol
and the arrival of the navy's latest prize.[15]

Easy to imagine is some heavy drinking by groups of New England
soldiers who were feeling very much victimized and therefore prone to
self-pity and helpless anger, their roistering about Louisbourg loaded
with emotional dynamite ready stacked and fused, their encountering
some seamen who doubtless pointed with high glee to their new prize
anchored under the guns of the Royal Navy and, without so much as

being asked, freely offered estimates of the vast bounty to be distributed among the men of the ships involved in her capture. There must have been a crescendo of shouting, then shoving, and finally blows. Other men of the army and navy, attracted by the uproar, came running, and the brawl intensified and spread. My description is imaginary, and I cannot be certain even of what triggered the trouble, but the account I have constructed seems highly plausible. We do not know how long it took the officers of the army and navy to restore peace among these infuriated brothers-in-arms. What is virtually certain is that New England fists had found a way to vent a vast accumulation of resentment against the attitude and the ways of Britain's professional armed forces.[16]

Pepperrell's men were fed up and eager to go home. Weary from a hard campaign, sick of their foul quarters and disintegrating apparel, disappointed in the material gains of victory, and galled by the attitude and behavior of Warren's men, the New Englanders now reminded their commanders that they had enlisted only for the duration of the campaign against Louisbourg. In their view that campaign was over, and all troops who had been present during the siege were entitled to a quick discharge and a free voyage back to Boston. Pepperrell and Warren, in spite of any personal differences they might have had, were united in recognizing that Louisbourg had to be garrisoned by New England troops until regular units eventually could be brought from distant bases. Could the increasingly restive men of the siege army be kept under control while temporary replacements were being assembled and transported from New England to relieve them? Letters from Louisbourg brought the problem home to Governor Shirley, who was becoming more and more uneasy over the whole situation, including the sensitive issues of command and the disposal of the rich French prizes.

Well before the outbreak of interservice violence Shirley had decided that the situation was grave enough to require his own presence at Louisbourg, and began making arrangements for an official visit. He arrived in mid-August, saluted by booming New England cannon, an honor that he himself had taken pains to arrange well in advance. Pepperrell and Warren greeted him warmly, eager to reassure him about their personal relationship and hoping, as the commodore put it, that Shirley would be able to "keep The Troops easy with regard to their Construction of his Proclamation, which assures them they should be only kept here till the Expedition was over, which they think is now."[17] The governor's visit stretched on for three months, as he sought to mollify the discontented New Englanders and deal decisively with incipient mutiny, promising the men that they would be released no later than the end of May. Finally, on 27 November Shirley and his entourage sailed for home, leaving behind Pepperrell, Warren, and an army not at all pleased with the prospect of spending the winter on wind-swept Cape Breton Island.[18]

In the meantime, important decisions had been made in England which would affect the New Englanders remaining at Louisbourg. Warren, promoted to the rank of rear admiral, was appointed governor of Cape Breton. Two regiments of redcoats were ordered transferred from Gibraltar to Louisbourg for garrison duty. They were to be supplemented with two new regular regiments formed by enlisting troops from among Pepperrell's army and other colonists, one to be commanded by Pepperrell and the other by Shirley. The raising of these two regiments proceeded slowly, as might have been predicted.[19]

Because the provincial garrison had hoped to be relieved before winter, the New Englanders had not been very thorough in preparing good, weathertight quarters for themselves, with the result that when the severe weather did come they suffered greatly. Inadequate diet together with constant exposure to the damp and cold opened the way for debilitating disease, which spread through the huddled companies like a plague. Conditions were made even worse by a shortage of fuel, forcing the men to scour the ruins for loose boards and other combustibles, and even to tear down portions of their living quarters so as to keep the fires going. Men sickened and died by the dozens, and were committed to shallow graves laboriously scraped out of the frozen earth. A total of at least 900, or approximately one of every three New Englanders in the garrison, perished.[20]

The appalling conditions at Louisbourg from December to April may have put a temporary damper on Anglo-American strife. On 30 December a joint declaration by Pepperrell and Warren urged upon all personnel the "maintaining and promoting an universal good agreement and friendly correspondance, without any distinction in respect of the different parts of his Majesty's dominions to which they belong, or to their being in the land or sea service, but all treating each other as loyal and brave subjects." Pointedly the two commanders went on to warn that their displeasure would fall upon anyone who should "cast any national reflections on any of his Majesty's subjects here, or use any other reproachful or abusive language tending to stir up disputes or quarrells."[21] This admonition, unmistakably implying previous difficulties between the navy and the New Englanders, may have had some beneficial effect. Perhaps by this time, too, all the men at winter-bound Louisbourg simply were too miserable to bother others in similar circumstances. And so the long winter dragged on.

By April the moderating weather and the decline of disease had begun to raise the men's spirits. On the 21st of that month arrived the bulk of the two regiments from Gibraltar, lending substance to a memory that had never long been out of the minds of the New England troops— Shirley's definite promise that they would be on their way home by the end of May. Nine days later came the first anniversary of the army's successful assault landing. While the impatient New Englanders were awaiting the next development, and possibly sizing up the redcoats at a distance, Commodore Charles Knowles, Warren's successor as governor of Cape Breton, arrived. As the reader may recall, Knowles had had previous experience with American provincial troops at Jamaica in 1740–41. Upon viewing the woeful New Englanders he found in and around Louisbourg, Knowles had no desire to delay their departure. Commenting that the town was "the most miserable Ruinous place I ever beheld," he proceeded to lay most of the blame for the difficulties of the past months upon the provincial troops. To the Duke of Newcastle he wrote that

> The confused, dirty, beastly Condition I found this Place in is not to be expressed, and I almost Suspect being credited when I tell your Grace, that these New England Folks were so lazy, that they not only pulled one End of the House down to burn which they lived in, but even buried their dead under the Floors and did their Filth in the Other corners of the House rather than go out of Doors in the Cold: They were of so Obstinate and licentious a disposition that not being properly under Military Discipline there was no keeping them in any Order, and as much as I rejoyce at getting rid of them, so do I pitty Mr. Warren who was Obliged to be so long amongst them.[22]

Obviously, Warren had been pouring all his frustrations into his successor's receptive ears.

In particular, Knowles was appalled at the quantities of rum being brought into Louisbourg by New England vessels, which led him to the hasty conclusion that profligate ingestion of the fiery beverage during the past winter had been the principal cause of the bad health and heavy mortality in Pepperrell's army. Acting decisively, the new governor revoked the licenses of all the sutlers, and ordered all rum to be deposited in the casemates of the citadel, under guard, with the result that many thousands of gallons were sequestered. Even with that, according to the commodore's observation, great quantities of liquor remained concealed among the troops, as evidenced by the prevalence of drunkenness for some time thereafter. Knowles, however, proved to be one of those great men not prone to worship the idol of consistency. His own subsequent experience of a Louisbourg winter, in 1746–47, helped give him a somewhat different perspective on the merits of New England rum. In January we find him writing to the Duke of Newcastle that allowing the men rum and spruce beer "I have found so necessary (and indeed it has proved so beneficial to them) that I am convinced the greatest part would have been dead without it."[23] Knowles must have been referring primarily to his own regulars, for by that time all the New England troops except those who had put on the red coat were far away from bleak Louisbourg, most of them probably at their own firesides and thankful to be there.

The Louisbourg experience in 1745–46 had only served to reinforce the long-developing, mutually antagonistic perceptions of men who served the king directly and those who claimed to be Americans. Shirley, Pepperrell, and Warren all had placed a high value upon harmonious relations at Louisbourg, but each had also been ambitious for personal gain, and correspondingly sensitive to apparent slights. Pepperrell's officers had gone into the operation hoping to increase their personal fortunes by acquiring French real estate and other property, their troops had expected rich booty, but all these dreams went largely unrealized while Warren and his men swept up valuable French ships and cargoes. In every respect, moreover, the long period of garrison duty after the conquest proved disillusioning for all involved. British regular officers once again perceived the provincials as undisciplined, unreliable, and sometimes cowardly. As soldiers the New Englanders seemed to reflect traits in colonial society that the disciplined professionals of the British army and navy later would condemn as irresponsible and even disloyal. At the same time, the leaders of New England saw once again how readily British authority was willing to subordinate provincial ambitions and economic interests to the demands of empire. Indeed, it was becoming ever more clear that New England's destiny rested no longer in the hands of the area's own God-fearing leaders, but rather in the hands of imperial administrators, military commanders, and politicians whose interests and values were at odds with New England's own desires and, above all, heritage.

CHAPTER 5.

THE GREAT WAR FOR

THE EMPIRE

MEETING THE ARMY'S NEEDS

 O far, we have observed the development of dislike, distrust, and occasional open hostility between the British professional armed forces and the American colonists they had been sent to protect and, if necessary, repress. As we have seen, this rather ominous alienation was largely the result of divergent expectations and needs in a variety of circumstances. By mid–eighteenth century the attitude of both sides had become almost traditional, neither expecting much good from the other, even as they continued interacting within the confines of the imperial relationship. The outbreak of a new and potentially more disastrous war with the French in North America, occurring in 1754, required the eventual involvement of the regulars to a degree never before experienced by the Americans, heightening all the old friction in a climax of Anglo-American tension. Thus our next task is to examine the ways in which the British army's demands upon American colonial government and society, in pursuit of victory, helped produce such a significant climax.

The Seven Years' War (1756–63), which many historians consider to be the first of the so-called world wars, began two years earlier in the western wilderness when Major George Washington of the Virginia militia unsuccessfully challenged a French thrust into disputed territory. Thereafter, during the early years of this expanding international conflict, the string of fourteen British coastal colonies from Nova Scotia down to Georgia trembled under the menace of rampant Franco-Indian military power. So immediate was the threat and so obvious the colonies'

own inability to cope that the ministry in London, backed by Parliament and the Crown, quickly decided to intervene. Accordingly, Britain began to send more and more regulars into the American theater of operations, regiment after regiment, thousands upon thousands of redcoats. Initially, because of the Franco-Indian menace, these fresh troops were welcomed by the Americans, who had been badly shaken by early defeats.

The increasingly heavy investment of regular forces by Britain, at great cost to the treasury, required reciprocal support by the several provincial governments and the colonial population in general. Indeed, the ministry, the various commanders sent over to lead the forces against the enemy, and all the other king's officers involved, believed that they not only were striving to uphold British imperial interests but also defending and, in a very real sense, rescuing the threatened colonies; therefore they had every right to expect wholehearted cooperation from grateful colonies, all sacrificing together in the common cause. That was the theory, the ideal, but previous experience since the time of Bacon's Rebellion and the Glorious Revolution should have prepared the British for a quite different actuality.

Even when confronted by the apparent menace of French conquest and Indian massacre, the various British colonies seemed incapable of burying their mutual antagonisms and rivalries. Wrote one American, with little exaggeration, "The strength of our colonies . . . is divided. . . . Jealous are they of each other—some ill-constituted—others shaken with intestine divisions—and . . . parsimonious even to prodigality. Our assemblies are diffident of their governors—governors despise their assemblies, and both mutually misrepresent each other to the Court of Great Britain. . . . Without a general constitution for warlike operations, we can neither plan nor execute."[1] In virtually every colony the tussle for dominant political power between the executive and legislative branches, which had been intensifying all during the first half of the eighteenth century, continued with a vengeance. Indeed, the elected assemblies, having already gained a very large measure of control over the purse strings of provincial government, were strongly inclined to use the extraordinary needs of the executive (and the military) in wartime as a fulcrum to gain yet more leverage. The adverse effects of such internal political competition proved extremely frustrating for British commanders standing in urgent need of what only the assembly could provide. Viewing these stultifying conditions, one impatient British officer hoped (in vain) that "for once in their lives, they will forget their jealousies and their petty provincial interests, for the general good of their fatherland."[2]

We are not surprised to discover at this time the existence of widespread profiteering, endemic to all societies at war, but its actual practice in America at the immediate expense of the British army infuriated officers who were hardpressed to meet urgent military requirements. One general, needing a large supply of lumber for military construction at Albany, New York, discovered to his dismay that the price of boards had jumped from 9d. to 15d.[3] Another officer encountered rampant profiteering in South Carolina, "the People having so immoderately imposed upon us, that there is no carrying on the service at such a Rate."[4] Accommodations for soldiers stationed in provincial towns, it was said, were "dearer than such Lodgings would cost in the Capital Street of London."[5] The commander of an important expedition in Pennsylvania deplored the "villiany and Rascality of the Inhabitants, who to a man seem rather bent upon our ruin . . . than give the smallest assistance, which if at last extorted is so infamously charged as shews the disposition of the people in its full Glare."[6] When British warships and transports arrived at Hampton Roads, Virginia, after the long Atlantic crossing and needed to replenish their depleted stores of fresh water, they discovered that the wells in the area were privately owned, with the owners holding out their hands for payment—otherwise, no water![7] In fairness, it should be recognized that prices of some goods and services normally were higher in America than in England, and that wartime conditions sometimes did justify even higher prices, but seldom were the British in a position to give the colonists the benefit of such a mitigating view. They saw the Americans only as grasping profiteers.

The governments of the various colonies were expected to appropriate money and raise troops for the successive campaigns against the French, a process that became in each colony an annual political battle. Usually the appointed governor was strongly inclined to support the demands of the ministry in London and the British commanders in America, while the representative assembly, reflecting only too clearly the parsimonious attitude of its middle-class constituents, typically struggled to minimize the colony's contribution to the war effort. "It is the constant Study of every Province here," reported one disgusted regular officer, "to throw every Expence on the Crown, and bear no part of the Expence of this War themselves."[8] At every step there were seemingly endless political maneuvers and delays, to the bewilderment and fury of the commanders charged with the awesome responsibility of defeating a powerful foe. Most British officers soon adopted the view that provincial politicians were shortsighted, selfish, and even maliciously unpatriotic. "I never saw such a sett of people, obstinate, and perverse to the last degree," exclaimed a disgusted general.[9] Another denounced the colonists as "a Sett of people whose Sole pleasure seems to be that of thwarting every Measure of Government, tho ever So beneficial to themselves."[10] That was precisely what was so puzzling and at the same time infuriating to the regulars—they asked only for colonial help in rendering the colonies safe from the French, yet received little but excuses and recriminations. Adding to British indignation was the fact that the colonies, even while loudly complaining about their burdens and sacrifices, were being at least partially reimbursed by the British treasury for the actual contributions they did make to the common cause.[11] The nature and importance of these issues will become more sharply focused if we now examine some actual developments during the course of the war.

Major General Edward Braddock's ill-starred expedition of 1755, using the colony of Virginia as its base for a conquest of the disputed western territory, experienced almost constant frustration because of colonial attitudes and deficiencies. In turn, Braddock and his men aroused the resentment of the colonists because of their constant demands and overbearing manner. Braddock himself was a professional officer of lengthy but undistinguished career, being nearly sixty years of age at the time of his designation for the American command. Blunt of manner and set in his ways, he habitually functioned by rule and, occasionally, instinct. Moreover, he could show disdain when overruling provincial leaders whose ideas did not match his own.

On 26 October 1754 Secretary of State Thomas Robinson had directed an official letter to the various provincial governors requiring them to assist in obtaining such essentials as supplies, transport, and quarters, in aid of Braddock's endeavor and other military operations being conducted simultaneously. It was expected that draft horses and wagons, for example, would be hired or, if necessary, impressed from local farmers, with appropriate compensation to the owners. Because this and other forms of aid would be costly, the ministry clearly expected the colonies themselves to bear at least a portion of the expense. Accordingly, in the interests of efficiency as well as fairness, Braddock was instructed to urge upon the various provincial governments the creation of a common war fund to which all would contribute. Upon such a common fund the commander in chief would be able to draw in order to meet some of the operational expenses as they occurred, with the individual legislatures and the British treasury itself bearing the remainder of the cost.[12] Unfortunately, the project of the common fund died at birth from lack of nutrition. "Though such a Method [of financing] would greatly facilitate the Service I am engaged in, . . ." Braddock wrote to Robinson, "I almost despair of their complying with it, from the Jealousy of the People, and the Disunion of the several Colonies, as well among themselves, as one with another. Indeed I am sorry to say," he continued gloomily, "that in all appearance, I shall have much Difficulty in obtaining from 'em, in their own way, such assistance, as His Majesty expects, and their general Interest requires."[13] Braddock's pessimism about the prospects for the common fund was not excessive; nothing ever came of the idea, and so the successive commanders in chief were forced to obtain whatever funds they could by means of separate appeals to the different assemblies, at best a haphazard and inequitable method.

As Braddock and his subordinates struggled doggedly to complete their preparations for the expedition against the French, they encountered what seemed to be a surging tide of colonial profiteering. Pennsylvanians, complained their own governor, had "no kind of Scruple to make as great an Advantage as they can of the Forces that are sent to protect them."[14] Braddock's deputy quartermaster general, Sir John St. Clair, was if anything even more blunt: "Every body laid themselves out to put what money they could in their Pocketts, without forwarding our Expedition." This same officer, after experiencing seemingly interminable delays and obstructions in his dealings with the Pennsylvanians, lost his temper completely and said things that still burn across the pages of the record. Meeting with a group of commissioners from the delinquent province, he "stormed like a Lyon Rampant," threatening to "march his Army into Cumberland County to cut the Roads, press Horses, Wagons, &ca.; that he would not suffer a Soldier to handle an Axe, but by Fire and Sword oblige the Inhabitants to do it, and take every Man that refused to the Ohio . . . ; that he would kill all kind of Cattle and carry away the Horses, burn the Houses, &ca., and that if the French defeated them by the Delays of this Province that he would with his Sword drawn pass through the Province and treat the Inhabitants as a Parcel of Traitors. . . ."[15] One of Philadelphia's leading citizens, hearing of St. Clair's explosive diatribe, reacted with sarcastic condescension. "The Horrors of our mountains, and The wildness of a long Uncultivated Country—Where no man Dwells, seems to be an untryed scene," he wrote. "And when the Indian Cruelty to Their enemies and the barbarous Custom of scalping is added to it with the Perpetual danger of being Liable to perish, perhaps by want, or in an Inglorious Manner I Cannot wonder that the officers, at least, such as have been of Note and Rank, should in The Course of Their Military Duty, Arrive among us in a very ill Humour." He concluded by predicting that "it may very Probably exceed every excuse of this kind, before we have done with our Military Protectors."[16]

In mid–April Braddock hosted a conference at Alexandria, Virginia, at which he discussed with five key provincial governors the plans and problems relating to impending military operations. During this discussion it soon became painfully clear that whatever material assistance was at last extracted from the various assemblies would be meager and grudging. Indeed, all the governors present advised Braddock to rely as heavily as possible upon his credit with the British treasury, not the generosity of the colonies.[17]

As the days continued to slip by with Braddock foundering in the maddening problems of preparation for his difficult enterprise, the parsimonious attitude even of Virginia, the colony most likely to benefit substantially if his expedition were successful, became painfully obvious. On 9 May Governor Dinwiddie had to inform the general that his legislature would not contribute to the subsistence of the regular regiments, as it had been implored to do, and probably could not be induced to appropriate any more money for the expedition. By early June Dinwiddie had become only slightly less pessimistic, reporting that "the Backwardness of our neighbouring Proprietary Governments of Maryland and Pensylvania make my Applications to our Assembly an up-hill Work." Three weeks later the governor was writing to the Earl of Halifax, president of the Board of Trade, that "Our Assembly meets To-morrow, when I shall endeavor to bring them to a due sense of their Duty, but I much doubt Success, they are so very infatuated and narrow in their Thoughts, pretending great Frugality to ingratiate themselves with their Constituents that I am heartily weary of their unjust Arguments at this Time of Danger." Braddock denounced the "Supineness, and unseasonable Oeconomy of the Governments and people" as simply inexcusable.[18]

One of the expedition's most pressing needs was overland transport, obtainable only from the colonists themselves in the form of draft horses and farm wagons for hauling bulky supplies along the rough road being cut through the mountainous wilderness. Virginia seemed unable or unwilling to provide all of the many wagon teams needed, so Braddock turned to Maryland and Pennsylvania. Everywhere, it seemed, the farmers were stubbornly reluctant. As late as mid–May, George Washington, writing from Fort Cumberland on the upper Potomac, could see no good prospect of the expedition pushing beyond that point "as we have neither Horses nor Waggons enough. . . ."[19] Those wagon teams that Braddock had been able to pry loose from the Marylanders, complete with drivers, had refused to cross into Virginia. For Braddock the only bright spot in an otherwise lowering situation appeared in the unlikely form of a shrewd Pennsylvania politician named Benjamin Franklin who, although no truckler to remote authority, was patriotically eager for the expedition to succeed. Contacting the frustrated general, Franklin boldly promised to obtain the needed transport. Then, in the extensive rural areas of Pennsylvania, he distributed a broadside advertisement soliciting wagon teams. In this carefully constructed message to the reluctant farmers Franklin skillfully combined the carrot and the stick—a convincing promise of monetary compensation on a daily basis, and a stern reminder that if the required wagon teams were not voluntarily offered the army was prepared to send groups of soldiers into the Pennsylvania countryside with orders to impress the horses and wagons wherever they might be found. This approach succeeded remarkably well, with the result that a highly self-satisfied Franklin was able to produce for Braddock about 150 wagons, each with a driver and four horses, plus a large number of packhorses. The grateful commander in chief cited Franklin's accomplishment as "almost the only Instance of Ability and Honesty I have known in these Provinces," certainly a severe indictment.[20]

The army's great difficulty in obtaining adequate numbers of horses and wagons in the colonies was far more than just a petty annoyance. Without such transport in far greater numbers than a mere Franklin was able to gather, the army simply could not begin, let alone sustain, its laborious advance across hundreds of miles of wilderness terrain. Many years after the event General Thomas Gage, a survivor of Braddock's stunning defeat at the Monongahela, was queried about the causes of the disaster. The first thing he mentioned was that very problem, arguing that the shortage of wagon teams had caused a fatal delay in the westward advance.[21]

Braddock's defeat contributed heavily to the worsening of relations between the regulars and the colonists. Many of the professional army officers salved their own sense of humiliation by blaming the colonists for being so niggardly in providing the essential support for the expedition, even as they condemned their own men for succumbing to panic in the face of the enemy. Then, as the tattered remnants of Braddock's regular regiments, under the command of Colonel Thomas Dunbar, beat a hasty retreat toward early winter quarters in New York, the frontier folk in the exposed areas of Pennsylvania, Maryland, and Virginia complained bitterly that the cowardly redcoats were leaving them unprotected, a helpless prey to the fury of the French and Indians. More and more Americans were becoming convinced that the king's regular troops were not only ineffective in wilderness warfare but also contemptuous of colonial capability and largely indifferent to colonial need. In short, any early sense of gratitude toward the redcoats in their role as rescuers proved to be short-lived as a result of Braddock's defeat and the bitter recriminations that followed. Thereafter, in the strain of a prolonged and wearing conflict with a tenacious enemy, the colonists and the redcoats viewed each other with distaste and distrust.

A considerable number of Americans had been persuaded, in the heady days of the preceding spring, to enlist in Braddock's regiments. Now, having survived the humiliating defeat at the Monongahela, many were deserting the service, doubtless finding concealment among their own kin, or friends, or the colonial population in general.[22] This large-scale desertion, coupled with the high losses suffered in action and immediately thereafter, impelled the regular officers to try refilling their depleted companies by a vigorous campaign of recruiting among the colonial population. The usual practice was for a regiment to send out several recruiting parties, each consisting of a commissioned officer, a few enlisted men, and a drummer whose vigorous beating would announce their presence in a community and attract potential recruits. While engaged in this activity, the recruiting party expected to be quartered at colonial expense, usually in a local tavern. This routine requirement, along with the methods of inducing young men to enlist and the kinds of persons actually enlisted, frequently aroused local resentment, which in turn invariably soured the attitude of the soldiery. Thus, the routine and necessary recruiting activity of the regular regiments in the colonies proved to be a frequent cause of Anglo-American tension.

Most men preferred to avoid a term of service in the regular army except as an unhappy alternative to something even worse. Unfortunately, in many parts of the colonies, especially the urban centers and the older rural areas, by mid-eighteenth century there were many young men at loose ends and having a hard time finding enough food for the table. A young man in dire poverty and without prospects of improvement, a bored or abused apprentice or servant, a criminal facing prosecution—these were likely candidates for enlistment in the British army when the recruiters came to town and the drummer began to beat.[23]

Few responsible colonists objected to the recruiting of criminals or the unemployed, for that removed a burden from the community. The major objection to recruiting, and it proved to be a very strong one, arose when the recruiters became especially receptive to apprentices and other bound servants who represented a substantial financial investment on the part of their masters. This problem was a familiar one in England, where many a master had struggled to prevent such a loss of costly labor; it became intense also in the colonies, where the cost of labor was relatively high.[24] Governor Shirley of Massachusetts, having succeeded the deceased Braddock as commander in chief, anticipated the opposition and instructed the army to avoid enlisting boys and men who were under indenture. The result was a dearth of recruits at a time when the regular regiments in North America needed to renew their strength for the next campaign. Confronted with this dilemma, Shirley eventually relented, reversing his earlier policy. Thereafter, the apprentices and servants were prime targets for the zealous recruiting parties.[25]

With active recruiting of servants there arose a storm of opposition on the part of the deprived masters. So intense was the anger that one provincial governor feared a possible "Insurrection of the People."[26] As servants began to consider the army a possible escape hatch from a boring or unpleasant existence, masters found it expedient to ease up on the conditions of servitude, even going so far as to humor the servants and tolerate their insolence lest they respond to the call of the drum. Some servants, it was said, gave it out that they were going off to enlist but instead simply absconded. In both Maryland and Pennsylvania, colonies heavily dependent upon the labor of indentured servants, public opposition to army recruiting reverberated in legislative chambers. The Pennsylvania assembly asked Governor Robert Hunter Morris to issue an official proclamation against the practice of enlisting servants, a request denied by the governor who, although recognizing the hardship experienced by the deprived masters, saw the problem as one that should be settled by individual litigation. According to Morris, any master who felt himself unlawfully injured by the activity of a particular recruiting officer should sue for damages. What this generally meant, in any colony, was that as soon as the complaint had been formally lodged with local civil authority the aggrieved master could have the offending officer arrested and held for trial. Similarly, the servant in question, as disputed property, could be securely lodged in jail so as to prevent further possibility of loss until such time as the suit had been settled in court. Naturally, the recruiting officers, and indeed all regular officers, were outraged by such proceedings, which they regarded as blatant obstructionism through unjustifiable litigation.[27]

Sometimes the coercive power of the British army, as an agent of the Crown, was sufficiently intimidating to prevail. At New Brunswick, New Jersey, for example, where a recruiting officer had been arrested, "the Person who brought the Suit was so frightened the next day at what he had done, that he paid the Cost and droped the Action."[28] Most masters, though, were not nearly so timid. On occasion, too, a recruiting officer had at least a chance to win his point by means of his wits. One British general relished the story about a certain recruiting officer in Philadelphia, where a large number of servants had been confined in jail to prevent their enlistment. When an irate group of masters complained loudly to the officer about the recruiting methods of his sergeant, he feigned sympathy and had the sergeant arrested. Just as the constable was about to lead the offender off to jail the officer slipped into the sergeant's pocket a good supply of money, essential to recruiting. That very night in the jail, so the story went, the sergeant managed to sign up seventy servants.[29]

The seriousness of the whole problem of recruiting apprentices and servants soon came to the attention of the ministry in London. As a result, Parliament, in an attempt to regularize the situation, extended to the colonies those sections of the Mutiny Act relating to enlistment procedure. Additionally, it was stipulated that masters were to be given financial compensation for any servant enlisted, proportionate to the amount of service lost. Funds for this purpose, it was hoped, would be appropriated by the various provincial legislatures. Some masters were mollified by this scheme, but many taxpayers and legislators were less enthusiastic. In practice, as experience proved, legislatures were reluctant to provide funds for compensation to masters, and even when funds theoretically were available, the process of acquiring compensation could be painfully difficult and time consuming, as many a deprived master discovered to his cost.[30]

The anger generated among colonists by the army's persistent attempts to enlist servants, as well as the army's resentment of all opposition, permeates contemporary accounts of actual cases. Take, for example, the complaint lodged by one Corbin Lee on 30 April 1757, characteristically laced with emotion and probable exaggeration. Lee, a man of considerable local standing, was overseer of a Maryland ironworks that depended heavily upon the labor of white indentured servants. Early in March a recruiting party led by Captain Abraham Bosomworth of the Sixtieth Regiment came looking for recruits. As Lee described it in his complaint, "they stole into our Plantations disguised like theives in the dead of night made our Servants Drunk forced them to inlist and carried them off." Later, when Lee demanded the return of his servants, he was rebuffed. Apparently the overseer then joined forces with one William Bennett, who also had lost some servants, to agitate against the recruiters and commence legal action. "It is not unusual with many of these Recruiting Gentlemen," Lee stoutly reported, "when they meet with a person that will not be bullied out of his Property and tamely give up his Servant without any sort of Recompence immediately to deem him an Enemy to his Majesty's Service."[31] That clearly was the view adopted by Captain Bosomworth when the doughty overseer was so bold as to commence legal proceedings against him, for he angrily denounced Lee and Bennett to the commander in chief himself, accusing them of stirring up antirecruiting sentiment in Maryland.

Jeremiah Gridley, a prominent Massachusetts lawyer and politician who was sympathetic toward the army, informed Lord Loudoun about the popular opposition to recruiting in his colony. "If any native of the Province inlists," he wrote, "the Inlistment is critically examind, every imaginary flaw is made a real one, and the Desertion of such a person encouragd. This is the popular temper, and the Magistrates, always in some shape or other dependent upon the people, are in my opinion too complaisant to it."[32]

This view was confirmed by Lieutenant George Cottnam of the Fortieth Regiment who was having no success recruiting in the seaside town of Marblehead. "The whole Country Are Against the Regulars," he complained, "And in Stead of Assisting a Recruiting Officer, Are at all times Ready to Lay Stumbling Blocks in His way." New Hampshire, it seems, was no more complaisant. Wrote Lieutenant Samuel Mackay from Portsmouth, "I have had my party out in the Country but they generally get Mobed; one of them was beat in the Streets the other Evening by five Sailors."[33] There can be little doubt that the recruiting parties, always under pressure to acquire new men for their regiments, often resorted to tactics that were rough and provocative. Even the royal governor of Massachusetts, who certainly was no rabble-rousing enemy of the British army, deplored the "imprudences" committed by some of the redcoats: "To see a Drunken Man luggd through the streets on a Souldiers back guarded by others wither it was or was not to carry him before a Justice to swear must certainly give a strang[e] impression of the method of enlisting and certainly have an ill effect on an inflamed Mobb."[34]

From New England down to Georgia the colonial complaints against recruiting by the regulars all had much the same ring. Colonel Henry

Bouquet's summary account of his frustrations in dealing with the inhabitants of South Carolina might well have come from any other commander in any one of a dozen other colonies. The people, wrote Bouquet on 25 August 1757, are *"extremely pleased to have Soldiers* to protect their Plantations," but will tolerate no inconveniences in return. They show little respect for the redcoats, "making no great difference between a soldier and a Negro." "The Lawyers, Justices of the Peace, and in general the whole people are eternally against us." "Everything goes here as slowly as in any other part of America and patience is the chief Qualitye to carry on Business." A lieutenant has been arrested by the civil authorities "for some Quarrel in recruiting not worth mentioning." "The Impositions of the public houses, the Denial of Quarters, Carriages and Ferryages make it very near impossible to carry on the Service."[35] In such remarks coming from an able and responsible professional officer we are able to detect the extreme sense of frustration that had arisen in the British army through its tortuous dealings with the American colonists.

Another issue that was just as pervasive and persistent as recruiting, and even more volcanic in its effect on Anglo-American relations, was the forced quartering of British officers and enlisted personnel in colonial communities, a practice long resented by the colonists. At the time of Bacon's Rebellion the Virginians, as we have seen, had been unwilling hosts to the soldiery. From South Carolina in 1727 an angry captain of one of the independent companies of redcoats complained bitterly of the "injurious treatment we receive from the Country, for whose assistance and relief H.M. was pleased to raise and pay the Company, they deny quarters to the recruits when landed, as likewise to any detachment on service, and refuse to supply the Garrison with either bedding, fire or candle. . . . I find I am not to expect assistance from the country, who I firmly believe (some few persons excepted) would sacrifice not only this unfortunate Company, but all H.M. Forces if in their power."[36] The complaint was characteristic, expressing bewilderment and deep resentment toward colonial people so niggardly and ungrateful as to deny the very necessities of life to the men whom the king had provided for their security. In the Great War for the Empire the earliest eruption of serious trouble over the issue of quartering coincided with the march of Dunbar's defeated redcoats through Pennsylvania to New York in the latter part of 1755.[37] Thereafter, the colonies experienced prolonged sequences of further eruptions, especially during the autumn season when the campaign-weary regiments were sniffing out snug quarters for the impending winter.

Why was the quartering of troops such a volatile issue in the North American colonies? In part, at least, because the American colonists, whether of British or continental European background, had retained a folk remembrance of how despotic rulers at home had used forced billeting as a form of economic, political, or religious coercion. Ever since the Petition of Right, which gained the royal assent in 1628, Englishmen had held fast to the belief that forced billeting in private dwellings was unlawful. Yet in England it had long been understood and accepted in practice that troops on the move through areas where royal barracks did not exist were entitled to demand shelter, along with certain provisions such as candles and firewood, in the civilian communities along their route. The process of arranging for such accommodation was specified in the annual Mutiny Act. Upon arrival the officer in command was to apply to the local magistrates, apprising them of his need. It was then the responsibility of the magistrates to designate the actual buildings in which the troops were to be sheltered, normally consisting of the local "public houses," that is, the establishments maintained as a public service by inn keepers and licensed victuallers. All such hosts were to be compensated for the accommodation at specified *per diem* rates, the money being drawn from the soldiers' daily subsistence allowance. Especially important to note is the fact that the Mutiny Act clearly prohibited the billeting of soldiers in any private dwelling without the owner's consent, a further reinforcement of the cherished constitutional liberty.

The situation was complicated, however, by the fact that in both Ireland and Scotland public houses or taverns were more scattered and scarce than in England, at least in the rural areas, with the result that in those two countries the army was permitted to take temporary quarters, when necessary, in private buildings such as barns and warehouses. Obviously, the young and still-developing North American colonies raised much the same problem as Ireland and Scotland, at least in the eyes of the British army. Furthermore, the soldier's daily subsistence allowance, which in England was used to compensate the owners, proved inadequate in America where prices and costs were higher. And because the quartering sections of the Mutiny Act had not been extended specifically to North America by Parliament, the question of the army's right to quarters in the colonies remained ambiguous. There was ample room for dispute.

It seems clear that most Americans who had to deal directly with the issue of quartering held to the view that an Englishman's home was his castle and forced billeting was a violation of the British constitution.

From that perspective, the prohibition was general and unqualified. Any attempt by the army to force itself upon a colonial community, therefore, was likely to be resented and even resisted. British officers, on the other hand, saw the matter in a totally different light. First of all, they tended to assume that whatever the army could do in Britain it could also do in the colonies, which meant that they could quarter their troops in public houses as in England, and, when necessary, in private buildings as in Ireland and Scotland. Beyond that, they also knew that they were engaged in a war with the French, which brought into play a time-honored tradition, namely, that in a time of extreme emergency such as war the normal legal restraints could be relaxed so that the armed forces might do whatever they must in order to succeed in their mission. This tradition, if valid, gave to the army in North America a virtual *carte blanche*, a condition that few if any of the colonists were willing to accept.

The commander in chief who encountered the quartering problem in its most virulent form was the Scottish Lord Loudoun, who had succeeded to the supreme command in 1756. Loudoun was a professional officer of considerable intelligence and broad interests, with practical field experience in both Flanders and Scotland. Coming to the American theater with the firm intention of correcting a deteriorating military situation while, at the same time, dealing firmly but fairly with the troublesome colonists, the new commander in chief found the latter task the more difficult of the two. Whenever thwarted by provincial intransigence, however, Loudoun always was prepared to fall back upon the one resource in which he had the utmost confidence—his authority as the king's chosen chief officer. Even before leaving England, Loudoun was aware of strong colonial opposition to the quartering of troops. Hoping to be able to get the problem quickly under firm control, he sought but failed to obtain from his superior, the Duke of Cumberland, a clear-cut delineation of policy. All he was told in this regard was that "Quarters must be taken in the plantations as they are in Britain in time of war," which hardly clarified the matter.[38] In effect, then, Loudoun came to the test in 1756 with little more than the terms of the Mutiny Act, along with his own sense of responsibility and right, to guide him in dealing with a most complicated and disruptive issue.

Generals James Abercromby and Daniel Webb had arrived at Albany, New York, accompanied by two regiments of regulars, nearly a month before the ship bringing Lord Loudoun to America dropped anchor in New York Harbor. They came to a town that was peculiar in its long-standing involvement in the sensitive fur trade as well as its persistent

Dutch heritage. Moreover, Albany's location near the junction of the Mohawk and Hudson rivers made it a natural base for military forces operating along the northern frontier in the direction of either Lake Champlain or Lake Ontario. Thus it is not surprising that Albany witnessed the coming and going of large numbers of troops, and that the local inhabitants displayed a tenacious opposition to quartering these strangers. As soon as Abercromby and Webb applied to have the newly arrived redcoats quartered in Albany, they encountered strong reluctance from many of the local inhabitants, including the town fathers. Nevertheless, the needed quarters were somehow obtained, and Abercromby was taking satisfaction in the thought that as yet he had heard "no complaint from either Burgher or Soldier."[39] Perhaps there was indeed a brief calm before the storm, but by the time Loudoun himself appeared upon the scene Albany's anger was intensifying ominously. Loudoun apparently did not make a good first impression. In an early conference with local leaders he undertook to lecture them rather loftily, reminding them that his authority was of royal derivation, warning them that because they were unfamiliar with military affairs they must expect to be mystified by some transactions, and "a Great Deal more of that Stuff," as one of the auditors put it. Unimpressed but obviously overawed, the town fathers then withdrew to the "City hall," where they "began to Converse with Each other about my Lords Abilities and that partly by Dumb Signs as if every word That was Spoken In derogation of his wisdom . . . and Judgment would be treason." Some thought Loudoun "very Shellow or very imperious."[40] It was, as Loudoun perhaps did not realize, an inauspicious beginning.

Basically, as Loudoun noted in a report to the secretary of state, the dispute over quartering arose because of the colonists' contention that the sections of the Mutiny Act relating to quartering had not been extended by Parliament to include America. "I should imagine," remarked the commander in chief with unjustified complacence, that "a few words in the Act, next Sessions, would clear up the dispute." Sometime later William Pitt informed Loudoun that a few words inserted in the Mutiny Act would not be sufficient. Instead, the ministry was considering "how far a Provision of that Sort may be framed by a Separate Act of Parliament." Obviously, then, the growing dispute over quartering in America was a matter of no little concern. Although the colonists were fond of falling back upon their constitutional right, Loudoun suspected, rightly it seems, that most Americans simply did not want to bear the cost and inconvenience of providing quarters for redcoats. "They will give you, not one Shilling, to carry on the War," he complained bitterly. "They will give you no one thing, but for double the Money it ought to cost. . . . I hope," the general added with a slight tinge of optimism, "a time will come, that with a little Sweet and a little Sower, they may be brought about."[41] As it turned out, of the sweet there was to be precious little, of the "Sower" enough to spoil the dish.

In the meantime, Albany continued to seethe with discontent, especially after the inhabitants learned of smallpox among the troops. Some of the soldiers, well aware of the hostile attitude of people upon whom they were billeted, reciprocated with loutish behavior. One of the town's leading fur merchants had "an officer and 6 private men Billeted upon me, we are not Master of our own houses, so that itt is Very hard Living here at present."[42] To the commander in chief the controlling consideration was military necessity. Writing to the royal governor of the province, Sir Charles Hardy, Loudoun conceded that under ordinary circumstances the quartering of troops was limited to public houses, but insisted that in time of war "the Practice has always been . . . that no house has been exempt from Quartering the Troops, the General thought proper to have in any Place for carrying on the Service, and from this rule the People of the first fashion in England have not been exempted."[43] As the winter of 1756–57 approached, with even more regulars needing shelter in Albany, Loudoun put his staff to work making a systematic tabulation of all suitable buildings. Listed were each house, the occupant's name and trade, the number of rooms with and without fireplace, and which rooms were actually occupied by the residents. From this, the staff officers calculated that Albany was easily able to quarter 146 officers and 1,448 men, numbers which, in case of extreme necessity, could be increased to 190 and 2,082 respectively. As a result of this survey and the relentless use of his own military authority backed by the threat of physical force, Loudoun managed to break down the opposition. His redcoats were sheltered for the winter with grumbling townsfolk who sullenly endured what they had to bear.[44]

Loudoun, having overridden the stubborn reluctance of the Albanians in the fall of 1756, had to turn his attention almost immediately to a crisis over quartering in Philadelphia, where the proprietary governor, Colonel William Denny, was in contention with the strong antiproprietary faction of the provincial assembly led by Benjamin Franklin and some of the leading Quakers. As early as September the commander in chief had informed Denny that some of the regulars would have to be quartered in Philadelphia during the coming winter. Accordingly, the

governor asked his legislature to pass a quartering act that would constitute a legal basis for what Loudoun required. In response, the assembly
in effect adopted those sections of the Mutiny Act that provided for the
quartering of troops in England in time of peace, thereby authorizing the
use of public but not private houses. The relatively inexperienced governor, who had arrived in Pennsylvania only the previous summer, felt
obliged to accept this limited provision, and so it became law early in
December. By that time more than 500 officers and men of the Royal
American Regiment, under the command of Colonel Bouquet, were im-
minently expected in Philadelphia for the winter. Because of anticipated
recruiting activity among the Pennsylvanians, that regiment would require quarters for more than 1,000 men, none of whom, if the new law
was strictly obeyed, could be forced upon private householders.[45]

The weather in Philadelphia was frigid when Bouquet and his regulars
arrived in mid–December. Unhappily they soon discovered that the local
inhabitants did not want them, even as paying guests, a disturbing reluctance that was reinforced by the presence of smallpox among the soldiery. Surgeon James Stevenson feared that unless a proper hospital were
provided, "every house in this place will be an hospital in a fortnight."[46]
Philadelphia did have a considerable number of taverns and other small
public establishments, but all of them together were not sufficient to
shelter all of Bouquet's shivering redcoats, and the assembly held fast to
its requirement that only public houses be used for quartering, as in
England during peacetime. In a communication to Governor Denny the
legislators managed to strike a telling blow by linking the problem to the
still lively issue of the recruiting of servants: "We cannot conceive it will,
when well considered, be thought adviseable, to quarter the Soldiers by
Force on private Houses rather than by Law on Publick-houses; and we
apprehend that if the bought Servants, which have been so lately taken
from the King's good Subjects here, and no Satisfaction made their Owners, notwithstanding the Act of Parliament so expresly requires it, are
now to be thrust into their Houses, and made their Masters, some Com-
motions may arise, dangerous to the King's Peace."[47] It was a telling
point: Servants turned into soldiers against their master's will and then
allowed to live in the domiciles they had abandoned, lording it over their
former masters.

Actually, as it turned out, most of the troops on hand managed to
cram themselves into the town's public facilities, but a minority remained
without satisfactory shelter while the harried governor duelled with his
stubborn assembly. The latter's "obstinate persisting in an open Neglect

of Humanity was the highest Instance I have ever met with of the Depravity of Human Nature," exclaimed Denny in complete exasperation.[48] If the taverns in Philadelphia really were insufficient, responded the assembly, then place the surplus soldiers in yet other public houses located in the outlying communities. Colonel Bouquet, on the other hand, insisted that his troops must all remain in the town, where they could be adequately supervised and disciplined. It was an impasse. At the time when Loudoun in New York became fully aware of the situation in Philadelphia, he was weary from wrestling with the town fathers of Albany over much the same issue, but had just won complete victory by threatening to billet his troops, if necessary, at the point of the bayonet. Therefore, he believed that he knew exactly the right method for dealing with the stubborn people of Philadelphia. To Governor Denny he wrote on 22 December, "If the Number of Troops now in Philadelphia are not Sufficient I will Instantly march a Number sufficient for that purpose and find Quarters for the whole."[49] That meant billeting in private homes—by force. An express rider carrying Loudoun's ominous threat reached Philadelphia on Christmas Day. At the earliest opportunity the governor shared the commander in chief's threat with a key group of legislators, Franklin among them, with the result that a solution was speedily found. Local authorities decided to make available to the soldiery a brand new municipal hospital capable of sheltering 500 men. Later, an even better arrangement was made with the construction of a military barracks. In a sense, both sides had won, but both also remained resentful.[50]

Colonel Bouquet was an officer who somehow seemed more often than not at a center of controversy with the colonists, even though he does not appear to have been naturally antagonistic. Perhaps it was just a matter of bad luck for a commander who really had the best of intentions. In June 1757 it fell to Bouquet's lot to lead five companies of the Royal American Regiment into Charleston, South Carolina. The arrival of these troops, along with two companies of Virginia provincials, did not take the town by surprise and, indeed, it seemed at first glance that the provincial legislature was in a welcoming mood, having made special provision for their accommodation. Although some barracks space was already available in Charleston, the Royal Americans set up camp outside the town because some of the soldiers were known to be carrying smallpox. Persistent rains soon turned the camp into a quagmire, to the intense discomfort of the troops, who lacked even an adequate supply of straw for bedding. Toward the end of July conditions in the camp were becoming so bad that Bouquet put in an urgent request for more adequate quarters, with the result that four vacant houses were made available to shelter some of the men. Governor William Henry Lyttelton and his legislature had agreed that the construction of additional barracks was the best way to solve the larger problem, and so that project was begun.[51]

Early in September a battalion of Highlanders arrived in Charleston, further complicating the problem. Some of the newcomers were lodged in an uncompleted church, others in hired buildings, but many simply had to wait for a better solution. Among the dispirited regulars, disease and death were increasing. Some compassionate Carolinians did voluntarily shelter a number of the soldiers in their own homes, which helped but did not solve the problem. Bouquet continued to prod with little apparent success. "I shall always prefer to make two Campaigns," he wrote, "than to settle the Quarters in any of our American Towns."[52] By October the urgency of the situation was apparent to nearly everyone, and the assembly even appropriated more money, although it would make no grant for the quartering of the captains and field officers, on the assumption that they had personal allowances sufficient to enable them to fend for themselves.

Bouquet and the other regular officers were increasingly angry, not because South Carolina was unwilling to do anything about quartering their troops, but rather because of the inadequacy of the arrangements and the maddening slowness of the progress made, while the soldiers continued to suffer, sicken, and succumb. The situation was beginning to seem even worse than at Philadelphia a year earlier. To Bouquet it was "the eternal Struggle in America." He and his military colleagues were "heartily tired of these eternal Disputes, which makes the Service so disagreeable in America." Again the assembly refused to defray the costs of lodging all the officers, but did consent to increase the allotment of firewood and double the number of blankets doled out to the troops. At the same time, the legislators took note of an apparent fraud attempted by one of the Highland officers, who allegedly ordered more firewood than was actually needed, with the intention of making a profit from the surplus. Such an allegation, of course, merely fed the antiarmy prejudices of disgruntled Carolinians. Once again Bouquet's exasperation exploded. "I am heartily tired of America," he exclaimed, vowing that "if I can once get rid of it, no Consideration in the World, would make me come again."[53]

By this time Loudoun, who had been hearing the reiterated complaints of his officers in Charleston, was ready to intervene once more. To Bouquet he wrote on Christmas Day, "You must remember I had a Dispute on that Subject last Winter both here and at Philadelphia which you know I got the better of, and have since had the Approbation of the King's Ministers of what I did, and I will follow the Same Measures in Carolina."[54] But Charleston was far distant from New York, and Loudoun was being replaced as commander in chief by General Abercromby, so the situation in Charleston continued without much real change. In fact, the much-harried Bouquet had to grapple with yet another urgent problem. Whereas formerly all provisions imported into South Carolina for the use of the regular troops had been exempted from the usual duty, now the colony treasurer was attempting to collect the tax. Naturally anxious to have the financial advantage of the exemption, Bouquet submitted a formal "remonstrance" to the provincial government, whereupon Governor Lyttelton informed him that in South Carolina any such request had to be in the form of a "petition" instead of a "remonstrance." Accepting the lesson with all the grace he could muster, the colonel altered the one offending word and resubmitted his request, this time with success.[55]

At long last the new barracks were completed, although not in a very workmanlike fashion. Likewise, the assembly did make some additional provision for the accommodation of regular officers, while continuing to insist that neither officers nor soldiers could constitutionally be quartered in a private dwelling without the owner's consent. In the spring of 1758 Bouquet and the surviving regulars were summoned to serve elsewhere, leaving the Charlestonians to ponder the cost of dealing with the British army. As for the troops themselves, they had ample reason to want to forget their experience in South Carolina. The officers especially, from Bouquet on down, must have carried away with them a firm conviction that the people of that colony, as represented by their assembly, were both grasping and stingy, but then, what colony had treated them any better?[56]

The dispute over quartering was likely to spring up wherever the redcoats appeared, and everywhere the disgruntled colonists were quick to cite their constitutional rights. When Loudoun was in Boston, Massachusetts, early in 1757, some of the leading politicians were so bold as to invite his attention to certain radical pamphlets published during the reign of the ill-fated Charles I, but the commander in chief would have none of it. In the manner of a learned professor he lectured them on the nature of military quartering both in time of peace and time of war. The latter now being the case, he was sure that he had an undeniable right to quarters for his troops wherever needed, at colonial expense. Loudoun probably thought he had made his point, but developments in Massachusetts the following autumn proved otherwise.[57] The general court had shown its willingness to provide barracks for regular troops, along with such necessities as beds, kettles, lamps, and firewood, on one or more of the islands in the harbor, but not within the town itself. Then, in November 1757, some recruiting parties arrived in Boston and routinely requested appropriate quarters for themselves and the recruits they hoped to gain. For purposes of effective recruiting, this meant in town, not out on some isolated island. When two of the officers formally asked the justices of the peace to obtain the needed accommodations, they were told that "no Act of Parliament relative to the Quartering of Troops extended to these Colonies and they had no Law of their own to enforce such a Measure, therefore they could not do it."[58] To make matters worse, one of the recruiting parties had arrived in a ship supposedly carrying smallpox, with the consequence that a lieutenant of the Forty-fifth Regiment found himself confined by local authority in the Boston pesthouse, even though there was no evidence that he himself actually had contracted the disease. In vain Governor Pownall ordered his release; the local health officer stood fast on the law.

The adamant behavior of the general court and the local authorities in Boston, especially their insistence that quartering be limited to barracks and not extended to include either public or private houses in town, was like a signal to other provincial governments all up and down the seaboard. In many places the aversion to quartering intensified. Loudoun was quick to sense the danger. Boston's evil example was like a contagion; in colony after colony where the redcoats were preparing to occupy winter quarters local authorities might decide to follow Boston's lead, thus leaving the troops without proper lodging. Therefore, Loudoun decided to act decisively once again, in order to stifle the contagion at its source. In a letter to Governor Pownall dated Albany, 15 November 1757, he stated that the messenger who brought it would wait no more than forty-eight hours for the reply. If that reply were unsatisfactory, the commander in chief would move three battalions from Connecticut and New York to Boston, and still more if necessary, to overawe the opposition and take the quarters demanded. A private letter two days later left no doubt concerning Loudoun's thinking. He was convinced that quarters wherever needed, at colonial expense, were owed to the army as a right, and that Pownall's rather conciliatory way of dealing with his legislature was counterproductive. "Tis the Nature of the People to do all in their Power to pull down every legal Authority," he lectured the uncomfortable governor. Be firm; demand that to which you have a clear right; accept nothing less.[59] Pownall duly passed along to his legislature the commander in chief's uncompromising threat, emphasizing Loudoun's insistence on having quarters in Boston as a matter of right. Then he sent to the general a defense of his own conduct in the controversy. "Such is the unhappy State of His Majesty's Governors on this Continent," he pointed out, "that although they be invested with every Power both Legislative and Executive of the Crown and have Commission to Exercise those, Yet on the other hand such is the State of the Governments that there cannot on the Continent be produced an Instance of the Governors being able to carry His Majesty's Instructions into Execution where the People have disputed them, nor has all the Power that the Crown has thought fit to add been able to support such,—But the people have Constantly maintained themselves in their Claims."[60] There was not a British governor in North America who could not identify with Pownall's plaint.

In the meantime, the general court of Massachusetts was hastily preparing a bill that, it was hoped, would meet Loudoun's expectations and prevent the massive influx of redcoats he had threatened. On the first day of December a more compliant legislature passed "An Act making Provision for the Quartering, and Billeting Recruiting Officers and Recruits in His Majesty's Regular Forces, employed for the Protection and Defence of His Majesty's Dominions in North America."[61] By the terms of this new law, selectmen and justices were required, upon application, to quarter recruiting parties and recruits in public licensed houses, as was done in England. Even this failed to satisfy Loudoun, because it failed to acknowledge the army's unlimited *right* to quarters. Only if Massachusetts would agree to quarter the regulars as the other colonies did, without limitation, would he change his mind and withhold the regiments. Under such continuing pressure the general court yielded sufficiently to satisfy the imperious commander in chief, at the same time flaunting its own obstinate adherence to principle by declaring that "the Inhabitants of this Province are intitled to the Natural Rights of English Born Subjects."[62]

That Loudoun really was willing and able to employ forced billeting as a means of coercing recalcitrant civilians was best demonstrated in Albany, the town that was almost never free of redcoats. There the high sheriff, a stickler for the fine points of civil law, annoyed the military authorities so intensely that they finally added to the six redcoats already quartered in his home another half-dozen, all of whom, according to the outraged sheriff, behaved like devils. Two other townspeople, for declining to sell wood to the army at a price deemed reasonable by the purchaser, had six soldiers apiece imposed upon them. For whatever reason, some of the quartered troops in Albany did make themselves more than a little obnoxious, bringing in their girlfriends, "Abuseing and Spoiling Peoples things . . . Breaking open Peoples doors Attemting to take the Beds from under Them altho upwords of 70 Years of age . . .," and much more.[63] Other towns, too, learned the possible consequences of being too insistent upon imagined civil rights. When a householder in Trenton, New Jersey, refused to accept a soldier, the billeting officer took a musket in hand and forced his way through the door. In Bordentown the local magistrates flatly declined to quarter 300 men of the Forty-eighth Regiment, whereupon the officer in charge, as he later recalled with satisfaction, formed up his men with bayonets fixed and had them "make good their Quarters," with especial attention to the dwellings of the magistrates themselves.[64]

Under Loudoun's successors the acrimonious dispute over quartering persisted but apparently with somewhat less intensity. In general, both sides seem to have reached a *modus vivendi.* Provincial assemblies continued to insist that the quartering sections of the Mutiny Act had not been extended by Parliament to the American colonies, and above all, that the forced billeting of soldiers in private dwellings was unconstitutional. But as a way of meeting the obvious needs of the army, colonial legislatures typically passed their own quartering acts in general conformity with the legal requirements for billeting soldiers in England. The general court of Connecticut actually did provide for the quartering of troops in private buildings, but only by virtue of the authority of the legislature and under the direction of local civil officials.[65]

It would be incorrect to assume that the presence of regular troops invariably meant trouble. Much depended upon a variety of circumstances including the economy, the state of civilian housing, the perceived importance of military protection, and the attitude of local civic leaders. Serious trouble was most likely to erupt where the presence of the soldiery was deeply resented, where civic officials were strongly inclined to resist, and where the military officers involved were angered by such attitudes. In extreme cases, as we have seen, an officer might lose his restraint and order his men to take by force the shelter they required. Most officers probably were anxious to avoid unnecessary confrontation with the civilian community upon which they were so dependent, and we can even ponder some examples of the military's sensitivity to local concerns. At Albany, of all places, on at least one occasion the commander remembered that in English tradition the soldiery was considered a potential threat to the free exercise of civil authority, and so took measures to allay fear on election day, as demonstrated by the following order: "Tomorrow being the Election of Representatives for the County of Albany; The Troops in the Garrison are to be confined to their Barracks from Troop Beating, till further Orders, Or may be marched out of Town to Exercise if the Commanding Officers choose it. The Captain of the Day and the officers of the Piquet to go frequently round the Street, and to order Patroles from the Guards to take up every Soldier they find in the Streets."[66] For some reason the town of New Brunswick, New Jersey, was very happy with the four companies of the First Regiment residing in barracks there, for when it was learned that the troops were to be withdrawn, the town fathers implored General Amherst to let them remain. A surprised commander in chief, unaccustomed to hearing such sentiments, readily consented. Upon receiving this good news, the mayor and aldermen thanked the general, assuring him that "the Engaging good Nature and politeness of the Colonel and the Officers as well as the Orderly behaviour of the Soldiers under his Command has been unexceptionable among us. We are therefore the more Strongly induced to Contribute all we Can to make the place as agreeable to them as posible."[67] Such sentiments were so exceptional that we may perhaps be forgiven for suspecting ulterior motives. More commonly the soldiery and the townsfolk lived uneasily and unhappily together, with occasional threats and even open violence.

At the highest levels of provincial government an almost constant battle was being waged between the elected assembly and the executive for control of provincial military policy and the conduct of military operations, as part of the assembly's long campaign to gain political parity with the appointed proprietary or royal governor. The Great War for the Empire raised this internal struggle to a new level of intensity, to the great discomfiture of the professional military establishment. Having already gained the power of the purse, the colonial legislatures now were increasingly insistent on exercising some degree of control over the actual use made of the funds they appropriated for the war effort, extending to such matters as the designation of provincial commanders, the definition of geographical areas beyond which provincial troops were not be be led against their will, the siting of new forts, and even the selection of military targets for attack. Inevitably, the assembly's determined intrusion into such previously exclusive preserves of the executive-military was facilitated throughout the war by the constant need for special appropriations that only the legislature could provide.

In New England it had long been customary for each legislature to appoint a "committee of war" charged with general oversight of the colony's military affairs. As these committees were responsible to the parent body making the needed military appropriations, they were strongly inclined to insist upon at least the right to advise and consent with regard to military operations. Hard-pressed governors, caught between the demands of the Crown, the royal commander in chief, and the legislature, often were forced to give ground. Lord Loudoun once found it necessary to lecture a New England governor on the folly of a commander in chief being expected to review his operational plans with each provincial government in order to obtain needed appropriations. Such a procedure, he correctly pointed out, was a sure way of getting those plans to the enemy.[68] Later the same governor found opportunity to remind Loudoun that "as Men are raised in this Colony as well as others by and in Consequence of the Votes . . . of the General Assembly . . . they must know at least the General Service the Men are to be raised for whether for Garrisoning or for attacking and reducing the Garrisons or Settlements of the Enemy or the like otherwise it will be Extreamly difficult to prevail on an Assembly to make provision for that purpose as well as difficult for them to know what provision to make. . . ."[69]

Often the colonies were insistent that their own militia could not be required to serve outside the bounds of their own colony without legislative consent. In 1756 the Massachusetts committee of war took pains to apprise Loudoun of this restriction, citing the royal charter of 1691. The general, in turn, informed an intercolonial meeting at Boston that the practice of restricting provincial contingents to the kind of service specified by an assembly was "a preposterous Measure" because "Our affairs are not in a Situation as to make it reasonable for any Colony to be Influenced by its Particular Interest." He could not promise, he told them, to employ their provincial soldiers "in this or that particular place only."[70] Despite this admonition, the Massachusetts assembly later took it upon itself to specify the locations to be occupied by certain provincial scouting units on the frontier, which the royal governor instantly recognized as an intrusion upon his executive authority. When he delivered an official protest, the assembly refused to budge, and so the governor was forced to acquiesce or lose the service of the troops in question.

Governor Benning Wentworth of New Hampshire was disappointed when his assembly placed a limit of nine months on the service of its provincial troops. The assembly, he reported ruefully to William Pitt, also had granted to one of its own committees the power of appointing certain military officials. Viewing that as a clear encroachment on the royal prerogative, reserved to himself, he nevertheless felt obliged to acquiesce. "As at this Critical Hour, all disputes and Controversys ought to Subside," Wentworth went on to explain, "I am hopeing I shall not Incurr His Majesty's displeasure by this or any other Condescention I may be under a Necessity to make for the good of the Common Cause."[71] Nor was the problem limited to New England. The Virginia legislature once went so far as to order a part of the Virginia Regiment then in garrison at the Forks of the Ohio to withdraw, at the same time threatening that if any authority (meaning a British officer) should try to prevent the move, Virginia would cease contributing to their support.[72]

The persistence of such issues as quartering and the role of the assemblies in military planning, and especially the strength and assurance with which some of the leading provincial politicians clung to their claims of right and power, show that by the midpoint of the war some of the dominant colonies such as Massachusetts, New York, Pennsylvania, Maryland, Virginia, and South Carolina had become firmly established in an adversarial relationship with royal authority. During the remainder of the war, even as the regular forces themselves became increasingly dominant in the drive for victory over the French, friction between the army and the colonial population continued to mar the relationship. In retrospect, this seems inevitable, for provincial interests and needs were not identical with those of Great Britain, even though British officialdom seemed to assume that they should be. Although the colonists were not unpatriotic, they were less interested in contributing to British glory and wealth than to their own gain. Victory they did desire, most sincerely, but not at the cost of their own well-being. And especially were they unwilling to humble themselves before arrogant outlanders wearing the red coat.

Albany remained a center of almost constant trouble. On the evening of 20 May 1758 a sentry of the Twenty-seventh Regiment, on duty at the south gate of the town, shot and killed a Dutch burgher who had failed to halt when challenged. Before the matter was settled, even Lieutenant Governor James De Lancey became involved. Litigation, apparently encouraged by the high sheriff, became for the Albanians an especially satisfying way of retaliating against the redcoats. Any time a regular officer took a step that was in some way disadvantageous to a local inhabitant, the consequence was likely to be a writ, an arrest, and a civil suit that could be hampering, involved, and prolonged. Local lawyers seemed happy to play along with this game.[73]

Captain Gabriel Christie of the Forty-eighth Regiment, who served for a time as deputy quartermaster general under Abercromby, found himself pestered with writs. One, for example, came after Christie had impressed a supply of oats for the army's horses. This particular case brought Abercromby's indignation to the boil. Christie, he stormed, had "mett with all the Obstructions and difficulties it was in the Power of the Inhabitants . . . to throw in his way," and the general went so far as to ask the governor himself to "put an immediate Stop to all these litigious and unwarantable Actions against him." That, of course, was beyond the power of the civil magistrate to do. Even the breezes at Albany brought an unpleasant reminder of the army's presence. One disgusted resident told of a large military stable "which Gives a stink and a Prodigeous noise of the stamping of the horses, the dung lies about it so high that some of the neighbours have Been oblidged to Lay Large Logs of wood before their doers to keep The dung out."[74] From one end of the horse to the other, it seems, there was little but trouble between the army and the townsfolk.

Later, Brigadier General Thomas Gage, when forced to deal with a multitude of formal claims by the residents of Albany and vicinity for goods and services not yet paid for by the army, quickly concluded that the people were naturally litigious and probably unscrupulous as well. "Oaths," he commented wryly, "are Swallowed by these People with as much Facility as by a Sett we have heard of who carry a straw in their shoes."[75] He was referring to an old English tradition that a man willing to perjure himself for pay signalled his availability by loitering near the courts of law with a straw in his shoe. It was not a flattering characterization for the inhabitants of an American community, but it did convey only too well what many of the regular officers had come to feel as a result of long and frustrating dealings with the colonists.

American farmers continued to serve as a prime example. Since the time of Braddock they had remained generally reluctant to help the army with its perennial problem of transport, fearing loss of their essential horses and wagons. In 1758, when Brigadier General John Forbes set in motion at Philadelphia a major expedition to advance westward and recapture the Forks of the Ohio, Pennsylvania again became a focal point for this problem. Forbes's expedition totalled nearly 7,000 troops, less than a quarter of whom were regulars. Because this large force would have to advance across a vast area of sparse settlement and mountainous wilderness, a plan had been devised for establishing a chain of fortified supply stations at intervals along the route. These were to be kept stocked by convoys of wagon teams and drivers hired from Pennsylvania farmers at a legally established *per diem* rate of fifteen shillings for each driver with four horses and a wagon. It was to be a contractual arrangement. Primary responsibility for acquiring the needed transport rested upon the already sorely tried shoulders of none other than Colonel Henry Bouquet. Unfortunately for Bouquet, the farmers still were more than a little reluctant to part with their equipage, not only because they needed the horses and wagons for working their land, but also because they considered the price offered too low for the risk involved. Indeed, previous experience with the army had convinced them that all too often that which was lent was never returned, and that obtaining the compensation owed was difficult and frustrating.[76]

As in the case of quartering, when thwarted and desperate the army would resort to sheer coercion. By the end of May, Bouquet was seeking and obtaining legal warrants for the impressment of horses and wagons. Because local officials such as constables often could be intimidated by groups of angry farmers, Bouquet routinely backed them up with parties of soldiers, wisely selecting for that duty not redcoats but provincials. In this way more wagon teams were obtained and the expedition was able to proceed.[77] Officers suspected that some of the farmers had managed to bamboozle the army by presenting strong, healthy horses at the time of official appraisal and later substituting "nags who were unable to drag themselves along."[78] Soon the route along which the army was advancing so painfully was littered with broken-down, abandoned wagons. At Shippensburg, Forbes was moved to denounce "the horrible roguery, and Rascality in the Country people, who did not at all fulfill their Contracts and agreements, neither in Carriages nor Horses."[79] Drivers sometimes hauled smaller loads than stipulated, and proceeded at a slower pace, probably in hope of preserving the valuable wagon teams. Eventually, Forbes appealed to Governor Denny for more assistance, threatening to employ force if necessary. In an anguished letter to the struggling Bouquet, he wished the Pennsylvanians "damned for their treatment of us with the Waggons, and every other thing where they could profit by us." The furious general even spoke of dispatching an officer with "possitive orders to call in the whole troops from their Eastern frontier, and to sweep the whole Country indiscriminately of every Waggon, Cart, or

Horse that he could find."[80] Fortunately for all concerned, the army did not go to quite that extreme.

Under the circumstances, one is not surprised to discover that many of the owners of the wagon teams used on the expedition were every bit as angry as Bouquet and Forbes. Three months after Forbes had gained his victory, a message from the Pennsylvania assembly to Governor Denny indicated that many of the wagons had never been returned, some of the horses had perished in the service, most of the others were broken and useless, and at least some of the owners still had not received their compensation. Moreover, in obtaining the needed transport, regular officers and soldiers had sometimes ignored the stipulated procedures, abusing and terrifying the colonists.[81]

The unpaid claims from the Forbes expedition became a nagging headache for one of General Amherst's subordinates, Brigadier General John Stanwix. As usual in Pennsylvania, such a problem became entangled in the seemingly endless tug-of-war between the proprietary governor and his antiproprietary assembly. The truth of the matter was that the British army in Pennsylvania simply lacked the ready cash to pay off its provincial creditors, and the assembly was in no hurry to pass an appropriation that would help the army clear its books. So the poor farmers had to persist. Stanwix suspected that many of the claims were fraudulent or at least padded, and quickly became irritated by the whining importunity of those demanding payment. The clamoring farmers, on the other hand, found themselves struggling in the miry bog of military bureaucracy, without any success. At first all claimants were required to press their cases in Philadelphia, a great hardship on many. It was reliably reported that one Virginian had spent some seven or eight weeks in the City of Brotherly Love trying to get reimbursed in the amount of £40. If paid in full, after deducting all his expenses he could expect to pocket only about £5. Such stories became common currency throughout the countryside. Later, after much grumbling because of the hardship, arrangements were made for hearings to be held closer to where the claimants lived.[82]

Once the British had established Fort Pitt at the Forks of the Ohio, the army required transport from eastern Pennsylvania on a continuing basis to sustain the garrison. The provincial assembly was indulging itself in blatant hyperbole when it assured Governor Denny, who must have known better, that "the same People, who, with so much chearfulness entered their Waggons and Horses into the King's Service last year, were they rendered capable by receiving their just Due from the Crown, would with the same Readiness enter into the like Service again."[83] Not likely! Under these circumstances the army's strategy was twofold: tempt with cash whenever it was available, and, where farmers were found to be unwilling, resort to impressment through the agency of local civil officials. Impressment sometimes worked, sometimes did not. In either case it created deep resentment. Occasionally, ingenious local officials who sympathized with their neighbors were able to delay or even thwart the workings of the law. A press warrant issued for Chester County somehow just disappeared. Justices of the peace could be quite slow and inefficient in performing their duty, and some showed unwonted reluctance to levy the stipulated fines. It was said that some farmers, anticipating a press, worked their animals at a furious rate to get as much farming completed as possible; consequently, the army acquired horses who were "extreme poor and low in Flesh."[84] Others either concealed their wagon teams or sent them outside the county. When owners were likely to be obstructive, the army tried sending soldiers along with the constables, but even that did not always suffice.[85] British officers struggling with the problem were infuriated by what appeared to be a wave of unpatriotic profiteering, which, by September 1759, caused Colonel Bouquet to contemplate prophetically the "degree of Insolence the Rabble of this Country will raise, if they are not brought down from home," meaning England![86]

In this chapter we have explored the various problems that bedeviled the British army wherever it went in the North American colonies—in recruiting, in finding shelter for the troops, in acquiring needed supplies and transport. Colonists in general seemed almost eager to hinder the military and take advantage of its urgent needs, profiteering whenever possible, standing fast on supposed constitutional rights, denouncing additional taxation or assessments for military purposes, undermining the efforts of recruiting parties, resorting frequently to litigation. These problems, complicated and intertwined as they were, seemed to go on forever, distracting and hampering the officers responsible for conducting the war against the French. Everybody seemed perpetually angry, and quick to suspect the lowest of motives. Such tension, obviously, was generated by clashing interests. The colonists, envisioning the wealth of British royalty and the national treasury, felt that the motherland could and should bear most of the cost of imperial conquest; seeing themselves as poor, they naturally sought to minimize any sacrifices they might have to make. British officers, on the other hand, were career soldiers always intensely conscious of professional reputation and the tortuous pathway to promotion; they were ever anxious to please their superiors and succeed in their missions, if possible at colonial expense.

Each side tended to view the other in an unfavorable light that seemed to become even worse with lengthening experience. Redcoats often seemed to regard the colonists with a condescension bordering on contempt, marking them down as unsophisticated and even crude outlanders, a bewildering conglomeration of ethnic and religious groups, selfish and unreliable, grasping, and even unpatriotic. Such highly negative judgments were constantly being relayed by the officers to their families, colleagues, and superiors back in England, with the result that a growing number of influential Britons, both in and out of government, were becoming more and more unfavorably inclined toward the Americans. Some even began to anticipate serious trouble ahead, trouble that might be averted only by the timely exercise of firm discipline and control. Conversely, most American colonists simply did not like the red coat or the man who wore it. The king's troops (excepting those drunken or simple-minded colonists who had given themselves over to the recruiting parties in America) were strangers who came from a distant land. Many spoke with a marked brogue or at least an accent and vocabulary that were different from local speechways. Pious Protestant Americans tended to be suspicious of those among the regulars who might be Irish Catholics, or high Anglicans, or perhaps altogether irreligious. To the independent-minded American civilians, the king's officers appeared to be arrogant and callous, the ordinary soldiers abject, brutal, mean, untrustworthy. Above all, the presence of large numbers of royal troops reawakened old traditional fears of a standing army, the tool of the tyrant, a potential threat to all civil liberties.

By 1763, as the result of constant, unhappy interaction throughout the long and trying war, these mutually unfavorable perceptions had become firmly established on both sides, creating a potentially dangerous atmosphere of antipathy and mistrust between the British professional forces and the American civilian population. The shared dangers of actual campaigning, however, might have had the effect of promoting a sense of comradeship among troops of diverse origin and character. What kinds of relationship did in fact develop between the British regulars and the provincial troops raised by the various colonies to participate in the struggle against the common enemy? That problem will be explored in the next chapter.

CHAPTER 6.

THE GREAT WAR FOR

THE EMPIRE

JOINT OPERATIONS

ESPITE all the disagreement, wrangling, and recrimination between Americans and Britons during the Great War for the Empire, there was one proposition on which all parties were virtually unanimous: provincial military manpower, in conjunction with British regular forces, was essential for victory over the French and their Indian allies. Actually, the British high command attempted to make effective use of provincial manpower in two ways. First, regular regiments were dispatched to the colonies undermanned, with orders to recruit to full strength after arrival by enlisting men from the general population. Second, the various colonies themselves were encouraged to raise regiments of their own, provincial regiments whose officers were commissioned by the governor instead of the king. Thus from the earliest phase of the war until the very end, provincials were joined with redcoats in joint operations, with results that were sometimes favorable to the enemy, sometimes otherwise, but nearly always destructive to Anglo-American relations.

The British army was a full-time, highly disciplined, professional organization whose ideals and tradition had been evolving during more than a century of varied experience. Its officers, drawn almost entirely from the upper classes and involved in a system of promotion that gave a distinct advantage to both influence and wealth, were accustomed to deference, and cherished authority. Many were prone to disdain not only the lower orders of society but all outlanders and provincials in general.

Rank-and-file redcoats were recruited from the lower classes, especially the drifters and losers. Toughened by hard training and severe discipline, and without much hope for any personal future beyond the army, they were little better than tools of destruction in the hands of their commanders. Some, no doubt, did develop a sense of regimental pride, taking satisfaction in the proficiency produced by arduous training. The companies and regiments, smartly uniformed and uniformly equipped with standardized weapons and accouterments, made an impressive appearance on parade. They were trained, according to standard doctrine, in linear tactics designed for the traditional open-field battles of western European campaigning, but in some circumstances were also prepared to function on wooded mountainous terrain, as in Scotland. On the whole, this was a career-oriented, consciously professional force held together by discipline, tradition, and pride.

Provincial forces, in sharp contrast, consisted almost entirely of military amateurs, essentially civilians temporarily involved in the defense of their homeland. They considered themselves obligated only to the colony from which they had been raised, and looked forward impatiently to the day of return. The officers, mostly drawn from the upper and middle classes of provincial society and, as we have said, holding their commissions from the provincial governor rather than the king, typically were actual neighbors of the men they commanded; often they retained a fairly strong sense of identity with their troops, even feeling some need to enjoy their affection as well as their respect. In fact, most provincial units did have a strong local or regional identity, consisting as they did of men who had enlisted to serve under a particular officer whom they knew either personally or by reputation. Discipline was somewhat more casual and less brutal than in the British army. Any occasional admonishing or punishing was almost paternal in nature; the troops could accept this kind of fatherly discipline at the hands of officers they knew and respected without feeling like despised slaves.[1]

For obvious reasons, provincial troops usually were less thoroughly trained than the regulars. On parade they seemed awkward and sloppy, unkempt and even ragged, with a variety of weapons that might defy classification. One American commander was frank enough to say that his "Officers and Men with very few Exceptions are not only Strangers to Military Life but show an averseness to Discipline and Regularity . . . ," adding that their muskets were all "of different Bores and sorts."[2] No wonder that in the eyes of professionals, the colonial troops seemed quite unsoldierly if not ludicrous. The provincials were not unfamiliar with at least the most rudimentary forms of drill, battlefield maneuvers, and platoon firing cherished by the British regulars, but years of hard experience in the wilderness environment had caused them to adopt a somewhat loose or fluid approach to field tactics, even though much of the militia training continued to rely upon standard manuals emphasizing the traditional linear evolutions. They recognized the advantage of spreading out when advancing across heavily wooded terrain, were alert to the possibility of ambush, and considered it no disgrace to take cover when the bullets flew thick and fast. Unlike the redcoats, they feared the enemy more than they feared their own officers, and were inclined to act accordingly, which is why most regular officers considered them not only ill trained, poorly disciplined, and inexpertly led, but generally unreliable.

Above all, as temporary soldiers the colonial troops held unshakably to the concept that they were serving under precise contractual terms, having enrolled under a particular officer for a stated period of time, for a specified purpose, at a definite rate of pay. Any deviation from those agreed-upon terms violated the contract, thereby dissolving the obligation. Thus any attempt to impose unfamiliar officers upon provincial troops was likely to mean trouble. Similarly, as soon as the stated term of service had expired, the provincial soldier felt justified in leaving his post and heading for home, regardless of the current military situation.

What has been said above regarding the provincial soldier applied generally to the troops raised in all the colonies, but most strongly and characteristically to New England, where the militia cherished a long-standing democratic tradition as well as a tenacious sense of communal identity and individual rights. New England soldiers repeatedly distinguished themselves by their stubborn insistence upon the contractual nature of their military obligation, their deep-seated reluctance to serve under any commanders other than their own, and their sullen refusal to submit any longer than absolutely necessary to unreasonable or abusive authority. During the long hard years of the Great War for the Empire the British regulars, officers especially, often had their limited patience stretched well beyond the breaking point by the attitude and behavior of colonial troops, most notably the New Englanders, and above all the flinty men who hailed from Massachusetts.[3]

Throughout the war there were occasions when British regulars and provincial troops were expected to operate in close conjunction, usually under the overall command of a British regular officer, so as to bring maximum strength to bear against the common foe. Sometimes those occasions would stretch out over a period of weeks or even months, under conditions causing strain for both groups, with consequent friction signified by volleys of criticism and complaint. It was during such times especially that mutually unflattering perceptions began hardening into biases that would persist for years thereafter. Such was not the desire of responsible British commanders, who had hoped for harmonious relations that would enable the combined forces to function with minimal friction and maximal effectiveness. General James Abercromby urged one of his regular officers to promote "the Strictest Harmony between the Regulars and Provincials," and General John Forbes caused the following reminder to be inserted in the daily orders for 28 September 1758: "Every one must be Sensible that a good Understanding and a Mutual Cement of Hands and Hearts will most Certainly be the most surest means of a Completion to all our wishes, that is success over our Enemys and the Support and prosperity of these Provinces."[4] Responsible provincial commanders felt a similar concern. Thus when General John Winslow of Massachusetts learned of incipient trouble between his men and the redcoats, he initiated an official inquiry by provincial officers "To Prevent Misunderstanding between the Troops Immediatly under his Majestys pay, and the Provincial Forces." Likewise, the colonel of a Pennsylvania regiment took pains to insist that "heats and quarrels with Regular Soldiers be carefully avoided as the Service the whole are engaged in is as one," adding the pious hope that regulars and provincials alike would "look upon themselves as brotherly Soldiers."[5] It was an ideal seldom realized.

Central to the problem was the question of military discipline, the very cement of any army. From the moment in 1754 when the ministry first decided to send regulars to North America against the French, British commanders had to face the problem of establishing effective disciplinary control over the provincial forces with which they would be operating and for whose behavior they, in the last analysis, would be responsible. They considered the problem critical because of previous and unhappy British experience with American troops, whose own lack of martial discipline had become almost legendary among the regulars. Unless the provincials could be effectively disciplined as were the redcoats, they would constitute a handicap and possibly even a hazard to the king's regiments.

Responding officially to an inquiry from Secretary of State Sir Thomas Robinson, the royal attorney and solicitor general advised that the only expeditious way by which provincial troops could be made subject to the disciplinary provisions of the Articles of War, when operating in conjunction with regular forces, was for Parliament to include such a provision in the annual Mutiny Act. Accordingly, this was done, stipulating that

> all Officers and Soldiers of any Troops being mustered and in Pay, which are, or shall be, raised in any of the *British* Provinces in *America*, by Authority of the respective Governors or Governments thereof, shall, at all Times and in all Places, when they happen to join, or act in Conjunction with, his Majesty's *British* Forces, be liable to martial Law and Discipline, in like manner, to all Intents and Purposes, as the *British* Forces are; and shall be subject to the same Trial, Penalties, and Punishments.[6]

Immediately, the Massachusetts agent in London offered a petition against this requirement, a clear indication of the reluctance of provincial troops, New Englanders in particular, to experience the extremely harsh discipline of the regular army. In the ensuing debate over whether or not the Massachusetts petition should even be received by the House of Commons, several important points were advanced. It was argued that even though the rigorous Articles of War were essential for regular soldiers because of the low character of the enlisted personnel, such was not the case with the Americans who might serve in time of war, for the latter were likely to be responsible men of higher quality. Indeed, it was said, few if any colonists would enlist if they knew that it made them subject to the Articles of War. Despite such arguments, the stipulation was passed and the various provincial governors duly notified. When provincial units joined the Braddock expedition in 1755, they were drawn up in formation to hear the Articles of War read, after which the men were tendered the oaths of allegiance and supremacy. Thereafter, they were fully subject to the disciplinary system of the British army. This condition prevailed throughout the remainder of the war whenever provincial troops were operating in conjunction with regulars under a commander bearing the king's commission, the provincials being formally reminded of that fact by occasional formal readings of the Articles of War.[7] Urged by the governors, some provincial legislatures reinforced the Mutiny Act by themselves stipulating that their troops were subject to the same discipline as the regulars, an action reflecting both a reluctance to concede that Parliament had jurisdiction in the matter and a recognition that there really was no practical way for a colony to exempt its forces when they were operating under British overall command.[8]

Like it or not, provincial units engaged in joint operations were in every respect subject to British military law. This meant, in practice, that any provincial soldier could be charged with an offense by any regular officer. If the offense were relatively minor, the case would be decided by a regimental court martial of the offender's own provincial regiment, but for any major offense the unhappy culprit would find himself facing a court whose membership, appointed by the British commander, included both regular and provincial officers. From such a court he could expect little sympathy. The sentence imposed was subject to the approval of the British commander, who could let it stand, reduce it, or even cancel it altogether as an act of mercy.[9]

British military punishments at that time, as is well known, were almost incredibly severe. Only a person made callous by long military experience could have failed to be horrified by the calculated, ceremonial, prolonged savagery. Routinely, these punishments were administered before entire bodies of troops drawn up in formation as silent witnesses. The victim's agony served as a stark reminder of the iron discipline under which they were required to exist and the awesome authority vested by the Crown in all officers holding the royal commission. For stealing a keg of beer, one British regular was sentenced to receive 1,000 lashes (subsequently reduced by the commander to 900, administered 300 at a time on three different occasions). Another soldier was condemned to 1,000 lashes for stealing some money from an officer. As a first installment of the punishment he was given several hundred lashes and then returned to confinement for recovery; the next morning he hanged himself. Two Highlanders drew sentences of 1,000 lashes each. As the first was being viciously flogged the other, awaiting his turn, impulsively "Drew his Knif and Cut His own throat to Escape the whip."[10]

The supreme penalty was ignominious death, by hanging or shooting. As in the case of lesser punishments, the commanding general had the power of pardon, a clemency he sometimes chose to exercise by withholding the word of mercy until the very moment of execution, thereby inflicting upon the victim a sickening combination of terror and desperate hope. There were cases in which several condemned soldiers were marched to the gallows together and then, with all preparations made, notified that some were to be spared and others killed. General Amherst's specific orders will serve to illustrate the method. Samuel Harris and David Rogers, provincial soldiers belonging to the Rhode Island

Regiment, had been convicted as deserters and sentenced to death, whereupon Amherst issued the following instructions:

> Samuel Harris is first to be shot by the Platoon of the Rhode Island Regt. in the Front of the Line.
>
> David Rogers is then to be brought to the Place of Execution and is there to be told that in hopes that one Example may be sufficient to put a Stop to any further desertion in the Regiment I pardon him.
>
> The comanding officers of the Provincial Troops will then acquaint their men with the orders I have given in regard to the infamous practise of desertion: that it is with the greatest reluctancy I find myself obliged to order this execution; that I now take upon me to pardon one out of two, being willing to think one example will deter others, which I hope from my heart it will do, for if after this any do desert, the good of His Majesty's Service will not permit me to shew mercy.
>
> The Regiments will then march back to their Camp.[11]

The above words are not those of an inherently cruel man, but rather one who was long accustomed to disposing of the lives of the king's soldiery in the cause of the king's victory. Much the same can be said of the other British commanders who wielded such enormous authority in North America.

Finding themselves subject to British authority and discipline, many provincial soldiers had little choice but to wait out their term of service. The experience did nothing to lessen their deep-seated, almost traditional aversion to the redcoats. One soldier from Salem, Massachusetts, who found himself under British military discipline at Louisbourg in 1759, undoubtedly spoke for many when he exclaimed that "although we be Englishmen Born yet we are debarred Englishmens Liberty therefore we now see what it is to be under Martial Law and to be with the regulars who are but little better than slaves to their Officers." When at last free, he concluded with fervor, "I shall take care how I get in again."[12] He was not the only soldier then or later to make such a vow.

To view more clearly the kinds of Anglo-American friction that did develop in joint operations we shall focus now upon two specific campaigns—in Nova Scotia in 1755, and at Lake George the following year. Neither example, as we shall see, reflects much credit upon the sensitivity and common sense of either party.[13] The joint expedition to seize Fort Beauséjour at Chignecto, Nova Scotia, consisted of about 280 redcoats and a contingent of some 2,000 New England provincial troops, all under the command of Colonel Robert Monckton of the British army. In an unusual arrangement, one of the provincial battalions was commanded by Lieutenant Colonel John Winslow of Massachusetts and the other by Lieutenant Colonel George Scott, a regular officer. For many of the younger New Englanders this enterprise was a first and somewhat intimidating taste of life with and under the redcoats.[14]

Once assembled in Nova Scotia, the expedition advanced toward its objective with little delay, the New Englanders putting their shoulders to the wheels of the artillery and wagons whenever the going became rough, and laboring hard with picks and shovels in the trenches. By the evening of 16 June 1755 the French fort was in British hands. Monckton had cause for much satisfaction, while Winslow was almost glowing in his praise of his fellow New Englanders. "The Troops in General have behaved Well and I Cant but be of opinion Equal to any New raised Forces in the World," wrote the New Englander to a correspondent in London, adding significantly, "and for Fatigues better then the regulars or at Least put to More Duty of that Kinde perticularly in Drawing the Cannon in all our removes and Solely ussed in advance Guards. . . . All Parties behave well and without Jaring," Winslow concluded.[15]

Soon, however, under conditions of deprivation the provincial troops became increasingly restive. Encamped in the open during unusually cold weather for July, and denied an allowance of rum to warm their bellies, the men of Winslow's battalion took up a sullen chant of "No rum! No rum! No rum!," keeping the noise going through much of one evening. Their officers went from tent to tent trying to still the clamor, with little success. It was not a convincing display of good discipline, and certainly made an unfavorable impression upon Monckton, who never would have tolerated such from his redcoats. Significantly, Scott's battalion of provincials refrained from contributing to the disturbance. Monckton was disgusted with not only the bad behavior of Winslow's troops but even their very appearance. "Many of them. . . ," he sniffed, "have Not Changed their Shirts Since their First putting them on at Boston." Recoiling from that gratuitous slap, Winslow grimly recorded in his journal the following disclaimer: "Mistaken as to the Fact of Shirts."[16] As the days passed, with the troops still quartered in a makeshift tent camp outside the captured French fort, Winslow's annoyance mounted. The red-coated commander seldom sought his opinion on military matters and seemed quite insensitive to the increasing hardships being experienced by his men. At one point Monckton, upon hearing that some of the hungry provincials had been out killing stray sheep for food, peremptorily decreed that no officer or soldier should leave the camp without his express permission. Such a drastic restriction, wrote Winslow, "Gave Umbrage not only to me but to the whole Regiment."[17] When Winslow informed his superior that he could find no basis for the allegation, he was told only that Colonel Scott had observed some provincials out roaming without supervision. Ironically, about a week later some of Scott's own provincials, yearning for fresh vegetables, made their way to a place where they found green peas growing, possibly an abandoned Acadian garden, and helped themselves. Discovering these miscreants, Monckton had them placed under arrest, which caused another uproar among the New Englanders.

One day four companies of provincials, drums beating and battalion colors flying, marched out of camp on an official mission. As the formation passed by the fort where Monckton had his headquarters, the British commander noticed the flying colors at the head of the little parade and hastily dispatched an aide to confiscate them. That, said Winslow in a masterpiece of understatement, "raisd my Temper Some."[18] When the Massachusetts officer protested in writing, Monckton coolly responded with a little lecture to the effect that colors must never be removed from camp without the prior knowledge of the senior officer, and besides, they must always remain in custody of the "Color Company," which, in this case, had not been a part of the marching formation. Perhaps, in terms of British custom and rule, the regular commander was teaching a valid lesson, but to the provincial commander, whose sense of pride and propriety had been wounded, the abrupt seizure of his colors seemed, as he wrote, "the most Ungentel Ilnatined thing that Ever I Saw."[19]

In September came a terrible gale that tore down many of the tents and rendered the remainder almost useless, leaving the provincial troops drenched and shivering with cold. Feeling for the men, Colonel Scott and Major Jedediah Preble, the latter a veteran Massachusetts soldier, made their way to headquarters and asked Monckton to permit the provincial troops to take shelter inside the fort. At first the commander replied that there was no room available, and when the two officers indicated actual space Monckton merely promised to give the matter his consideration. Furious at this apparent indifference to the deplorable condition of the provincial troops, the major, no stranger to wilderness hardships, blurted out that "if we were to be Treated in this maner these were the Last Troops that it would be Possible to raise in New England."[20] Later Monckton did decide that one-half of each of the New England battalions, with all the officers, could be admitted to the shelter of the fort, but one New England captain was so disgusted that, rather than take advantage of the offer, he chose to spend a sleepless night in his sodden tent.

To top it all, Monckton proceeded to recruit for the regular regiments by soliciting enlistments among the two provincial battalions. It is difficult to see why any of the New Englanders would have found the offer attractive, but unquestionably some did. On one occasion the dauntless Major Preble actually ordered the recruiting sergeants off, which produced another warm exchange with a furious Monckton. Needless to say, the recruiting continued. When news of this activity reached Massachusetts the assembly itself took umbrage, feeling that the regular army was taking advantage of the provincials. Angrily, the legislature demanded the immediate release of those New Englanders who had been persuaded to enlist in the regular units and the return of the two provincial battalions. To Governor Charles Lawrence of Nova Scotia, who probably was the moving force behind the recruiting campaign, the unreasonable opposition to it had been stirred up by "the base misrepresentations of Lieut. Col. Winslow and some of his Creatures who wrote the grossest Falsehoods to their Friends in New England that ever were penned."[21] In due time, at least some of the recruits were discharged and the two battalions sent home, thereby terminating a generally miserable experience. Especially perceptive, perhaps, was a comment made at the end of September 1755 by Lieutenant William Jacobs of HMS *Success*, a man familiar with the New England contingent in Nova Scotia. After referring to "the unkind Behaviour of the Regulars to the Irregulars [provincials]," Jacobs said that "The Resentment has run so high, that I believe the New England Troops will not serve . . . the Regulars any more, and perhaps will not serve at all." That, he went on to remark, would be a great loss, "for the Americans are a brave honest people. I do not pretend to say, whose fault it is; but this is certain it ought to be looked into."[22]

Here we should acknowledge that attempts by the British army to recruit from provincial units are certainly understandable, given the difficulty of maintaining the regiments at full strength in North America. Nevertheless, such activity could breed resentment on the part of provincial officers and governments when it succeeded, and on the part of the regulars when it failed. New Englanders were hard nuts to crack. General James Wolfe once tried to recruit for the Rangers from among the Massachusetts troops in garrison at Louisbourg. "The Men were asked if they chose to go, and as it seldom happens, that a new-England Man prefers service to a lazy life, none of them seemed to approve of the proposal," he reported with obvious disdain.[23] Under some conditions, on the other hand, a potential recruit might have little choice in the matter. At Crown Point in October 1760, for example, nine recaptured provincial deserters were persuaded to enlist in the Inniskilling Highlanders as the only way of escaping the lash or the firing squad.[24]

New Englanders did not soon forget the Nova Scotia experience. Tales of hardship and abuse, exaggerated no doubt in the telling, spread through the whole region, with the result that all males of military age were further reinforced in their strong determination not to come under the direct authority of any British regular commander. That reluctance was unmistakably demonstrated during the ensuing summer, when a large army of provincial troops, based at Albany, was preparing to advance against the important French bases at Ticonderoga and Crown Point on Lake Champlain. Commanding that intercolonial army was none other than John Winslow, now bearing the title of major general. "The state of these Troops," claimed one observer, not without bias, was "much more orderly then I believe Provincials ever were before. Winslow has the faculty of managing them much better than I could have expected. I was at their Grand Camp . . . , and I do assure you they are very Regular."[25]

Then Generals Abercromby and Webb arrived on the scene, preceding the new commander in chief Lord Loudoun, thereby raising the haunting issue of a conjunction of regulars and provincials for the impending operation. This placed General Winslow in a nice dilemma, for he knew and shared his men's aversion to the redcoats, yet needed the additional strength that the Forty-fourth and Forty-eighth Regiments of regulars would bring. It was Abercromby who took the initiative in the matter by arranging a meeting with the provincial general. When asked directly if the provincial army would object to a joint operation, Winslow replied that although he personally had no objection, he was unable to dispel a contrary attitude on the part of his subordinates. As a result, it was decided that the two regular regiments should follow the provincial advance at a distance, occupying the various posts along the upper Hudson Valley as they were evacuated by Winslow's troops. In this way the redcoats, although not actually operating with the provincials, would be in a position to provide support in case of a serious reverse. Winslow apparently believed that the question had been fully resolved, for he informed Admiral Sir Charles Hardy, governor of New York, that a commingling of redcoats and provincials, "a thing our people are strong-ley disafected too," had been prevented. Abercromby, who was not so sure, wrote to Loudoun, apprising him of the problem.[26]

In the large accumulation of contemporary correspondence about the question of a joint operation in the summer of 1756 may be discovered at least four reasons why the New Englanders were set so strongly against it. One was perhaps a rationalization: if the regulars actually assisted the provincials in capturing Crown Point, they would take to themselves all the glory of victory, which, argued some New Englanders, was exactly what had happened in Nova Scotia the previous year. "Shoud there be a Junction [of regulars and provincials], and Success Attend the Army, the Provincial Troops must do the buisness, and others will reap the honours and Advantages," was the way Colonel Israel Williams of Massachusetts put the case. Others saw a daunting dilemma: "We run a great Resk if we go on without em for if we should then not succeed we shall never be paid from home [England] and if we go on with em it seams we shall loose the Glory if we Do succead."[27] Most of the provincial soldiers were willing to take that risk. Second, the contingents from the several colonies had been raised by the authority of their respective governments. The men who had accepted commissions, and those who had enlisted under that arrangement, believed that their only direct obligation was to their own colony, which meant that they were required to serve only under their designated provincial officers, with Winslow as the agreed-upon supreme commander. A conjunction with the regulars would dissolve that limited arrangement, for British command would then prevail. Third, virtually all of the enlisted personnel in Winslow's army, and many of the officers as well, were determined not to run the risk of becoming subject to the harsh disciplinary system of the British army.

The fourth cause of American opposition to a joint operation was the current system for ranking commissioned officers, a matter of particular concern to all provincials whose commissions derived from a governor rather than the king. This distinction above all else was the dividing line between regular officers and their provincial counterparts. The latter, by and large, were amateur soldiers who had learned the art of war by poring over any available military manuals, drilling periodically with the local militia, and engaging occasionally in actual operations. Many were men of reputation and social standing who had gained some experience in earlier conflict, perhaps at Cartagena, or Louisbourg, or in some of the expeditions along the wilderness frontier. During King George's War

some provincial officers who had served well against the enemy anticipated royal recognition by the granting of permanent commissions in the
British army. When such commissions were not forthcoming, the disappointment felt by these officers did not readily subside.[28] Such officers
had taken responsibility, exercised leadership, and learned much about
the practical problems of combat in the American environment. Now,
with a new and greater war underway, they and other colonial military
leaders had been feeling the sting of discrimination as a result of official
British policy. Secretary at War Henry Fox put the matter quite bluntly in
1754 when he said that "no Officer who has the Honour to bear The
King's Commission can be required, or ought, to Act under the Orders of
a person who does not bear the King's Commission without His Majesty's particular Order for so doing."[29] That placed every provincial officer below every regular officer, regardless of rank, date of rank, or
experience.

Then, in the fall of 1754, as the ministry was preparing to send
Braddock's two regiments into Virginia, it was realized that the standing
policy regarding rank would have to be modified in the interests of
provincial cooperation. After considerable discussion at the highest levels of government, a royal proclamation dated 12 November 1754 announced that

Whereas some Doubts have arisen with regard to the Rank and
Command, which Officers and Troops raised by the Governors of
Our Provinces in *North-America*, should have, when joined, or
serving together with [the regulars]. In order to fix the same, and to
prevent for the future all Disputes on that Account, We are hereby
pleased to declare, that it is Our Will and Pleasure that all Troops
serving by Commission signed by Us, or by Our General commanding in Chief in *North-America*; shall take Rank before all Troops,
which may serve by Commission from any of the Governors . . . of
Our Provinces in *North-America*: And it is Our farther Pleasure,
that the General and Field-Officers of the Provincial-Troops, shall
have no Rank with the General and Field-Officers, who serve by
Commission from Us; But that all Captains, and other inferior Officers of Our Forces, who are, or may be employed, in *North
America*, are on all Detachments, Courts-Martial, or other Duty,
wherein They may be joined with Officers, serving by Commission
from the Governors . . . of the said Provinces, to command and take

Post of the said Provincial Officers of the like Rank, though the Commissions of the said Provincial Officers of the like Rank, should be of elder Date.[30]

What this meant, in effect, was that a provincial captain would now outrank any regular lieutenant or ensign but would stand below any regular captain regardless of his date of commission. Similarly, provincial colonels and majors would have to defer to their British counterparts.

The policy was quite unsatisfactory to the provincials. Those who had learned their soldiering the hard way in earlier combat with the French and Indians especially resented being made subordinate to British officers who had purchased their commissions and knew little about the peculiar difficulties of wilderness campaigning. As Winslow himself explained, "The grand Debate with the Officers in regard to the Junction arises from the General and Field Officers losing their Rank and Command which they were Universally of Opinion they could not give up." As for the common soldiers, they continued to insist that they had enlisted to serve under specific provincial officers, and would not serve under any others whom they did not know. This, said Winslow, "is a Principle so strongly Imbibed that it is not in the Power of Man to remove it."[31] And that is exactly where matters stood following Abercromby's conference with the Massachusetts general.

The new commander in chief, Lord Loudoun, finally arrived at Albany, and promptly set about dealing with the impasse, for time was growing short and the whole campaign seemed jeopardized. By this time the provincial army had advanced as far as Fort Edward, about forty-five miles north of Albany. Convinced that Winslow and his stubborn provincials had been prejudiced against him by his predecessor in the supreme command, Governor Shirley, Loudoun was determined to have the matter out, overcome provincial opposition, and get on with the war.[32] In his hand he held one trump card, a new but relatively minor royal concession in the matter of rank, giving provincial generals, colonels, and majors the status of eldest captain when operating in conjunction with regular officers.[33] Loudoun now sent a conciliatory message up to Winslow at Ford Edward, referring to the modified policy and urging the general to bring some of his leading officers down to Albany for yet another conference.[34]

Winslow, apparently deeply apprehensive and feeling uncomfortably trapped between his own officers and the new commander in chief, delayed his response, thereby infuriating Loudoun, who now sent up to Winslow a steaming missive literally ordering him to Albany. Down Winslow hurried, accompanied by a number of his subordinates.[35] For the better part of a week the regular high command and the provincial high command discussed, explained, and argued, making little or no progress toward agreement. The new royal concession was simply inadequate to dispel the New Englanders' deepest reservations, but no one seemed willing to say bluntly that the provincials would have nothing to do with the redcoats. At last, his patience nearing exhaustion, Loudoun decided to end all equivocation and evasion. "I desire to be informed by you, in writing," he notified Winslow, "whether the Troops now Raised by the several Provinces and Colonies of New England, and Armed with His Majestys Arms, will in Obedience to His Majestys Commands . . . Act in Conjunction with His Majestys Troops, and under the Command of His Commander in Chief, in whose hands he has been pleased to place the Execution of all those Matters."[36] The response was a carefully drafted letter from Winslow and his field officers, dated 12 August 1756, in which they all acknowledged Loudoun's authority over them, but then went on to remind the commander in chief regarding what was "with them and their constituents a Tender Point," namely, that they had entered the service of their respective colonies to serve only under recognized provincial officers. Therefore, they respectfully requested the commander in chief "to allow these Troops to act Seperately, from His Majesty's Regular Troops, upon all occasions; so far as may be consistent with His Majestys Service." To this, the frustrated Loudoun apparently agreed. It was no more than bowing to necessity, a face-saving way out of what Winslow aptly called "this Knotty affair."[37]

Then, suddenly, disaster intervened. The French, under the Marquis de Montcalm, unexpectedly captured and destroyed Fort Oswego at the western vestibule of the Mohawk Valley, thereby threatening Winslow's rear. Swallowing their pride, Winslow and his provincials now accepted redcoat reinforcement at Fort Edward. As the possibility of a British offensive northward against Ticonderoga and Crown Point evaporated, the army looked instead to its defenses, fearing what Montcalm might next attempt. Loudoun's engineers recommended substantial strengthening of the fortifications at Fort Edward, a project requiring long, hard labor by the provincial troops, who by now were thoroughly disillusioned and eager to return home. The sour comment of one soldier reveals the prevalent attitude: "As we have Submitted our Selves to the Regulars expect we must do all their drudgery which will not be Small, as the Plan of Works laid out here will hold our Men in full Employ 'till near winter, when I suppose those few that are not dead, if able to creep may crawl to Winter Quarters or die on the road getting there."[38] So it was that Winslow's provincials found themselves grudgingly wielding pick and shovel under the direction of royal engineers. It was an unhappy end to a once-hopeful campaign.[39]

After 1756 the problem of rank and command continued to affect the relationship between the regular and provincial officers, causing the latter to remain wary. Further experience in 1757 finally convinced the British government that some further concession had to be made if the provincials were to be brought under effective military control. Accordingly, at the very end of December the Crown promulgated another decree:

> For the future, all General Officers, and Colonels serving by Commission from Any of the Governors . . . of Our Provinces and Colonies in North America, shall . . . take Rank next after all Colonels serving by Commissions signed by Us, though the Commissions of such Provincial Generals, and Colonels should be of Elder Date; And, in like manner, that all Lieutenant Colonels, Majors, Captains, and other Inferior Officers, serving by Commission from the Governors . . . shall . . . have Rank, next after all Officers, of the like Rank, serving by Commissions, signed by Us, or by Our General Commanding in Chief in North America. . . . [40]

As for the imperious Loudoun, he continued to depreciate provincial military leaders, doing everything in his power to assure that actual control of any important military effort remained in the hands of an officer bearing the king's commission. Writing to Governor Pownall of Massachusetts on 6 February 1758, the commander in chief stated in no uncertain terms that "the Youngest Major in the Service, that I should send would take the Command from any Person they could appoint to command the Troops they should raise."[41] Obviously, any dispute over rank could have serious consequences affecting individual officers. On one occasion, when Lieutenant Colonel Adam Stephen of the Virginia Regiment actually defied the authority of Lieutenant Colonel Sir John St. Clair of the British army, the latter had the provincial officer arrested for mutiny.[42]

The special units of scouts or "Rangers" employed by the British, largely American in composition and headed by the redoubtable Major Robert Rogers of New Hampshire, further complicated the problem.

Strictly speaking, as General Thomas Gage was at pains to explain, the Rangers had "no Rank at all" relative to the regulars, but because the rank of other provincial officers had been given a form of official recognition, the Rangers assumed the same right. Gage counselled a colleague facing that issue to avoid any dispute if at all possible, but went on to say that "if you are forced to a Decision, you must decide against the officers of the Rangers as they have certainly no Rank in the Army."[43] This despite the fact that the specially trained, woods-wise Rangers had become widely recognized by regulars and provincials alike as among the most valuable of soldiers in the dangerous wilderness. The whole thorny problem of rank continued to fester throughout the course of the war, as the redcoats assumed an even larger share of the burden of actual campaigning, with the provincials being relegated increasingly to a secondary role. Although some American leaders did aspire to regular commissions and all the advantages that came with them, few were content to be subject to the authority of a British regular officer of lesser rank, especially if the redcoat seemed less experienced and less capable in wilderness warfare.[44]

In American campaigning, even more than in European campaigning, an enormous amount of hard physical labor was required for any kind of progress. Brush had to be cleared, rocks blasted, earth moved, streams unclogged, roads built, trenches dug, earthworks raised, acres of trees felled and shaped for construction, bulky supplies manhandled along forest trails or poled upstream in bateaus. Most of this hard labor had to be done by the ordinary soldiers, whether regulars or provincials. The problem was, should the men be given extra pay for performing such tasks, and if so, how much? British officers were accustomed to demanding much from their own men, without extra compensation; under the repressive disciplinary system of the regular army few of the soldiers ever dared voice any objection. American provincial troops, on the other hand, believing that they had enlisted under the terms of a contract that called for soldiering, not menial labor, were inclined to be much less reticent. In fact, they sometimes simply dug in their heels and flatly refused to work until assured that extra pay would be given. Virginia troops with General Forbes's expedition in 1758 made clear their position in the matter of extra pay for extra work, forcing the hard-pressed commander to concede the point. Later he remarked in private, however, that he would never accept the proposition that "the soldier in America should be paid for his work on campaign. That can be done in Europe where they have no provisions, and there is little work to be done," he explained, "but here where not a step can be taken except by work, if things were put on that basis, this army would cost the government more than three armies in Europe."[45] At Lake George the provincial soldiers simply refused to labor without a guarantee of two extra shillings per day.[46] This widespread attitude on the part of the Americans, along with their stubborn resistance to the authority of the regulars, made it always difficult for the two groups to work in harmony.

Nothing bewildered and infuriated regular officers more than outright defiance on the part of provincial units, a defiance that sometimes went so far as mass desertion. Generally, colonial soldiers became defiant whenever they came to believe that the terms of their enlistment were being breached. In such cases they might simply decline to perform assigned duty until the matter were rectified, or, if the condition persisted and morale became sufficiently undermined, they might turn their backs on the army altogether. Mass desertion by provincials might even be triggered by a routine expiration of the term of enlistment, for it was typical for an entire provincial unit to be enlisted at approximately the same date and under the same terms. Often the British officers under whose overall command the recalcitrant provincials were operating suspected that such defiance was being condoned or even encouraged by resentful provincial officers.

The problem began with Braddock's expedition in 1755, and reappeared with nearly every subsequent major campaign. Not unexpectedly, New Englanders were often at the forefront of defiance. During the winter of 1755–56 troops from that area were garrisoning Fort William Henry at the southern end of Lake George, under promise that they would be relieved early in the spring. Toward the end of April the men grew restive and declared that if no relief appeared by a certain date they would abandon their post, which could have been disastrous. A detachment of redcoats was accordingly sent forward to maintain the security of the fort. The following July, at Fort Edward, a provincial sergeant, two corporals, and about forty other men deserted as a group, but were apprehended and returned. By September, with the supply of food diminishing rapidly at these bases, the threat of mass desertion became more intense. Placed on limited rations doled out from the king's stores, the provincial troops "would not take none of it and made a grate noise and Cried hom hom hom . . ." making, as another diarist described it, "a Great Ruffill through out all the Camp."[47] The next day several hundred angry provincials actually headed for home, without leave. Most were rounded up and brought back under guard.[48]

Shortly after the French captured and destroyed Fort William Henry in August 1757, whole units of provincials took it upon themselves to place more miles between themselves and the enemy. One Massachusetts lieutenant was court martialled for "exciting desertion."[49] There were clear signs of panic among the New York militia. Reported one observer, "The Militia by all Accounts have behaved most shamefully. . . . One of the Dutchess [County] Serjants who retreated without orders, was ordered by a regular Officer . . . to return to Fort Edward the fellow behaved Insolently was Shot and 70 of them taken Prisoners and put in Albany Goal." Colonel James Montrésor, reporting on this same unauthorized withdrawal, stated with disgust that the militia "Deserted and went away to their Respective habitations by Bodys with their Officers at their heads," simply forcing their way through any line of sentries placed to stop them.[50] In midwinter a unit of Massachusetts provincials, their time of enlistment having expired, determined to remain in garrison no longer. When a regular captain warned them against leaving, their leaders flatly informed him that they had no further obligation to serve, and off they went, some seventy of them, all on snowshoes.[51]

John Appy, secretary to General Abercromby, complained at length about the stubborn refusal of American colonial units to leave Albany and proceed on up to Fort Edward, as ordered. "Their dilatoriness," he wrote, "and the constant trifling demands they make, of sundries not provided by His Majesty, and that with no other view than Cloaking their tardiness; is almost incredible, to those who have not the opportunity of being an Eye Witness to it."[52] Several months later, at Fort Edward, a colonial diarist recorded yet another example of American intransigence. When the commander of the fort came to the writer's regiment about sunrise and ordered the men out on a mission, many of them began grumbling that they hadn't yet eaten breakfast. Some even refused to move, whereupon the officer began belaboring the laggards with a stick, "which Caused a Great Uproar among us—Our people in General declare if in case we are so Used To morrow, Blows shall End the Dispute."[53]

One of the most revealing examples of mass desertion by provincial troops occurred along the Mohawk River in July of 1758. Several regiments of New England and New York provincials, among them the Massachusetts regiment commanded by Colonel Thomas Doty, were stationed in the vicinity of Fort Herkimer, where Colonel John Stanwix of the Sixtieth Regiment was in overall command. These provincial troops not only resented the authority of the regulars, but disliked having been sent as far west as the Mohawk Valley to build fortifications, which caused much grumbling and talk of leaving. Then, when the men learned that they were being ordered to move still farther west to the Oneida Carrying Place, their anger burst its bounds; in droves they shouldered their packs and headed eastward toward home. Colonel Stanwix was powerless to stop them. By 6 August the tally of "immence desertion" from Fort Herkimer included 250 from Johnston's regiment, 190 from Doty's, 50 from Babcock's Rhode Islanders, 52 of the New Yorkers, and 120 from the New Jersey regiment.[54] Captain Charles Cruickshank, commander of an independent company of redcoats, encountered a flock of the deserters encamped near the mouth of the Mohawk preparatory to crossing the Hudson, and tried to stop them. Instantly he found himself in a dangerous tussle, and was lucky to get away without being shot. "The men are intirely out of all Command and the Mutineers Cannot be Apprehended. . . . The Guard and Centrys placed to prevent Desertion go off themselves," Cruickshank reported ruefully.[55] General Abercromby, learning of the mass desertion and the threat of more among the provincials, sent units of light infantry to intervene, and requested the various provincial governors to have the deserters apprehended as they arrived home. But the general had learned something from experience, for he proved generous with pardons, having concluded, as he said, that "Rigor and Strictness with those Kind of Gentry, may have quite different Effects than upon Regular disciplined Troops."[56]

Autumn 1759 produced yet more cases of near-mutiny and mass desertion, even as the British cause seemed closer than ever to ultimate victory. At Lake Champlain, General Amherst tried to stifle an incipient uprising among the provincial units by the threat of armed force, which worked momentarily, but desertion continued.[57] Farther west, at Onondaga Falls, some fifty New York and New Jersey bateaumen fled the service.[58] The captured fortress of Louisbourg on Cape Breton Island was being guarded by three regiments of regulars plus Colonel Jonathan Bagley's Massachusetts regiment, all under the command of Brigadier General Edward Whitmore. Among the men of the provincial regiment there was serious discontent, for their time of enlistment had expired; Whitmore felt it necessary to retain them for the time being. Apparently it came to the point where the entire regiment simply refused to perform any further duty, and many of the malcontents sent a "round robin" message to their colonel requesting an early voyage home. For this "mutiny," Whitmore had a large number of the most vocal dissidents confined, leaving the remainder angry but nervous. The following day he had the four regiments drawn up on parade, after which the arrested delinquents were brought forth under guard and placed before the assembled troops. An officer read aloud the Articles of War. Then Whitmore addressed the men, announcing forgiveness for the offense committed and promising to send the provincials home as soon as possible. In this case, it seems, discretion was the better part of discipline, although the stony-faced officers of the three regular regiments may have wondered.[59]

When men were determined to escape from the army, even the most extreme penalties sometimes failed to deter. On 29 May 1759 a Rhode Island soldier was shot for desertion.[60] A Connecticut deserter was led forth to be shot on 15 June, "but was Pardoned after being ordered to his Knees and the Cap pulled over his face. . . ."[61] At Lake George a soldier of the New Hampshire regiment deserted, was captured, and then, under cover of darkness, managed to get away again.[62] On 7 April 1760 a captain stationed at Oneida Lake reported sarcastically that "Our Gentlemen Rangers (their time's being out) having got the Notion of deserting so much in their heads, I am obliged to keep constantly on the scout to prevent them going off—two of them made their elopement about five days ago in the night, and were pursued about five minutes afterwards, but could hear nothing of them. . . . Indeed it would be no great detriment to the Service," he concluded inconsistently, "should their Lieut. and all his party follow their example."[63] It was like an epidemic, spreading everywhere, as disillusioned colonial troops became convinced that they had no further obligation to the British command.

At this point it may be instructive to turn away from the generally somber record of official relations between regulars and provincials, in order to examine whatever personal perceptions and relationships evolved as a result of the conjunction. Contemporary evidence, especially in the form of letters and diaries, is quite plentiful. Some puritanical-minded provincials, for example, gained the impression that the redcoats were careless about religion because they made frequent use of strong language and seemed to ignore the Sabbath. Joseph Nichols of Massachusetts heard little profanity among his fellows but "among the Regulars much profaness." One Sunday he observed that "the Regulars Followed Theire business as Brief as any Common Day Building of small Houses and other Affairs" in marked contrast to the provincials, who "some what Restrain them Selves from Work." Thus, in Nichols's view, the "Lord's Day is much more regarded by the Provincials than the Regulars."[64] Another New Englander, Samuel Jenks, could see "no distintion paid to the day except the flags flying and more men put on duty, and almost always sum develish pranck playd. . . ."[65] Even some of the high-ranking American officers, it seems, succumbed to British influence, to the neglect of their religious duty. A Connecticut chaplain stationed at Fort Edward described a "Scene of wickedness" during the time of formal worship, involving the provincial generals Winslow and Lyman:

> The General and Head officers with Some of the Regular officers— in General Lyman Tent, within 4 Rods of the place of Publik prayers; None came to prayers; but fixing a Table without the Door of the Tent. where a Head Col, was posted to make punch in the Sight of all they within Drinking, talking and Laughing During the whole of the Service to the distrubance and disaffection of most present This was not only a bare neglect but an Open Contempt of the Worship of God, by the Heads of this Army Twas but last Sabbath that General L——n spent the Time of Divine Service in the Afternoon, in his Tent Drinking in Company with Mr. Gourden a Regular officer.[66]

As the above quotation makes obvious, provincial officers sometimes did enjoy the company of regular officers, apparently gaining a comfortable feeling of self-importance from their society.[67] All too often, however, regular officers and provincial officers simply disliked and distrusted each other. One provincial officer, disgusted with the duty to which his men were assigned at Lake George by Brigadier General William Haviland, wrote in his diary, "I heard that Colonel Haverland, going round the fort, fell down and broke his leg. Poor man! I am sorry it was his leg."[68] Mutual animosity could go much further than critical remarks. Witness the case of Colonel James Grant of the British army and Colonel Thomas Middleton of South Carolina. On the joint expedition against the Cherokee Indians in 1761, Middleton became so angry with Grant that he finally took his leave and returned to Charleston. Later, when Grant also came to town, the two fought a duel, without fatal result. Grant carried his animus against Americans back to England with him, and continued to cherish it during the ensuing years, as demonstrated by his derogatory remarks in the House of Commons on 2 February 1775.[69]

Personal relationships between regular and provincial officers varied appreciably, but inclined toward the negative. The same was true with enlisted personnel. One provincial soldier who seemed to have a talent for striking up friendships with individual redcoats was Jabez Fitch, Jr., whose diary affords numerous glimpses of such passing relationships: "I Got acquainted with one Issac Sims of the Regulars"; "In the Evening John Bennet of the Regular Troops Came to our Tent again Staid Some time"; "I Went to Visit John King of the Inniskillingers and Had Considrable Discorce with Him about one Daniel Fitch that he Knew in Corke."[70] Possibly such friendly intercourse was more common than the surviving records would lead us to believe. If so, it was unhappily counterbalanced by all-too-frequent antagonism and even hostility, a condition fairly common among allied troops, but in this case unusually significant for the future. Occasional arguments or fights between individuals need not detain us here, but a more general brawl may be taken as clearly symptomatic of serious tension. On 13 July 1760, at Crown Point, matters came to open violence, as recorded by two provincial diarists. A regular soldier showed disrespect toward a provincial officer, who had the offender arrested and confined in the provincial guardhouse. News of this quickly spread to the regulars' camp, where sympathy for a fellow soldier broke the bounds of military discipline. Soon a mob of determined grenadiers armed with clubs made their way to the provincial guardhouse, overwhelmed the provincial sentries, and rescued the prisoner. Provincial soldiers, responding to the alarm, poured out in hot pursuit. Gunfire erupted, and the eager provincials, doubtless exhilarated by a chance to work off their longstanding frustrations, managed to capture two of the fleeing grenadiers. Rhode Islanders had the satisfaction of collaring the released prisoner himself. "This affair," wrote Captain Samuel Jenks of Massachusetts, "put the whole of the line in commotion; all the regular regiments were turned out in an instant and drawn up in order, supposeing it was an enemy."[71]

There can be no doubt that just as the provincial troops feared and resented the authority of the regular officers, British regular soldiers sometimes chafed under the authority of provincial officers who seemed ill qualified or inconsiderate. During one cold winter some of the redcoats stationed in Pennsylvania lacked adequate clothing. Expecting to solve the problem, Captain Alexander McKenzie of the Seventy-seventh Regiment obtained authorization from General Forbes to draw blankets from the royal stores at Fort Bedford and convert them into jackets for the troops. As it happened, the fort was under the command of a provincial officer, Lieutenant Colonel John Armstrong, who flatly refused to release the blankets because McKenzie could not show the order in writing. For the moment, there was nothing the disappointed captain could do. Later he claimed that Armstrong had seemed "timerous and Confused," which suggests that the provincial commander was fearful of making a misstep for which he could be held accountable. McKenzie, on the other hand, stressed the importance of having the troops well supplied, a consideration "our Proventeal Gentlemen unaquainted with service does not attend to."[72] There it was again, the regular's judgment that provincial officers lacked military competence, just as their men were deficient in subordination, precision, and even raw courage.

Harsh derogation of provincials by regular officers, the result of endless frustration with a people whose basic assumptions about military obligation were markedly different from their own, reverberated throughout the years of a long and trying war. It was a litany of condemnation. In order to reveal the intensity of such criticism I propose to assemble a number of British regular officers in an imaginary drawing room somewhere in the colonies, and listen in on their conversation as they discuss among themselves their perceptions of the provincial soldier. Words within quotation marks are authentic, as indicated by the citations; the remainder have been supplied as a means of providing context and continuity.

General Edward Braddock: These Americans! Of what practical use are they to us when their "slothful and languid Disposition renders them very unfit for Military Service"?[73]

Deputy Quartermaster General Sir John St. Clair: I agree with you completely, Sir. The Virginians with whom I've had to deal are "totally ignorant of Military Affairs: Their Sloth and Ignorance is not to be discribed."[74]

James Montrésor (military engineer): "A proud indolent ignorant self sufficient Set."[75]

General James Abercromby: In my experience the troops sent to us by the New England colonies are no better; indeed, they are "mostly vagabonds pickd up by the N[ew] Englanders at Random . . . in order to save themselves from Service."[76]

Lord Loudoun: You're not telling me anything I don't already know by my own unhappy experience. Those so-called soldiers are "the lowest dregs of the People, on which no dependance can be had, for the defence of any particular Post by themselves."[77] Absolutely undependable.

Lieutenant Alexander Johnson: If I may say so, Sir, not only undependable but "Naturely an Obstinate and Ungovernable People, and

Uterly Unaquainted with the Nature of Subordination in Generall."[78]
James Montrésor: Let me give you an actual example from my own experience. It's almost unbelievable—until you know these Americans.
When the army was up at Ford Edward in the summer of 1757, General Webb ordered me to assign campsites on an advantageous piece
of ground north of the fort to the various provincial units. After I had
done it, the provincial officers "seemed to dislike the situation and
encouraged their men so to do, Murmuring that there were no
Springs of Water at hand though the River not 200 yards from their
Right, and that it woud be immense labour to fell the Trees." Well, in
my opinion the chief reason for their discontent was that I had placed
them "on the same side of the River that the Ennemy was on, and
coud not so conveniently run away."[79] Cowards they are; soldiers
they are not.
Brigadier General James Wolfe: I agree, I agree. "The Americans are in
general the dirtiest most contemptible cowardly dogs that you can
conceive. There is no depending on them in action. They fall down
dead in their own dirt and desert by battalions, officers and all. Such
rascals as those are rather an encumbrance than any real strength to
an army."[80]
General John Forbes: "A gathering from the scum of the worst of people." They haven't "the smallest Idea (neither Officer nor Soldier) of
the business they have undertaken." The provincial officers, with few
exceptions, are "an extream bad collection of broken Innkeepers,
Horse Jockeys, and Indian traders." A contemptible lot indeed. Take
it from me, when dealing with those fellows "you must drop a little
of the gentleman and treat them as they deserve, and pardon no re-
missness in duty, as few or any serve from any principles but the low
sordid ones."[81]
Colonel Henry Bouquet: Sir, you are absolutely right. "I know of but
one way to overcome the indolence of the provincial officers, which is
to break one of them when the army is assembled."[82]
Captain Charles Cruickshank: A disgraceful lot, Sir, officers and men
alike. "There's nothing to be found among them all but Laziness, Neglect Disobedience and Disorder, all ill and eating Constantly."[83]
They're more trouble than they're worth.
Sir John St. Clair: It's almost better when they don't show up, which is
often. They are "an Army in the Clouds. I never expected them and if
we had them they are good for nothing."[84]
Lieutenant Colonel James Robertson: May I make a serious suggestion:

In computing the strength of our forces, reckon the provincials "sufficient to work our Boats, drive our Waggons, to fell Trees, and do the
Works that in inhabited Countrys are performed by Peasants."[85]
That's exactly what these Americans are good for, and nothing else.
General Jeffery Amherst: Gentlemen, I've been listening to all of you,
and I yield to none in the extent and frustration of my experience
with provincial troops. In general, I quite agree with all that you have
said. "The Disregard of Orders, and Studying their own Ease, rather
than the good of the Service, has been too often Just Grounds for
Complaint Against Some of the Provincial Officers, and all their
Men."[86] But we do require their services, ill performed though they
may be, and so must endure their indolence and insolence until this
cursed war is over. Then good riddance to them all.

Rarely could a regular officer bring himself to utter words of praise for
colonial troops, who, when measured by European professional standards, continually seemed to fall far short. The contempt and disgust so
frequently expressed by the British officers inevitably were detected and
resented by the provincials, especially those officers who had some regard for their own ability, experience, and worth.[87]

It certainly does appear that, in contrast to the British regular soldier,
the provincial soldier was slovenly, careless of duty, and often simply
unwilling to endure prolonged hardship and peril. Was he, then, a less
dedicated and therefore a less admirable soldier? With some qualifica-
tion regarding the virtues and dependability of the redcoat, most regular
officers probably would have replied in the affirmative. Yet in all fairness
it must be said again that the British and the American soldiers brought
to their military assignment quite different outlooks and expectations
arising from quite different backgrounds and experiences, to say nothing
of training. The ordinary redcoat knew and accepted his lowly status,
existing with only a bare hope of continued survival through undeviating
obedience to authority. His duty was his life, and his life his duty. In
contrast, the provincial musket-sloper was on purely temporary service,
being essentially and always a civilian. Even though enlisted directly
from indentured servitude, or driven into the army by poverty, he knew
himself to be, at least potentially, a free inhabitant in a land of opportunity, where the future could become better than the past. Additionally, he
was accustomed to thinking in terms of laws and rights, civil procedures
and civil liberties. From these two quite different backgrounds, that of
the British redcoat and that of the American provincial, it proved diffi-

cult to converge. The two groups viewed each other with something less than complete understanding, and all too often with deep prejudice reinforced by unpleasant experience. And so there was friction accompanied by mutual recrimination.

Possibly, just possibly, if the British had been able and willing (which they were not) to integrate the provincial officers more fully into their regular command structure, at the same time performing the political miracle of integrating the various provincial regiments into the organizational structure of the British army in North America, the attitude and behavior of the provincials would have been different. Nothing like that happened, and so the gulf remained essentially unbridged. The deep-seated feelings of dislike, mistrust, and contempt that so often characterized relations between the regulars and provincials during the Great War for the Empire were not readily forgotten by either group. Such a sense of alienation lingered strongly in the minds of numerous Britons and Americans, especially those who had exercised command, coloring perceptions and affecting judgments during a momentous period that was to culminate in the American Revolution.

CHAPTER 7.

THE NAVAL DIMENSION

O study of the deterioration of Anglo-American relations in the eighteenth century would be complete without some attention to the role of the Royal Navy
in offending the mercantile community. The mutual
antagonism that developed over many decades corre-
sponded closely and sometimes merged with similar feelings already examined in the case of the British army; the friction generated was, if
anything, even more intense and the consequences equally significant. In
the principal American seaports such as Boston, Newport, New York,
Philadelphia, and Charleston—breeding grounds of revolutionary sentiment after 1760—the leaders of the mercantile community were among
the most influential in local and provincial politics, men ready and able
to play an important part in shaping public opinion.[1]

From the latter part of the seventeenth century on, ships of the Royal
Navy were seen fairly frequently in the coastal waters of North America.
Singly or in squadrons, sometimes en route home from the Caribbean,
they would stop in at some colonial port for needed supplies and repairs.
Also, the admiralty found it increasingly useful to assign a few small
men-of-war, typically sloops and frigates, to serve as station ships based
in one or another of the principal havens from New England down to the
Carolinas and, later, Georgia. Often remaining in the vicinity a year or
longer before being relieved, these station ships performed at least three
important functions: they protected shipping and coastal areas from hostile marauders, they helped enforce the Acts of Trade, and they stood
forth as a highly visible symbol of British sovereignty.

It was in the first of these roles that the Royal Navy gained its highest
degree of popularity among the American colonists, in particular the
mercantile community; at times when enemy privateers or marauding
pirates were known to be lurking along the sea lanes it was not unusual
to hear a threatened colony pleading for yet more of the king's ships.[2]
Beyond that, naval officers might be personally welcome both for the
money they had to spend in local trade and the enhanced glamor they

might contribute in local society. Occasionally, too, the personnel of the ships were able to perform extraordinary service for the community, as, for example, during the devastating fire at Charleston in November 1740, when detachments of sailors from HMS *Phoenix, Spence,* and *Tartar* helped fight the spreading conflagration, thereby earning the unfeigned gratitude of the inhabitants.[3] Gratitude owed for another reason was publicly expressed in the *South Carolina Gazette* of 23 January 1744 by a shipmaster who declared that the preservation of his grounded vessel was "entirely owing to the speedy and extraordinary Assistance given him by Capt. *Frankland* of his Majesty's Ship *Rose,* and Capt. *Henry Ward* of his Majesty's Ship *Tartar*," both of whom had declined any reward. Captain Frankland, in a later issue of the same paper, actually received the supreme accolade of "our Hero and our Friend" and "CHAMPION OF AMERICA," for services performed.[4] Most naval officers, however, were not so enthusiastically appreciated by the colonists.

It is important to remember that in the time of which we are speaking Britain lacked the advantage of a military or naval academy, or any other centralized system for shaping the outlook and official conduct of its professional officer corps. In this regard the navy was especially at loose ends, with its widely scattered officers pursuing their careers very much in accordance with their own individual perceptions and personalities. The typical captain was of middle-class origin, with some means and, usually, some connections in higher places. He had entered the navy as a youth, probably as a captain's servant or a midshipman, to spend long years at sea learning the ways of fighting ships while clawing his way up the teetering ladder of promotion. Toughened by the hardships, dangers, and rigorous discipline of the navy, it was an extraordinary officer who, during that precarious upward climb toward command, was able to retain the gentler qualities. Indeed, by its very nature the sea service tended to attract men who were bold and tough minded, while weeding out those of weak constitution and gentle disposition. The survivors—those who did eventually rise to positions of command—were likely to be arrogant, irritable, hard-fisted men unaccustomed to tolerating any opposition from their inferiors. Such commanders, when stationed in the colonies, inevitably meant trouble.

The captain of a navy ship in North American waters bore the heavy responsibility of operating a costly fighting machine, with all her personnel, in accordance with standing orders and the occasional instructions of a distant admiralty or royal ministry. Unless a squadron commander was nearby, there were few if any official personages anywhere in the vicinity able to say him nay, and because written orders from home might be months in transmittal, a captain on a colonial station really had virtually no immediate and effective check on his behavior. Colonel Robert Quary, a prominent administrative official in America, spoke knowingly of "the temper and ill Conduct of these Captains that command Her Majesty's ships," adding that such an officer "thinks himself above all Her Majesty's Governors, and even above Government itself," quite an indictment.[5] There is, in fact, much evidence to suggest that the professional naval officer viewed his career as a pathway to eventual riches that would enable him to retire honorably and comfortably. Such riches, however, never could be accumulated solely from an officer's salary; rather, any real wealth to be gained had to be raked in through activities tangential to the profession. As one expert on the subject has reminded us, these enterprising naval commanders "considered themselves soldiers of fortune."[6]

In wartime, a captain who captured a richly laden enemy merchant vessel received a large fraction of the proceeds when the prize was sold. Consequently, men-of-war sometimes spent valuable time on the prowl for such prizes when they could have been rendering better service in some other way, such as shepherding a convoy of colonial ships or patrolling a colonial coast. Seldom could they resist the temptation of chasing after a likely prize. In peacetime, captains could profit in similar fashion by arresting colonial vessels for infractions of the trade and navigation laws, because a vessel found to be in violation was subject to confiscation, with a large fraction of the proceeds going to the arresting officer. The *Boston Evening-Post* for 8 June 1741 reported sarcastically that Captain Pearce of HMS *Flamborough* had "gallantly" seized two suspected merchant vessels in New York Harbor "without the loss of a man," and was taking them to England for trial, in anticipation of a profitable judgment. Such ventures naturally contributed to worsening relations between the navy and the American mercantile community.

Far less dramatic and more insidious was the navy captain's penchant for engaging in profitable commerce as a sideline. Having available manpower without personal cost, and being in a position to avoid customs inspection, a captain could also be a trader with extraordinary advantages over American merchants who had to hire hands, pay freight, and satisfy royal customs officials. Apparently it was not unusual for such a captain to assign seamen from his own ship to man a trading vessel in his charge, feeding them from naval supplies, and of course paying them from the naval purse. In some instances those very men might earlier have been impressed from a commercial vessel owned by a local businessman with whom the captain now was in unfair competition. The latter could ride comfortably at anchor in port, while awaiting the profits that would roll in with the return of his trading vessel. "These gentlemen," complained William Byrd II of Virginia, "pay neither freight nor custome, nor run any risque, by which iniquity they are in condition to undersell all those that do. . . . They love to keep snug at their stations, where they have their trading sloops, which they man with the kings men, and victual with the kings provisions, and hardly ever pay any duty. This is not only a shamefull breech of duty as to the king," concluded Byrd, "but a certain ruin to all the lawfull trade of his subjects."[7]

If the king's ships seemed at times only too zealous in making arrests in harbor, their captains often appeared strangely reluctant to venture out onto the open ocean in defense of colonial shipping. It was a common complaint on the part of American merchants that the station ships simply were not providing the protection needed. Presumably the captains had many reasons, some sound, some more frivolous or selfish, for prolonging their stay in port, and perhaps Colonel Quary was exaggerating slightly when he told the Board of Trade that "they will lye in a Harbour for a year together without once going out to cruize." The *South Carolina Gazette*'s fulsome praise of the vigorous activity of Captain Frankland of HMS *Rose* is most revealing in its implied condemnation of the other captains on the same station:

> Ne'er in a Harbour is the *Rose* confined,
> By blind Excuses, or, *the Female Kind*.

Charleston merchant Robert Pringle, admittedly a biased observer, put it even more bluntly: "The Commanders of the Kings Ships here doe not doe there duty," he stated, and that in a time of war. Yet another complainant informed the House of Commons in 1742 "that during this war the station ships were not five weeks in a year at sea; sometimes going out in a morning, and returning back the same night." That the wave of criticism rolling from the American seaports to the shores of the mother country did not fail to reach Whitehall is shown by the admiralty's frank admission that "the captains of his Majesty's ships stationed in America have, of late years, taken a very unwarrantable liberty of lying in port with their ships for the greatest part of the time they have remained a[b]road, to the dishonour of his Majesty's service and the disservice of the colonies for whose protection they were appointed."[8]

Also occasionally discomfiting to provincial seaports, with less justification, was the navy's insistence upon the right to send seriously ill personnel ashore for recuperation in quarters selected by the captain for convenience and security. This was especially disturbing when highly contagious disease was a factor. Charleston, for example, always in dread of yellow fever, became incensed in 1749 when sick seamen from warships in the harbor were brought ashore and "crowded into some old rotton Punch Houses without either tolerable Accomodations or Attendance."[9] Such was the degree of care, apparently, for which the captains were willing to pay. Feeling threatened by an epidemic, however, the provincial legislature took matters into its own hands by passing an act requiring that diseased seamen be accommodated in a designated building outside the town, with the ship's captain obliged to give security for the payment of their board and lodging. Any captain who placed his sick personnel anywhere else was made subject to a substantial fine. From the provincial point of view this was an arrangement that made good sense and protected the community, but Captain John Reynolds of HMS *Arundel* felt so strongly about the intrusion upon his authority that he made official complaint not only to the royal governor but also the admiralty. Presumably this particular issue subsided and disappeared with the disease.[10]

Made tough by the hardships and dangers of the seafaring life, often frustrated and wearied by seemingly endless and perhaps unreasonable demands on their time and skill, proud and jealous of their supreme authority on their own quarterdecks, these captains sometimes proved to be dangerously arrogant and aggressive in their relations with American colonists. Take, for example, the notorious case of Captain John Jennings of HMS *Experiment*. On a certain day in May 1691 a boat from that vessel approached the courthouse landing on the Elizabeth River not far from the site of Norfolk, Virginia. Stepping ashore with an air of determination, Captain Jennings glanced briefly at the curious bystanders and then, sword at his side and stout cane in his hand, strode directly toward the county courthouse, followed closely by a rough-looking gang of his own men variously armed with guns, swords, and clubs. Behind them trooped the curious idle whose descendants, even to the present time, seem always on hand whenever a county court is in session. On this particular occasion the trial in progress involved one John Porter, Jr., possibly a deserter from the *Experiment*, who was charged with having slandered a friend of Captain Jennings. Before the angry captain was able to reach the courthouse he was accosted by the high sheriff, who tried to interpose. Not to be deterred by any such trifling, the determined Jennings threatened to brain the sheriff with his cane, pushed on by, and marched into the courtroom, his ruffians waiting by the door.

Instantly the captain perceived John Porter testifying at the bar. With not so much as a word to the startled court, Jennings strode directly up to the witness, seized him "by the hinde part of his hair of his head, and threw him backwards upon the flore."[11] As the wide-eyed justices half rose in their places and the under sheriff hastened to intervene, the captain started to draw his sword, while six or seven armed sailors rushed in as though on cue and began laying about them, belaboring spectators and even some of the cowering jurymen. Almost before the court realized what was happening, two tough seamen had Porter in their grip and were rushing him outside and down to the waiting boat, accompanied by the captain and the other sailors. One of the justices, perhaps more courageous or foolhardy than his colleagues, caught up with Jennings and urged him to release the terrified defendant, but received in reply only defiant oaths. Once on board the *Experiment*, the hapless Porter was dragged below decks and secured in irons.

Highly indignant at this affront to law and order, the justices lodged a strong complaint with the royal governor and his legislature. In turn, the governor and council issued a warrant for Porter's release, but when the sheriff rowed out to the *Experiment* to serve the order, he was told that Captain Jennings was elsewhere, and no one else on board had authority to relinquish the captive. Following that rebuff, both houses of the legislature joined in a protest to the king himself, a complaint that eventually was referred to the admiralty, by which time the imperious Jennings had had his way. This case well illustrates a captain's ability to take the law into his own hands and then avoid the consequences by shielding himself with armed power and delay, knowing full well that distance and time were acting on his behalf.

Boston tasted the angry impetuosity of another captain, Richard Short of the frigate *Nonesuch*. Soon after the ship arrived at Boston in the spring of 1692 the crew began deserting. Short, who already was at odds with Governor William Phips, believed that the deserters were hiding in the town, perhaps with the connivance of prominent inhabitants. Well aware, no doubt, that only three years earlier the townspeople had been so bold as to imprison Captain George of HMS *Rose*, he must have known the mettle of those Bostonians. Regardless, Short led a party of his men ashore, determined to find and arrest the fugitives. Knocking at the door of the Green Dragon Inn late that evening, he demanded to know if any of the king's sailors were within. Despite the landlord's

emphatic denial, the captain ordered his men upstairs to search the bed-
rooms. Throwing open a door, they found John Tomson, a representative
to the general court from Middleboro, snug in bed but wide-eyed at the
sudden intrusion. Short ordered this official downstairs with such quarterdeck authority that the startled representative made his way down, as
he said, "without my Stockins." When Tomson tried to identify himself,
the captain swore and "called me Hulver headed dog, old Rogue and
Assembly dog and [said] that he had a good mind to Slatt out my
brains."[12] Ordering his men to haul Tomson away, Short favored the
landlord with a few cuffs before joining his men and their prisoner in the
street. Strangely, after taking Tomson some distance, the captain let him
go. Next, at another dwelling, he assaulted Peter Woodbery, also a member of the general court, caning him until his head was bloody. The dazed
Woodbery then was hustled out of doors and along the street, only to be
released a short time later. If Short really was looking for deserters, he
had a remarkable talent for flushing the wrong game.

Tomson and Woodbery, at the first opportunity, complained to Phips
and his council, providing the energetic governor with more ammunition
to use against the already despised Captain Short. Matters between Phips
and Short finally came to a head on one of Boston's wharves, in full view
of all and sundry. The captain's insolence, apparently, provoked the governor into striking a blow, whereupon Short retaliated with his ready
cane, and the waterfront onlookers came running to see history made.
Phips managed to hurl the captain to the boards and beat him into
submission, after which he had him thrown into the common jail. It was
the second such humiliation of a Royal Navy captain in Boston town.

For yet another example of high-handed behavior on the part of a
naval commander we return to Virginia. Early in 1702, it seems, both
Captain James Moody of HMS *Southampton* and Colonel Miles Cary, a
prominent local widower, were amorously inclined toward an attractive
widow, Mary Roscow, daughter of Justice of the Peace William Wilson.
When the lady in question finally chose Cary over Moody, the disappointed captain conceived that he had been deeply wronged by both the
successful suitor and the lady's distinguished father, and sought to make
his frustration a matter of personal honor. According to one account, he
thereupon challenged Cary to a duel and, when the latter contemptu-
ously declined the encounter, affixed a notice to the public pillory pro-
claiming Cary a coward. Still unsatisfied, he boasted of his intention to
cane or horsewhip both Cary and Justice Wilson. On 19 December 1702,
when Wilson and his fellow justices were hearing cases in the county

courthouse at Hampton, Captain Moody and a party of men from the *Southampton* arrived outside the building, obviously in a mood for trouble. While the court continued in session, the volatile captain, armed with cane and sword, paced to and fro before the door. Then, when the court finally adjourned and the justices emerged, Moody confronted and threatened Wilson, but probably disappointed some of the assembled onlookers by stopping short of actual mayhem. Some months later Colonel Quary summarized this curious case in a letter to the Board of Trade, stating that

> It would take a quire of paper to particularize the several rude, Barbarous, and extravagant actions of one Captain James Moody. ... He neither spared the gentlemen of the Country the Queen's officers, Nor the Governor himself, because they would not suffer him to marry a gentleman's daughter, when at the same time he hath a wife and children in London. This was a sufficient ground for him to attempt the lives of the gentlewoman's father, several of her relations, and especially ... one Colonel Cary that courted the young Lady. The Governor was forced to secure the peace the Country being all in an uproar by this mans extravagant actions.[13]

Isolated cases such as those of Captains Jennings, Short, and Moody may not typify the behavior of royal naval officers in America, but they do illustrate the kind of self-assured arrogance that naval authority seemed to generate and that was so offensive to many colonists.

On the other hand, naval personnel sometimes felt victimized by malicious or self-important provincials. At Boston in June 1749 two prominent civilians tried to intimidate a boat crew from HMS *Viper* and became involved in a violent quarrel with the mate. When the *Viper*'s captain, Cornelius Smelt, heard of the affray he angrily decided to uphold the navy's dignity at all costs, and actually prevented a certain merchant vessel from leaving the harbor until he was satisfied that one of the offenders was not on board. Later, after having gone ashore to lodge a strong complaint with the royal governor, Captain Smelt was served a writ commencing a lawsuit against him for having delayed the ship. Unable to raise bail, the unhappy captain was required to remain in custody for the next fifteen days, which gave him ample time to ponder the rotting of royal authority.[14]

Far more serious was the case of HMS *Greyhound* at New York in 1750. At that time the province was an arena of intense competition between rival political factions, one headed by George Clinton who was the royal governor and an admiral in the navy, the other by James De Lancey, chief justice of the supreme court. The former was intent upon upholding the royal prerogative, and the latter sought to increase the power of the representative legislature at the executive's expense. So skillfully had the chief justice pursued his policy that by 1750 his own effective power virtually matched that of the king's governor. In particular, De Lancey enjoyed widespread support among the merchants as well as a large number of ordinary colonists who relied upon the legislature to protect their interests against those of the Crown. Among Governor Clinton's supporters was his son-in-law, Robert Roddam, captain of HMS *Greyhound*, currently stationed at New York.

Customarily, ships of the navy, as visible symbols of royal authority, expected and required a certain deference from ordinary vessels. For example, any civilian craft seen flying the union flag at sea was subject to arrest and prosecution. Likewise, a civilian vessel passing in the vicinity of a king's ship was required to salute by lowering its own pennant.[15] On the afternoon of 7 June 1750 a small sloop belonging to William Ricketts of Elizabethtown, New Jersey, put out from Manhattan Island and headed for home, a pennant gaily flying from her masthead. The party aboard included Ricketts and members of his household, among them a servant girl named Abigail Stibbins who was sitting in the stern sheets with a small child in her arms. Their route lay between the Battery and Governors Island, a stretch of water where HMS *Greyhound* rode at anchor. As it happened, Captain Roddam was not on board at the time, having left Lieutenant John How in charge. As Ricketts's sloop approached the *Greyhound*, Lieutenant How and Gunner's Mate James Parks stood by a swivel gun to see if her pennant would be lowered in salute. It was not. Deeming this to be "in Contempt of the Kings Colours," How resolved to bring the sloop to by firing a warning shot.[16] He took aim and ordered Parks to apply the match. The half-pound ball went tearing through the air. Even though Ricketts must have heard the report, he continued on his way as though nothing had happened. Lieutenant How, his annoyance increasing, now ordered a second shot, and again the gunner's mate put match to powder. By this time the offending sloop had opened the range considerably, perhaps to as much as a mile or more, which made the shot extremely chancy. The iron ball whistled in hot pursuit, tore through the sloop's mainsail, and struck Abigail Stibbins just above her right eye, smashing in her skull. Immediately, the horrified Ricketts put about and returned to town, where the wounded girl died.

In almost no time the news of this terrible accident (for How almost certainly had not intended to hit the sloop) spread through the streets and byways of New York, amidst mounting public anger. Captain Roddam hurried back on board his ship to deal with a serious crisis. Clearly How and possibly Parks would have to answer for the killing, but the question was—to whom. The *Greyhound*'s anchorage was situated within the jurisdictional bounds of New York, and a crime committed within those bounds, even on water, normally would be dealt with in the provincial courts. But by royal decree, incorporated in the governor's commission, any crime committed by naval personnel on board a ship of the Royal Navy on the high seas or even a river was reserved for the jurisdiction of the admiralty. Roddam was convinced that his two men were not subject to trial in the courts of New York, and so was Governor Clinton.[17] At once, the De Lancey faction began insisting that the case must be tried before a local jury, a stance that clearly worked to their political gain and Clinton's disadvantage. The governor could do little more than publish the jurisdictional clause in his royal commission and send a copy to the provincial attorney general. Should he be unable to prevent a trial, however, he did have the power to reprieve upon conviction for any crime, and pardon for any except treason and willful murder.

Roddam placed Lieutenant How under arrest on board the *Greyhound*, for later trial by the admiralty. In the meantime, New York authorities scheduled a coroner's inquest for the day after the killing, and to that the captain sent Gunner's Mate Parks as witness, presumably in the belief that because he had acted under orders he was not personally culpable. When questioned, the gunner's mate readily admitted applying the match for the fatal shot. Learning of this, Chief Justice De Lancey, although himself not directly involved in the inquest, took the initiative to have Parks clapped into jail to await trial in the provincial court. The coroner's jury duly returned indictments against both Parks and How, a verdict that subsequently led Clinton to fire the coroner.

At this point the political battle lines may be clearly discerned. The civil authorities, with the approval of De Lancey, demanded that How also be turned over to them; Roddam, with Clinton's backing, refused. Roddam repeatedly asked that Parks be restored to the custody of the navy; the civil authorities refused. Neither side gave an inch. Politically, the advantage went to De Lancey, for the populace was aroused against the navy and its apparent attempt to undercut local justice. Many New Yorkers suspected that Clinton and Roddam, if given a chance, would provide a route of legal escape for the two killers. While Parks languished in jail, How remained under naval arrest but, with his own consent, on 18 June was transferred to HMS *Hector*, which soon sailed for England. After arriving in the Thames, How was transferred to the *Somerset*, still under arrest, and eventually was lodged in Marshalsea Prison to await trial.

Parks's trial took place in New York in August 1750. Although convicted of the lesser charge of manslaughter, he was discharged as a result of Clinton's intervention. How's trial was long delayed, but finally took place in the Old Bailey in February 1752. In addition to the defendant, the principal witnesses who appeared were five of the *Greyhound*'s men who had been on deck when the fatal shot was fired. Under questioning, they agreed that people had said that a girl had been killed by the shot, but they had not seen a body and could not say of their own knowledge that a death had occurred. "Whereupon," as one attorney reported, "the Judge Observed to the Jury, that there was no Murder proved, and therefore they must Acquit the Prisoner."[18]

A naval officer did not have to be an unscrupulous entrepreneur or even an arrogant bully to alienate American colonists; quite frequently a straightforward attempt just to fill vacant berths on board a king's ship was sufficient to arouse intense opposition. Indeed, probably no other aspect of the British naval presence in the colonies so constantly exacerbated Anglo-American relations as the common practice of impressing seamen, an irritant so persistent and pernicious as to require extensive discussion here. At the heart of the problem lay the navy's inability to recruit willing deck hands. As one authority on the subject has said, Britain's able-bodied males "recognized the king's service for what it was; they refused to enter it willingly and deserted it whenever opportunity offered. Ships became floating prisons."[19] Certainly few if any American males showed any inclination to join the crew of a British man-of-war; on the contrary, the great majority would do almost anything to escape such a fate. Because the recruitment of volunteers was next to impossible, and with ship's crews being so frequently diminished by disease, death, and desertion, the navy saw no alternative to the time-honored practice of impressing men for the service.

In theory, only seafaring men were subject to naval impressment, but likely hands might be grabbed by the press gang nearly anywhere they could be found, including wharves, waterfront taverns, ships in harbor, and even vessels just arriving at the end of a voyage. All Americans having any connection with the sea hated the system. For ordinary seamen it was a chronic menace over and above the usual dangers of disease and shipwreck. Local shipowners and merchants generally deplored it because whenever the navy was pressing in their own areas employable seamen scampered elsewhere, thereby inflating wages and increasing the difficulty of manning the merchant vessels essential to local prosperity. A town such as Boston, which depended so heavily upon not only seaborne commerce but also many small fishing and coastal craft as carriers of foodstuffs, firewood, and other needed supplies, could be put in serious straits whenever heavy impressment frightened seafarers away. The very pattern of ocean-going trade could be distorted. Certainly one reason why American ships preferred trading with the French rather than the British islands of the West Indies was their desire to avoid the press gangs active in the latter.[20]

After 1708 the American colonists rejoiced in an Act of Parliament known familiarly as the "Sixth of Anne" (6 Anne, c.64), a wartime measure intended to encourage mercantile shipping in American waters by prohibiting impressment in that area. So positive was the prohibition that naval captains whose crews became seriously depleted in America had orders to return to England for recruits rather than attempt to impress men in the colonies. Naturally, the Sixth of Anne was heartily disliked by the captains. "I fear I shall find great dificulty in geting men," complained one, "for since this late act of Parliament . . . men dayly disert, and Masters of Merchant Vessells . . . Encourage and Intice them away with great wages soe that hardly a vessell sayles hence but carryes away one or more notwithstanding all our search."[21] To sympathize with the captains in this regard is not beyond reason.

When Queen Anne's War ended in 1713, many naval officers assumed that the Sixth of Anne expired, thereby opening the way for the resumption of impressment in the colonies. Unfortunately, the act itself was not explicit on that vital point. As late as March 1715, a set of instructions from the admiralty to the captain of HMS *Diamond* sounds very much as though the Sixth of Anne was still operative. Yet it wasn't long before the attorney general himself expressed his opinion that the law had expired with the war. No wonder there was confusion. Of at least one thing we can be certain—the American colonists believed and insisted that the Sixth of Anne did remain in effect after 1713, and that any impressment in North America was consequently unlawful.[22]

Be that as it may, the navy captains in North America did resume the practice of impressment after 1713, which in turn inspired the affected colonists to raise the charge of illegality, and resist with every means available. Some leading men who suffered loss as a result of impressment began resorting to the colonial courts for redress, thereby forcing the captains to defend themselves at law, at considerable inconvenience and cost. The problem became so bothersome that in 1740 the admiralty sought the legal opinion of the attorney general and solicitor general, who concurred in stating that the Sixth of Anne had indeed expired in 1713. Even that was not enough to convince the colonists or prevent their angry resistance.[23] The merchants of Charleston, led by Robert Pringle, acting in collusion with some of the shipmasters, made notably effective use of legal action, to the great chagrin of the navy captains affected. "I beg Leave to Accquaint thier Lordships," wrote Captain Charles Hardy of HMS *Rye* to the admiralty in 1743, "that this Spirit of Prosecuting on that Statute [the Sixth of Anne], reigns here more than ever; Insomuch that I am Informed the Merchants have Entered into a Subscription, to Prosecute Captain Hamar . . . for every Man he Impressed." Their intention, Hardy added, was to prosecute every captain who impressed any seamen from their vessels. When the irritated Captain Hardy snapped at one protesting master that he "*had something else to mind than any little Rascally Merchant-men,*" Pringle showed that he meant business by taking legal counsel and effecting the release of an impressed seaman. On another occasion, when Hardy stepped ashore on business, he was arrested by the local marshal on complaint of Pringle for having refused to release a man said to be illegally detained on board his ship. After consulting an attorney (at some expense) and paying the marshal's fee, the outraged captain found it expedient to let the man go rather than remaining himself in the toils of colonial law.[24] Parliament further confused and angered the Americans in 1746 by passing an act forbidding impressment in any British West Indian colony without the prior consent of the governor and council, a prohibition that did not apply to the mainland colonies. North American colonists, naturally, resented such discrimination that left their coastal communities all the more vulnerable. As one commander later explained to the admiralty, the act of 1746 had filled the New Englanders not only with "a Hatred for the King's Service but a Spirit of Rebellion each Claiming a Right to the same Indulgence as the Sugar Collonies and declaring they will maintain themselves in it."[25] Whether legal or illegal, impressment was an arbitrary outrage, producing violence and tragedy. The true nature of the system is clearly exposed when we begin to examine actual cases.

Captain Robert Jackson of HM sloop *Swift* was a genuine sea dog who stumped around on a wooden leg and employed a vocabulary that would have shocked the elders of Puritan New England. In 1702 he was at Boston, preparing the *Swift* for a voyage back to England, when ten members of the crew deserted. This was a serious loss for such a small ship, and Jackson was most anxious to recover his men. Soon he picked up word that the deserters, attracted by higher wages, had signed aboard several merchant vessels then preparing for voyages, where they were being concealed by the masters until the *Swift*'s departure. Evidence concerning subsequent events is sharply conflicting, but the general course may be readily discerned.[26] Governor Dudley being away from the colony, Jackson notified Lieutenant Governor Povey of his critical need for additional men, and was disappointed by the casual response. So, without bothering to request a warrant for impressment, the determined captain proceeded to obtain men by his own devices. The most obvious sources were the several merchant vessels in the harbor. Accordingly, Jackson himself led his press gang from ship to ship, taking one man from each of eight. According to one of the victims, a ship's cook, he was the only soul on board when Jackson and his gang appeared. When the cook was ordered into the *Swift*'s boat, he asked for time to douse his fire burning on an iron hearth, but Jackson would brook not a moment's delay, roaring "Come into the boat and be dammed, you Sorry Son of a Whore."[27]

Later that same day several Boston merchants, personally affected by what Jackson had done, complained to Lieutenant Governor Povey, who ordered the offending captain to relinquish the men. Jackson refused to comply. As the *Swift* now was ready for sea, Povey gave positive orders to Lieutenant Nathaniel Holmes, commander of the garrison on Castle Island, not to permit the sloop to proceed down the channel. Undaunted, Jackson sailed his little ship down toward Castle William and the Atlantic. As the *Swift* approached the fort, Holmes had his gunner fire a warning shot, which caused the sloop to come to and drop her anchor. Seeing this, Holmes with a party of his men rowed out to explain his orders and, presumably, take off the impressed sailors. As his boat drew near the *Swift*, according to the lieutenant's later testimony, Jackson "catcht up a Musquet cockt it and presented it at me," shouting, "God damm my blood if I do not Shoot you through the head you dog, if you come nigh my Ship."[28] The conference was cancelled.

Jackson now had himself rowed to nearby Governor's Island, apparently to survey the situation and decide what to do next, leaving the *Swift* still riding at anchor beneath the guns of the fort. A messenger from Povey sought out the captain and delivered to him a written order for the release of the impressed men. Although Jackson abused the messenger, he did send back his promise not to sail from Boston without official permission. About 6 P.M. he returned to the *Swift*, having decided to take her back toward the town. Even before reaching the sloop, Jackson shouted for the crew to begin hauling up the anchor. This sudden activity did not go unnoticed by Lieutenant Holmes, whose orders were to prevent the *Swift* from departing, even if that meant sending her to the bottom. Hardly had the captain gained the deck when a cannon ball came whistling in from the fort and carried away the main brace. Then, very quickly, there came a second shot, which struck the capstan at which the crew were laboring, killing one man and wounding several others. That stopped all effort to raise the anchor, and the sloop continued riding placidly under the guns of the fort.

Jackson, now almost beside himself with rage, had himself rowed to Boston, where he soon found himself face to face with Povey and several other officials. Angry words were exchanged, with Jackson calling the lieutenant governor a liar and a murderer, threatening a judge with his cane, and offering to kick the shins of a councilor. This intemperate behavior, as two of those present later wrote, was "the most insolent and wild that we remember to have observed in any man."[29] Povey was not a man to take such insubordination lightly. Drawing up his full (if temporary) gubernatorial authority, he removed Jackson from command of the *Swift* and had him locked up in the prison to await transportation home. Efforts by some of the captain's local supporters to have him released on bail were unavailing. Jackson himself, apparently, saw his plight as a continuation of the same rebellious spirit that had overthrown Andros in 1689. "All good men here who Value's a crowned head and a church of England," he wrote indignantly, "knows that it is a very open Affront done to her Majesty's Coullers."[30] Presumably, in this instance the impressed men did gain their freedom. As for Captain Jackson, he eventually faced a court martial, at which he continued to insist that he had only done his duty.

Another notable case occurred in Charleston Harbor in May 1740, when a press gang from HMS *Tartar*, led by one Samuel Bathurst, set out to board the merchant vessel *Caesar* and take her crew into the Royal Navy. The intended victims, having gotten wind of the stalker, had themselves locked in the ship's cabin shortly before the press gang arrived, leaving the ship's master and a pilot on deck to confront Bathurst and his armed men. As soon as the press gang arrived and swarmed aboard they noted the absence of the crew. At once there was a heated exchange between Bathurst and the master, with the former drawing his sword and thrusting at his antagonist. When the pilot protested at this aggressive act of violence, he became the target for another angry thrust and was bloodied for his interference with the king's business. At this point the master and the wounded pilot scrambled down into the ship's boat, rowed off to town, and reported what was happening on board the *Caesar*. In the meantime, Bathurst and his men forced their way into the cabin where the ship's crew had taken refuge. Somebody opened fire, a series of shots rang out, and when the smoke had cleared it was seen that one of the *Caesar*'s men had been mortally wounded.

Upon investigation, a local coroner's jury indicted Bathurst for murder. Backed by a warrant from the royal governor and the chief justice, the coroner sent a boat out to HMS *Tartar* for the purpose of arresting the accused, only to have the boat "repelled by force, and threatened to be sunk, in case it did not stand off." Obviously, the *Tartar*'s captain, George Townsend, had decided to protect his subordinates from prosecution by the colonial government. Some time later, after learning that the governor was preparing to act decisively in the case, Townsend simply sailed away from Charleston to some safer resort. Months later a naval court of inquiry consisting of three captains did look into the case, and ended by exonerating Bathurst, which caused one indignant member of Parliament to declare that "the military power set the law at open defiance."[31] A navy captain in a colonial seaport had refused to subject his command to colonial civil jurisdiction, and had gotten away with it. The impression left with the South Carolinians was that the Royal Navy intended to have its own way regardless. This case and others reveal that the navy captains were at odds not only with the colonists but sometimes also with royal provincial governors and government. There were, it seems, strong contending riptides and crosscurrents of interest and power in this remote imperial channel, involving a navy that was not under any close control by higher authority, a condition extremely dangerous to civil liberties.

In the spring of 1741 Captain James Scott brought HMS *Astraea*, a navy supply vessel, from Jamaica to Boston in order to obtain naval stores for Admiral Vernon's fleet in the Caribbean. As could have been predicted, soon after the ship's arrival her crew began disappearing. By the end of May, Scott had lost between fifty and sixty of his men, including the quartermaster and a brace of midshipmen. Fearing that without some remedy he would be unable to complete his important mission, and suspecting that the Bostonians were concealing his deserters, the captain appealed to Governor Jonathan Belcher. The governor readily perceived the serious nature of the problem and ordered his sheriffs to conduct a search. That failing, they were to impress for Scott other seamen who were not inhabitants of Massachusetts and not crewmen of fishing or coastal vessels. The carrying out of these orders, on top of Scott's own vigorous efforts to right himself, infuriated Boston's waterfront population.

At the time, Scott was residing in town. During the evening of 8 June a mob of several hundred men and boys wielding cutlasses, clubs, and axes, marched up to the door of his lodging and tried to force their way in. The door being shut fast against them, they milled around in the street, shouting dire threats, for more than an hour. Finally, after re-peated assurances from within that Captain Scott was elsewhere, the mob broke up into smaller groups that went prowling off in quest of their prey. It was an ugly affair, but not the first instance of an American mob threatening a British naval officer. Scott again appealed to local authority for support. Toward the end of the month, having gained some hands by impressment (and lost others by further desertion), the *Astraea* departed for the West Indies. She went, exulted one Boston newspaper, "to the great Joy of the Inhabitants of this Town, as well as the Owners of Vessels and Sailors, having greatly stop'd the free Course of our Navigation and prevented Supplys from coming to Town, by impressing Men out of Vessels inward bound, Coasters and Fishermen not excepted, for several Weeks past."[32]

Through the winter of 1741–42 Boston was relatively tranquil, but by March the *Astraea*, with Captain Scott, was back from the Caribbean. Again shorthanded, the captain was in no mood to trifle with a community that he had found to be stubbornly obstructive. Approaching Governor William Shirley, who was new in office and anxious to please, he persuaded him to order the local authorities to impress men for the *Astraea*, excepting inhabitants of Massachusetts, men serving in coastal vessels or fishing boats, and seamen with berths aboard outward-bound ships. This arrangement apparently did not work to Scott's satisfaction, for the next day he sent his own press gang in the *Astraea*'s longboat to obtain men from the various craft in Boston Harbor. At the end of two days of this activity, Scott had on board a miscellaneous bag of new, very angry or despondent recruits. One had been master of a coaster, two were Massachusetts men from a sloop supplying Boston with firewood, another was a local fisherman with a wife and children in Boston. There was even a master housewright who had taken passage on a coastal vessel bound for Maine where he was to obtain timber for new construction. As it happened, the master housewright was under contract for this construction to none other than Thomas Hutchinson, a young but prominent Boston merchant and legislator. When Hutchinson learned of the man's fate, he hurried out to the *Astraea* only to be rebuffed by Scott, who by now was ready to assert that he was subject to orders from no authority but his naval superiors. Angered by this, Hutchinson returned to town and began circulating a petition, which he soon was able to lay before the governor and council. After that, things moved quickly. Both houses of the legislature sent a joint complaint to Governor Shirley, denouncing *"the intollerable Violence and Injury done to the Liberties of His Majesties Subjects of this Province, their Trade and Business."*[33] They specifically asked the governor to order the commander of the fort on Castle Island to stop the *Astraea* if she tried to depart, rescue the impressed men, and bring Scott before the governor and council for a hearing. By that time Scott, realizing that he was in water too hot for comfort, had begun releasing some of the impressed men. Direct pressure from the governor quickly brought about the release of the others about whom Hutchinson and his fellow legislators had been so concerned. The sequel must have been balm to the people of Boston. Shirley notified Admiral Vernon of Scott's arbitrary behavior, with the result that the erring captain found himself transferred to an inferior ship.[34]

The Royal Navy's involvement in the New England expedition against Louisbourg in 1745 not only contributed enormously to the success of that bold venture but also, unfortunately, further intensified the issue of impressment. On 29 April, the day before the actual landing, Commodore Peter Warren on board HMS *Superbe* announced to all personnel in the expedition that they and all persons who later became involved in the enterprise would be exempt from impressment by navy ships under his command. Coming, as it did, only four years after the Cartagena experience, that was a welcome word of reassurance to every New England sailor and soldier. It did not solve the navy's problem of recruitment, however, and as Boston was the nearest British base of any appreciable size, Warren's men-of-war stopping in there for repairs and supplies inevitably tried to obtain seamen as well.[35]

On 2 November 1745 the general court of Massachusetts complained to recently promoted Rear Admiral Warren regarding the activity of Captain Richard Farrish of HMS *Bien Aimé* who, it was said, had impressed fishermen, sailors from coastal vessels, and even several men who had served in the Louisbourg operation. "This Proceeding has struck such a Terror into those People who have been employed in Coasting," asserted the legislators, "that while a Man of War lays in the Harbour impressing Men no Body will venture to bring Provisions and Fuel by Water for the Supply of the Town of Boston, since no Assurances are a Security from the Impress."[36] By that time the *Bien Aimé* had departed, but HMS *Wager*, Captain Arthur Forrest commanding, and HMS *Shirley*, Captain William Rouse commanding, both were at Boston, with tragedy impending. On 26 October Captain Forrest had informed the colony government of his need for additional men, a need both legitimate and urgent. At that time Governor Shirley was away on a prolonged visit to the garrison at captured Louisbourg, and so the responsibility of providing men for the *Wager* fell upon Lieutenant Governor Spencer Phips. To Forrest's dismay, Phips and the council, in arranging to acquire men by impressment, gave the broadest possible interpretation to the standing exemptions, with the result that merchant vessels newly arriving from sea were very nearly the only remaining source of manpower. Even that potential source was seriously compromised, for the exempted coasters took it upon themselves to warn incoming vessels that a press was underway, thereby giving those ships an opportunity to sneak their vulnerable seamen ashore at Marblehead or some other place along the coast before finally nosing into Boston Harbor.

In aid of the captains, the colonial government issued a press warrant to a deputy sheriff named Nathaniel Hasey. Contrary to his instructions, Hasey accepted the help of a small group of navy personnel consisting of Captain Rouse and his servant together with three men and a boy from HMS *Wager*. Armed with cutlasses and clubs, Hasey's party proceeded to a certain dwelling suspected of concealing some merchant seamen. Forcing their way in, they found and arrested seven sailors from a recently arrived ship. These unfortunates were then lodged in the local jail pending transfer to the waiting men-of-war. Next, Hasey's group hurried to a house in the North End of Boston. It was evening, and darkness had fallen upon the town. The men knocked, a maid opened the door, and they pushed on past her to begin their search. Hiding in an upstairs chamber were three crewmen of Captain Richardson's merchant sloop—Pierce Katon, William Conner, and John Bryan—all of whom were exempt from the press by virtue of prior service in the Louisbourg operation. Somebody went to fetch Richardson, who soon came hurrying to vouch for his men. This seemed to satisfy Rouse, for he then departed. Hasey, too, appeared willing to drop the matter. But the *Wager*'s four men lingered, and apparently decided to make their way upstairs to confront the three merchant sailors. Again and as usual there is conflicting testimony about what happened next. Apparently, when the *Wager*'s men burst into the upstairs chamber, candles were suddenly extinguished, and in the darkness a desperate fight began, ending only after two of the exempt seamen, Conner and Bryan, had been mortally wounded. Seeing the result of their work, the navy men fled the scene. Two of them soon were apprehended and jailed to await trial. The others escaped and went into concealment, probably on board the *Wager* or another man-of-war.

When Captain Forrest, who was ashore, learned of what his men had done, he decided that prudence required a speedy return to his own quarterdeck, a withdrawal he succeeded in making just ahead of a posse bearing a warrant for his arrest. Captain Rouse, even more than Forrest, experienced at first hand the fury of the outraged Boston mob, being saved from serious abuse only by prompt and decisive action on the part of the sheriff. Months afterwards, at Louisbourg, Rouse confided to Admiral Warren that in Massachusetts he had "dared not set his foot on shore . . . for fear of being prosecuted on the . . . [Sixth of Anne], or murthered by the mob for pressing."[37] Still insisting that the *Wager*'s men in Hasey's party had not acted without justification, Forrest spoke feelingly of the Bostonians as "an incensed unmercifull People governed entirely by their passions and prejudice. . . . He is the most Popular Man who can bellow lowdest or contrive most Ingeniously how to distress His Majestys Ships."[38] To the admiralty Forrest sent a detailed report, urging the lords to intercede with the king so as to save the lives of the two men being held as murderers, they having acted, he said, only from "a real sense of their Duty."[39] In an important communication to the Earl of Granville, conveying information for the king himself, the lords of the admiralty showed that Forrest's appeal had had its impact:

My Lord, The violent Spirit that reigns in all his Majesty's Colonies in America to oppose and obstruct the Officers of His Majestys Ships in their endeavouring to put those Ships in a condition to serve and protect those very Colonies and their Commerce, would appear very Surprizing, if we had not so many melancholy Instances of it, that if some Check is not put to that inveterate Humour among them, we fear it will get to such a Head, when they find it Attended with Impunity and Success, that it will be impossible to recruit the Mortality incident to Seamen, in those parts, and consequently our Ships will become useless to His Majestys Service. We annex hereto a Copy of the Narrative of Captain Forrest, which clearly sets forth the particulars of the late Transaction, and shews the Temper of the People of Boston.[40]

This case involving Captains Forrest and Rouse is of particular interest and significance for several reasons. First, it reveals how far the provincial authorities often felt obliged to go in assisting the navy with its recruiting problem, despite very strong local feeling against it. Also, it demonstrates the violent brutality that characterized impressment, and the tragic consequences that sometimes ensued. We see, in addition, the tendency of navy captains to excuse and protect their press gangs no matter how outrageous their conduct. Finally, this case establishes the fact that by 1746 the seaport of Boston was identified as the foremost center of American resistance to impressment, a community whose people were dangerously insubordinate. Thereafter, Boston did little to dissolve that reputation.

In November 1747 a squadron of ships under the command of Rear Admiral Charles Knowles was at anchor in Nantasket Road preparing to sail for the West Indies. As usual, the captains were shorthanded, and the public mood in Boston made the recovery of deserters next to impossible. Knowles decided to impress the men he needed without further delay, perhaps intending to release some of them later in exchange for deserters. On 16 November he sent the armed schooner *Achilles* into Boston Harbor with a strong-arm press gang on board. Very early the next morning, while most of the town still slept, this gang began boarding the merchant vessels in the harbor, and perhaps also swept along the dock area, seizing altogether about forty-eight men and boys. With the dawn the news of what had occurred spread quickly, swelling into a wild rumor that as many as three hundred had been taken, some out of their very beds in the town itself. Soon a crowd of several hundred angry seamen and dock workers were casting about for revenge. Coming upon a navy lieutenant ashore on business, they made him their prisoner, with the intention of holding him and any other officers they could find as hostages. By this time the sheriff had been alerted to the mounting danger, and with some deputies took to the streets in hope of restoring order. Encountering a group of four isolated rioters, they collared two, which quickly brought the whole mob on the run. The sheriff lost not only his two prisoners but also one of his deputies, and was himself "glad to get off with a Broken Head, tho was in danger of loosing it."[41]

Three days of turmoil ensued, during which naval officers ashore were compelled to take refuge in Governor Shirley's residence, the general court was terrorized by a surging mob that hurled stones through the windows of the townhouse, and the militia neglected to respond when the governor called for their assistance.[42] At one point Shirley actually withdrew to Castle William, not, as he insisted, for his own safety but to show his resentment at Boston's failure to uphold royal authority. Admiral Knowles even threatened to bring his squadron in from Nantasket to bombard the defiant town. The tide began to turn on the 19th, as increasing numbers of the colony's leading inhabitants realized how seriously the reign of law was being challenged. Aligning itself with the governor's council, the house of representatives officially deplored the rioting. Perhaps even more significant was the action taken the following day by the Boston town meeting, unanimously denouncing the violence while at the same time expressing hope for a cessation of impressment. By the afternoon of 21 November royal authority had been fully restored. With naval officers once again able to walk the streets in reasonable security, Knowles relented and gave up at least some of the impressed men, including most of those identified as local inhabitants. Then, on the last day of the month the squadron got underway for the West Indies, so that, as one Boston newspaper put it, "there is now Peace to him that goes out, and to him that comes in."[43]

On the very day of the squadron's departure there was published in Boston *An Address to the Inhabitants of the Province of Massachusetts-Bay in New-England, More Especially To the Inhabitants of Boston: Occasioned by the late Illegal and unwarrantable Attack Upon their Liberties, And the Unhappy Confusion and Disorders consequent thereon*, an anonymous pamphlet whose author probably was young Samuel Adams. With this publication and *The Independent Advertiser*, a newspaper begun by Adams and some of his friends a few weeks later, the future leader of Boston revolutionary agitation launched an attack upon Shirley's administration. Utilizing the issue of illegal impressment, Adams boldly summoned forth the concept of natural right, arguing that violence was justifiable when constituted authority failed to defend the rights of the people. According to Adams, the Shirley administration had so failed and then, compounding the fault, had tried to blame the dregs of Boston waterfront society for the recent rioting when, in fact, it had been the town's responsible citizenry who had risen up against naval tyranny. This significant foretaste of American revolutionary argument takes on additional interest from the fact that the speaker of the Massachusetts house of representatives in 1747, a merchant and politician who stood with the majority against arbitrary impressment, was none other than Thomas Hutchinson, later royal governor and political foe of Adams at the time of the Stamp Act crisis. Adams may have run with the mob in 1747, Hutchinson certainly did not, but both learned much about the confrontation between British authority and American resentment during those three unforgettable days of outrage and violence.[44]

As a result of the Knowles Riot and other confrontations ashore in North American ports, the Royal Navy preferred, when possible, to do its pressing offshore, which usually meant lying in wait not far from a harbor entrance to intercept vessels arriving at the end of a voyage. What is important to remember, however, is that Americans in general had come to consider any form of naval impressment "a Thing abhorrent to the English Constitution," and therefore unlawful.[45] If unlawful, then loyal subjects had a right, even a duty, to resist.

The log of HMS *Hunter*, Captain William Adams, reveals that impressment was in full swing during the late summer of 1758. From 30 August to 9 September the ship was lurking in the vicinity of Nantasket Road, impressing seamen from passing vessels including fishing boats. One example demonstrates quite dramatically that merchant seamen did not always submit. On 7 September the *Hunter* sighted an inbound ship and stood out to intercept. Sensing what was afoot, the intended victim headed for an alternate channel. Captain Adams hastily dispatched a boat with orders to board, whereupon the other vessel "fired at the Boat and Kept them off. . . ." An ebb tide prevented the *Hunter* from pursuing further, and so the merchantman was able to proceed and drop anchor in King Road. The next day, determined to seize the men he needed, Adams ran the *Hunter* up to King Road, anchored near the fugitive vessel, and sent his boat to board. Too late—all hands except one black man had prudently disappeared ashore. Later the *Hunter* voyaged on down the coast. At New York the ship fired a swivel gun and a six-pounder in order to make a privateer strike her pennant. On 18 November at Hampton Roads, Virginia, she "prest a man out of a Cannue." Near Charleston, South Carolina, two days after Christmas, Captain Adams "sent the Boats ashore pressing and Impressed 16 Men."[46] It seemed almost like a sport (to the *Hunter* but not the prey).

At New York in May 1757, preparatory to his intended amphibious attack on Louisbourg, Lord Loudoun gathered an army of about 3,500 men, together with a large fleet of warships and transports commanded by Admiral Sir Charles Hardy. The latter, who also was governor of New York, discovered to his dismay that large numbers of his seamen were deserting from the king's ships in order to sign aboard the privateers, where living conditions were more favorable and the prospects for enrichment more bright. Without sufficient hands to man the ships, the expedition could not sail. Many of the deserters, Hardy knew, were presently loafing in town, mingled with the civilian population, so he turned to Loudoun for help in recovering them. A plan was quickly devised and secret orders issued. Sometime after midnight on 20 May three battalions of regulars, about 3,000 men in all, marched quietly to predesignated points all around the perimeter of the town, completely investing the place. Numerous parties of armed sailors then began advancing along the streets, systematically searching taverns and other likely resorts, taking into custody all suspects. So sudden and effective was the search, that there appears to have been little resistance. Within a span of four hours nearly 800 men altogether, many of them blacks, were thus swept up in this massive dragnet; of these, about half were retained as deserters or impressed as new hands. By 6:00 A.M. the job had been completed. Those retained were rowed out to the ships under guard. On every transport to which these crestfallen men were sent was posted a subaltern with a sergeant and about twenty soldiers to suppress any incipient mutiny and prevent escape. Even after that successful sweep, the navy found it necessary to continue impressing sailors from incoming vessels almost to the very day of departure.[47]

To observe the possible complications of impressment, and the way in which local officials could become involved, we turn to the records of the admiralty itself, selecting another case in which, typically, the facts were in dispute. It seems that a youth named John Brown had been sent to school in New London, Connecticut, where he boarded with one Singleton Church. On New Year's Day 1760 Brown and Church started for New York in a small sloop. Unfortunately for them, HMS *Fowey* under the command of Captain George Tonyn was at New York pressing. As the sloop from New London arrived at its destination on 5 January it was boarded by the *Fowey*'s press gang, who forcibly impressed the young student. Two days later Tonyn's gang struck again, this time boarding a craft commanded by Peter Vail carrying wood and provisions to New York. From Vail's vessel they impressed one Seth Griffin. Both Brown and Griffin were retained on board the *Fowey*, much against their wishes.

Church and Vail, angered by their losses, appealed for help to the local authorities, who proved sympathetic. From Lieutenant Governor De Lancey and Mayor John Cruger, Church obtained official letters addressed to Captain Tonyn, but when he showed these to Tonyn the captain angrily threatened to impress him also. Subsequently, Tonyn let it be known that if Church and Vail wanted Brown and Griffin back they would have to provide substitutes. This they did, for a price, but when the two substitutes were presented, Tonyn demanded two more. After failing to find another pair of seamen willing to sell their liberty, Church and Vail obtained a warrant for Captain Tonyn's arrest, bearing the signatures of Mayor Cruger and Aldermen John Morin Scott, Philip Livingston, and Henry Cuyler, Jr.[48]

When Tonyn went ashore he was taken into custody, but released on bail. Because a convoy of ships awaited HMS *Fowey*'s protection, the chastened captain found it expedient to release both Brown and Griffin, the original cause of the dispute, but he did retain the two substitutes. Explaining himself to the admiralty, Tonyn claimed that Brown, who had been "represented as a Gentlemans son going to a boarding School proved on examination to be a strong lusty Seafairing fellow upwards of twenty five Years of age." Denying that he had beaten either Brown or Griffin, as charged, the captain insisted that he and his subordinates had in no way violated the official instructions regarding impressment. Indeed, he considered that the whole imbroglio had been politically inspired. "I look upon this [affair] as an Insult and indignity offered to their Lordships authority," concluded Tonyn, "and am very certain that the Men [Church and Vail] were Spirited on and privately encouraged by the corporation of New York who on several occasions have shewn themselves very fond of mortifying Gentlemen in His Majesty's Service."[49] He may have been correct.

If the impressment of seamen was a major cause of Anglo-American antagonism during the Great War for the Empire, another of even greater long-range impact was the attempt made by royal military and naval forces to stamp out illicit American trade with the enemy. Before General Braddock had even sailed for North America and disaster, the lords of the admiralty took cognizance of the problem in their instructions to Admiral Augustus Keppel: "It having been represented to His Majesty, that an Illegal Correspondence and Trade is frequently carried on, between the French and the King's Subjects in the several Colonies, You are to take all possible Measures to prevent the Continuance of such dangerous Practices, and more particularly to hinder the French being supplied, on any Account whatever, with Provisions, or Naval or Warlike Stores." Upon arriving in Virginia, Keppel began taking steps to block the traffic, ordering his captains on station to "act for the security of the

Colonies . . . and . . . prevent the French from being supply'd from any of his Majesty's Colonies with provisions or warlike stores. . . ."[50] There can be no doubt that American merchants and traders in such colonies as Massachusetts, Rhode Island, New York, Pennsylvania, and South Carolina were engaged in almost constant, systematic, and highly profitable exchanges of provisions and other goods with the French enemy, a form of economic activity that to the British professional forces seemed little short of treason. Military commanders were especially incensed when they discovered that the abnormally high prices charged the army for colonial provisions were attributed to shortages which, in turn, had been occasioned by the extensive export trade to the French.[51]

The extensive seaborne traffic between British North American ports and certain French areas—notably Louisbourg to the north and the French West Indies to the south—was a major annoyance to the British government in London. British officials, including military and naval commanders, became convinced that this illicit traffic, which was helping sustain the French colonial economy, was to some degree actually condoned and protected by colonial assemblies and other local authorities who themselves were profiting from it. American trade with the enemy seemed to the British regular forces, and the ministry as well, a prime example of the selfish, unpatriotic attitude of the colonists. As G. L. Beer has said, "To a large extent, the colonies neutralized the advantages arising from British naval activity, both supplying the French colonies with the sorely needed provisions, and also furnishing a market for their produce." The traffic "frustrated the policy of the British government, and prolonged the war; it aroused intense indignation and was unquestionably a potent factor in the subsequent alienation."[52] So pervasive was the traffic that in the summer of 1756 a bold French sloop actually tried to enter the port of New London, Connecticut, in expectation of trading her cargo of molasses for needed provisions. This, according to Captain Arthur Forrest of HMS *Rye*, was "a Custom much practised in this part of the World." In his report concerning the navy's interception of the French interloper, the captain went on to charge that the New Londoners themselves were prepared to falsify the sloop's papers in order to cover the illicit operation.[53]

American merchantmen voyaging to the West Indies found it easy to stop in at certain neutral islands such as Dutch Curaçao and St. Eustatius, or Danish St. Thomas, where they could exchange their cargoes for French goods, the contraband then being conveyed in neutral shipping to a French destination. This kind of traffic the Royal Navy found almost impossible to prevent, especially when false papers and other subterfuges were so skillfully employed. One method of evasion that proved remarkably effective and difficult to combat was the so-called flag of truce. Whenever there was legitimate need to make contact with the French by means of a ship as, for example, in an exchange of prisoners, the governor of the colony involved could provide to the vessel special authorization to sail to and from an enemy port under a flag of truce, which prevented interference by the navy. If challenged, all the captain had to do was show his official authorization from the governor. Such passports readily came to serve as a cover for illicit trade, often with the connivance of the governor himself. Governor William Denny of Pennsylvania actually made a practice of selling his official authorization to outbound ships, a most flagrant example of bureaucratic profiteering.[54]

About the end of 1758 a new development on the island of Haiti further enhanced the North American trade with the French. The eastern part of Haiti was Spanish territory and therefore technically neutral; the western part was a French colony. Now the Spaniards declared their small haven of Monte Cristi, situated conveniently close to the French settlements of Cap François and Port Dauphin, to be a free port. Immediately, Monte Cristi became a magnet for North American vessels bringing lumber and provisions to be traded for French sugar, molasses, rum, and coffee. Admiral Thomas Cotes, apprised of this state of affairs, dispatched Captain Usher of HM sloop *Viper* to investigate. In one day's close observation of the shipping at Monte Cristi the captain compiled a list of twenty-nine vessels, mostly from New England and New York, busily engaged in trading indirectly with the French enemy. A copy of that list giving the ships' names, masters, owners, and cargoes, was sent to the Board of Trade as evidence of American perfidy.[55] For months thereafter, trading at Monte Cristi remained a highly profitable activity for North American merchants. It was estimated that in 1760 some 400 to 500 colonial ships had visited the conveniently free port. As late as February 1762 John Watts, a prominent New Yorker, testified that "We have an odd kind of Mungrell Commerce . . . calld the Mount Trade, a Spanish Port near Cape Francois, the Lawyers say it is legal and contrary to no Statute, the Men of Warr say it is illegal. . . ." Apparently the question was indeed much in dispute, for, as Watts added, "No two Courts pursue the same Measure."[56]

British officials felt a deep sense of outrage and frustration at the colonists' relentless pursuit of trade with the enemy and their own inability to stamp out the traffic. Some colonial legislatures, apparently in recognition of the harm being done to the war effort, did pass prohibitive laws, which were rendered largely ineffective by the temptation of profit and, especially, the refusal of neighboring colonies to restrain themselves. As Governor Hardy of New York pointed out to the Board of Trade, "It is to no purpose for one Colony to lay a prohibition, if the others are not obliged to do the same."[57] Instructions issued by the Board of Trade, and legislation passed by Parliament, likewise proved less than totally effective. And so the traffic persisted, a virulent poison to Anglo-American relations.[58]

One fairly effective but localized and temporary means of suppressing colonial trade with the enemy was the embargo, more or less routinely employed by British commanders in chief during the later stages of the Great War for the Empire. By proclamation, all ships in designated ports were forbidden to sail so long as the embargo was in effect; obviously, preventing ships from leaving a guarded harbor was much easier than trying to intercept them anywhere on the high seas. Such embargoes might be imposed whenever preparations for an operation against the French had reached an advanced stage, ostensibly to prevent any leakage of information. But there were other effects as well, also advantageous to the British regular forces. The resulting stagnation of trade, for example, tended to depress prices in the immediate area affected, giving a distinct advantage to military commissaries and denying inflated profits to provincial suppliers. Also, whenever an embargo was in effect seamen tended to accumulate in port, readily accessible to the press gang. The colonists generally deplored such an embargo, especially when prolonged, because of the adverse effect on business.[59]

Lord Loudoun's embargo in the spring of 1757, when preparations for a major amphibious operation against Louisbourg were underway, serves as a prime example. Prices of colonial products plunged, enabling the military commissaries to stock their larders at bargain rates. In New England, howls of anguish were heard from the whalers and fishermen who could not get out to sea, and from the exporters of lumber. Massachusetts shippers were grumbling loudly that vessels from certain neighboring colonies had managed to clear port for the West Indies.[60] Some Philadelphia merchants became painfully entangled. Before notice of Loudoun's embargo had become official there, several ships had taken on valuable cargoes of provisions in preparation for their outward voyages; some of them had even obtained their clearances and were awaiting only a convoy or a favorable wind. After the embargo was clamped down and the weeks began passing, there was a mounting prospect of spoilage in the provisions, with consequent loss. When the venturers petitioned for a special authorization for the ships to sail, citing the conditions, Loudoun was unsympathetic, believing they were the very men who had been enriching themselves by trading with the enemy. By mid–June the anchorage at Philadelphia was crowded with nearly forty fully laden merchant vessels waiting to begin their voyages. At this point the Pennsylvania assembly took up this "inexpressible Grievance," pointing out that already the embargo had been lifted in neighboring colonies, which apparently was the case.[61] Such a severe disruption of the colonial economy as Loudoun's embargo of 1757 seems to have achieved relatively little when measured against the damage caused: weakening of the colonial export trade, unemployment, intercolonial suspicion, colonial resentment against British officialdom, and further reinforcement of the British impression that Americans in general were self-seeking, self-pitying, and deviously unpatriotic.[62]

Probably the illicit traffic with the French reached its peak in 1759 to 1760, declining gradually thereafter. Starting about 1759, the Royal Navy felt able to devote more attention to the game of seeking, intercepting, and arresting suspected vessels, with increasing success.[63] Yet as late as 1762 General Amherst was complaining about "the Infamous Trade Carried on with the Enemy, in Supplying them with Provisions, from almost Every Port on this Continent."[64] American traders, it seemed, were simply irrepressible. Their almost constant economic dealing with the French during the Great War for the Empire was, from the perspective of the British professional armed forces, a shameful stain. Using the Royal Navy as a principal tool of repression, the government persisted in its determination to bring the North American colonies into conformity with the imperial system as defined by Parliament. This continuing attempt led directly into the controversy over the writs of assistance in 1761, raising the pregnant issue of the constitutionality of parliamentary legislation, which opened the way for the American Revolution.

CONCLUSION

OSTON on 5 March 1770 as well as Kent State on 4 May 1970 serve as stark reminders that whenever armed soldiers are sent into a civilian community where they are not welcome the consequence may be tragic. There can be no doubt that nearly a hundred years before the Declaration of Independence, redcoats in a colony were viewed by Americans as the arm of repressive authority. It was in 1677 that Colonel Herbert Jeffreys implanted this perception by leading more than a thousand British soldiers into Virginia to restore royal authority in the wake of Bacon's Rebellion. "This extraordinary show of force," as Wesley F. Craven has called it, could have been viewed by the many former adherents of Bacon only as a manifestation of the iron fist.[1] Thereafter in America redcoats represented authority, and distant authority at that. Every colonist, whatever his political stance, understood that the king's forces were there to prevent civil insurrection.

In performing that function, as we have seen, the royal forces were not always successful. A British frigate and a small garrison of troops were at Boston in the spring of 1689 when the despised Andros regime was toppled by a popular uprising. One notes with interest that in this affair the companies of local militia in and around the capital were active participants against the royal forces, showing that their deepest loyalty was to their own people, not the regular military establishment. A similar uprising occurred in New York a few weeks later. There too the insurgents, although carefully avoiding anything resembling a renunciation of the monarch, dealt with the redcoats as enemies to American aspirations. Months later, when normal government was restored, it was accomplished with the backing of the Royal Navy and a large contingent of regular troops.

After these episodes, the army's repressive role tended to be obscured by the more urgent requirements of the colonial wars. Theoretically, this should have promoted a harmonious relationship between the British armed forces and the American colonists, for the immediate objectives of the two groups seemed to coincide. Instead, mutual antipathy continued to develop, although along somewhat different lines. Reviewing this significant development, we can readily distinguish two major elements—a conflict of attitudes related to differing military practices and standards, and a conflict of material interests. Both, embedded in the matrix of psychological hostility mentioned in the introduction, were actively undermining the relations between Americans and Britons.

The aristocratic professional officers from Britain tended to look down upon the provincials as something of an inferior breed—crude, uncultured, undisciplined, and largely untrained in the science of civilized warfare. Their disdain often extended beyond the obviously unprofessional rank and file to include colonial officers, who were amateurs at war and largely self-taught. Even the British private, one suspects, entertained a certain contempt for his provincial counterpart, he of the unkempt locks, the drooping stocking, and the bastard musket. The professionals prided themselves on the smartness of their appearance, the quality and uniformity of their accouterments, and their mastery of complex evolutions; whereas the provincials, unable to achieve such standards, sometimes may even have flaunted a certain casualness of military style that to the regular soldier was simply a mark of inferiority. Quite naturally the provincials, officers and common soldiers alike, were quick to resent every manifestation of professional contempt.

British officers attempting to organize military operations during the colonial wars frequently were baffled and infuriated by what appeared to be stubborn noncooperation on the part of colonial legislatures. We know that often such stubbornness was simply a manifestation of either intercolonial rivalry or else an internal power struggle between the executive and the assembly. But an impatient British commander was in no position to appreciate such maneuvering when its practical effect was to deprive him of the resources necessary for an impending expedition. To all this was added the factor of colonial reluctance to risk either body or goods in a dubious cause, as well as colonial eagerness to profit at the expense of remote and, presumably, wealthy royal government. Not only were funds withheld and galling restrictions imposed by stubborn legislatures; the population in general was inclined to hoard goods and services, or else provide them only at inflated prices. Under these conditions, British regulars naturally concluded that noncooperation was being developed by the Americans to the level of a fine art. Occasionally they spoke even of rampant obstructionism.

It is important to recognize that by mid–eighteenth century, American leaders, if not the masses of the common people, had their own provincial agendas quite firmly in mind, agendas they preferred not to submit to London's control. Even though they were councilors and assembly-men, they were first of all capitalistic businessmen, land speculators, planters, traders, and shipowners, with everyday greed and need. In or-der to protect and promote their own clearly perceived material interests, these influential men were determined to consolidate and, if possible, extend the gains already made against the royal prerogative. Thus their stubborn refusal to bow even to the demands of British military necessity. They wanted to shape their own destiny, and intended to do just that, even while enjoying the substantial benefits of the British connection. So, in a sense, they were trying to have the best of both worlds, and that was exactly what so baffled and infuriated the British regular forces.

Nor was that all. The staggering defeat suffered by General Edward Braddock's army in 1755 had released in the colonies a heady idea that some American provincials had been secretly nourishing. This was that Americans, through long experience in fighting both the stealthy Indians and the shrewd French in a wilderness environment, had acquired a special expertise in wilderness warfare that was neither possessed nor appreciated by the regulars. This idea led slowly but inexorably to an-other, even more heady—that under certain favorable conditions a small force of well-armed and woods-wise colonists could rout a much larger, more ponderous formation of professional European soldiers. It was an intriguing proposition, not easily forgotten.

Exaggerated or distorted images of both regulars and provincials now were rapidly hardening into stereotypes and traditions, each group per-ceiving the other as hostile and perverse. Aristocratic regular officers were strongly inclined to think of provincial officers as crude amateurs, incompetent in a demanding profession, ineffective in disciplining or leading their slovenly, unreliable troops. That image was to have impor-tance later as British authorities prepared to cope with rising disobedi-ence in the colonies. And, of course, the stubborn defiance displayed by the colonists at that time simply reinforced the unfavorable impression previously gained by regular officers who had experienced during the colonial wars the full measure of American noncooperation. Provincial troops tended to view British officers as aristocratic snobs, and their men as mere puppets who marched impressively at the word of command but had no feel for the kind of fighting that prevailed in the deep wilderness of North America. That view, too, was to be important as Americans contemplated the prospect of armed resistance to the mother country. Finally, the colonists in general were led to believe, partly through their unhappy experience with British military personnel, that royal authority was inclined to be careless of civil rights and oblivious to the real interests of America. It is not difficult to discover in such firmly shaped impressions living seeds of revolution and separation.

ABBREVIATIONS

USED IN CITATIONS

AAS *Proc.*	American Antiquarian Society *Proceedings*
BL	British Library, London
Add. Mss.	Additional Manuscripts
CL	William L. Clements Library, Ann Arbor
Conn. CR	J. H. Trumbull, ed., *The Public Records of the Colony of Connecticut*
Conn. HS *Coll.*	Connecticut Historical Society *Collections*
CS Mass. *Pub.*	Colonial Society of Massachusetts *Publications*
CSP Col.	*Calendar of State Papers, Colonial, America and West Indies*
CSP Dom.	*Calendar of State Papers, Domestic*
EI *Hist. Coll.*	Essex Institute *Historical Collections*
Ga. CR	A. D. Candler, ed., *Colonial Records of the State of Georgia*
Ga. HS *Coll.*	Georgia Historical Society *Collections*
HL	Henry E. Huntington Library, San Marino
HS Pa.	Historical Society of Pennsylvania, Philadelphia
LC	Library of Congress, Washington
Md. Arch.	*Archives of Maryland*
Mass. Arch.	Massachusetts Archives, Boston
Mass. A and R	*Acts and Resolves, Public and Private, of the Province of the Massachusetts Bay*
Mass. HS	Massachusetts Historical Society, Boston
Mass. HS *Coll.*	Massachusetts Historical Society *Collections*
Mass. HS *Proc.*	Massachusetts Historical Society *Proceedings*
Mass. JHR	*Journals of the House of Representatives of Massachusetts*
NMM	National Maritime Museum, Greenwich
N.S. HS *Coll.*	Nova Scotia Historical Society *Collections*
N.Y. CD	E. B. O'Callaghan, ed., *Documents Relative to the Colonial History of the State of New York*
N.Y. HS	New-York Historical Society, New York City
N.Y. HS *Coll.*	New-York Historical Society *Collections*
N.Y. PL	New York Public Library, New York City
Pa. Arch.	*Pennsylvania Archives*
Pa. CR	*Colonial Records of Pennsylvania*

PRO   Public Record Office, London
 Adm.   Admiralty Papers
 CO   Colonial Office Papers
 SP   State Papers
 WO   War Office Papers
 30   Chatham Papers
S.C. Arch.   South Carolina Archives, Columbia
S.C. CR   J. H. Easterby, ed., *Colonial Records of South Carolina:*
               Journals of the Commons House of Assembly
S.C. HS   South Carolina Historical Society, Charleston
Va. EJ   H. R. McIlwaine, ed., *Executive Journals of the Council of*
               Colonial Virginia
Va. JHB   H. R. McIlwaine, ed., *Journals of the House of Burgesses*
Va. LJ   H. R. McIlwaine, ed., *Legislative Journals of the Council of*
               Colonial Virginia
WMQ   *William and Mary Quarterly*

NOTE: Alternative copies or published versions of cited documents are indicated
with parentheses.

NOTES

INTRODUCTION

1. Firth, *Cromwell's Army*; Childs, *The Army of Charles II*.

2. Webb, "Officers and Governors," p. 136.

3. The case against the standing army was hammered together by a corps of radicals and visionaries such as James Harrington, Henry Neville, and John Trenchard, whose challenging publications were savored and cheered not only in England but in the American colonies as well. Notable examples of such works are Harrington, *Commonwealth of Oceana*; Neville, *Plato Redivivus*; Trenchard, *An Argument, Shewing, That a Standing Army is Inconsistent with a Free Government*, and *A Short History of Standing Armies in England*. During the 1720s Trenchard collaborated with Thomas Gordon in publishing *Cato's Letters*, which similarly denounced standing armies. As Caroline Robbins has convincingly demonstrated in *The Eighteenth-Century Commonwealthman*, American thinking was significantly influenced by such arguments. See also Schwoerer, *"No Standing Armies!"*

4. Social Science Research Council, *Social Sciences in Historical Study*, p. 45.

CHAPTER I

1. CO 1/39, f. 54. Book 1 of Webb, *1676* emphasizes the revolutionary character of Bacon's Rebellion, thereby underlining also the repressive role of the military-naval force sent to deal with the uprising.

2. Among the sources relating to preparations for the expedition, the following have been especially helpful: BL, Add. Mss. 25120, ff. 82–83, 88–89, 94–95, 136; Adm. 1/5138, ff. 512–31, 540–47, 550–57, 562–77, 594–601; CO 5/1355, ff. 30–34, 38, 48–50, 52–55, 57–58; WO 26/3, ff. 213–27, 229–30, 232, 234–35, 249, 253; WO 55/391, ff. 38–43; *CSP Col.* 1675–76, nos. 1051–64, 1083, 1087–92, 1099, 1104, 1109–14, 1118, 1130–32, 1140; Tanner, *Descriptive Catalogue* 3, nos. 3261–62, 3293, 3330, 3368, 3391, 3439, 3443, 3553.

3. Webb, "Officers and Governors," pp. 52–54. See also Webb, *Governors-General*, pp. 122–37.

4. *CSP Dom.* 1677–78, p. 180. Moryson had foreseen some of the difficulties long before the expedition left England. Writing to Attorney General William Jones, he inquired: Where will the troops live, as there are in Virginia no towns and the plantations are scattered? With sickness so common among new arrivals in the colony, who will take care of sick soldiers? What will be the source of pay

for the troops? Lacking funds, will they not attempt to extort them from the colonists, thereby increasing Virginia's difficulty? Pepysian Library, Magdalene College, Cambridge, vol. 2582. Another copy of this letter is to be found in CO 5/1371.

5. Copy of Berry and Moryson to H.M. Principal Secretaries of State, 2 February 1677, Pepysian Library, vol. 2582. Another copy of this letter is to be found in CO 5/1371. See also *CSP Col.* 1677–80, nos. 32, 49, 58, 65, 66, 72, 82; Neville, *Bacon's Rebellion*, p. 60.

6. *CSP Col.* 1677–80, no. 196.

7. Ibid., no. 994; Jeffreys (prob.) to Williamson, 8 June 1678, *Virginia Magazine of History and Biography* 5 (1898): 50–52; Shea, *Virginia Militia*, pp. 118–19.

8. Quoted in Washburn, "Bacon's Rebellion," p. 599.

9. Jeffreys (prob.) to Williamson, 8 June 1678, *Virginia Magazine of History and Biography* 5 (1898): 50–52.

10. *CSP Col.* 1677–80, nos. 542, 591, 619; Neville, *Bacon's Rebellion*, pp. 154, 158–59; Childs, *Army of Charles II*, pp. 160–61; Foote, "American Independent Companies of the British Army," pp. 285–93.

11. Leach, *Flintlock and Tomahawk*, pp. 59–60, 176–77, 236–37, 255.

12. *Andros Tracts*, 7:34–38, 74–75; *CSP Col.* 1689–92, no. 913.

13. *Andros Tracts*, 5:153, 170; and 6:49–50, 54.

14. Ibid., 6:194–95; and 7:236–37; *CSP Col.* 1689–92, nos. 664, 745, 774.

15. *Andros Tracts*, 7:145n.

16. Andrews, *Narratives of the Insurrections*, p. 189.

17. Palfrey, *History of New England*, 3:584–85n.

18. *CSP Col.* 1689–92, no. 1429. The important post at Pemaquid was an exception, as Foote has pointed out in his "American Independent Companies," pp. 234–35.

19. *Andros Tracts*, 5:151–71.

20. Archdeacon, *New York City*, pp. 106–15.

21. N.Y. CD, 3:591, 636, 763; N.Y. HS *Coll.* (1868): 245, 273.

22. Archdeacon, *New York City*, pp. 108–12; Lovejoy, *Glorious Revolution in America*, pp. 105–6, 253–54, 281–86.

23. N.Y. CD, 3:640; *CSP Col.* 1689–92, nos. 160, 458; N.Y. HS *Coll.* (1868): 287; McCormick, "Leisler's Rebellion," pp. 230–31.

24. N.Y. CD, 3:593–94; *CSP Col.* 1689–92, nos. 160, 190, 221; N.Y. HS *Coll.* (1868): 292–93; O'Callaghan, *Documentary History*, 2:408.

25. N.Y. CD, 3:637, 708, 710, 727–28; *CSP Col.* 1689–92, nos. 878, 886, 929, 1001, 1069–70; O'Callaghan, *Documentary History*, 2:3–4; N.Y. HS *Coll.* (1868): 288; McCormick, "Leisler's Rebellion," pp. 233–36, 271–72, 277; Foote, "American Independent Companies," p. 248.

26. *CSP Col.* 1689–92, no. 1840 (Translated in N.Y. CD, 3:809); N.Y. HS *Coll.* (1868): 300.

27. *N.Y. CD*, 3:757. See also *CSP Col.* 1689–92, no. 1484.

28. *N.Y. CD*, 3:758; O'Callaghan, *Documentary History*, 2:328–30, 333–34, 340–45; N.Y. HS *Coll.* (1868): 305–9, 315–16; Leder, "Captain Kidd and the Leisler Rebellion," pp. 51–52.

29. *N.Y. CD*, 3:758, 760, 765; N.Y. HS *Coll.* (1868): 316; O'Callaghan, *Documentary History*, 2:410; *CSP Col.* 1689–92, nos. 1463–65, 1469.

30. *N.Y. CD*, 3:758–59, 767; O'Callaghan, *Documentary History*, 2:358–59.

31. *N.Y. CD*, 3:767, 794; N.Y. HS *Coll.* (1868): 310–11.

CHAPTER 2

1. *CSP Col.* 1696–97, no. 27.

2. *CSP Col.* 1700, nos. 850, 880, 882, 953.

3. The only modern biography of Vetch is the excellent study by G. M. Waller.

4. Warden, *Boston, 1689–1776*, chaps. 3–4.

5. Details concerning the plan and the preparations are to be found in various documents abstracted in *CSP Col.* 1708–9. See also Leach, *Arms for Empire*, pp. 139–42, and Waller, *Samuel Vetch*, chap. 7.

6. John Marshall, Diary, 1689–1711.

7. *CSP Col.* 1708–9, nos. 612, 658, 670, 794; Snyder, *Marlborough-Godolphin Correspondence*, 3:1467n., 1467–68, 1489; Waller, *Samuel Vetch*, pp. 154–56.

8. BL, Add. Mss. 32694, ff. 108–18; *CSP Col.* 1708–9, nos. 794–98.

9. *CSP Col.* 1710–11, no. 81.

10. Webb, "Officers and Governors," p. 332.

11. *CSP Col.* 1710–11, no. 879. It is worth noting that in 1710 the ministry again alerted New England to prepare for a major expedition against Canada, and again failed to provide the promised assistance. This time the official excuse was "contrary winds which happened, when the season was proper for the fleet to sayle, and in regard of other important services which intervened." Graham, *Walker Expedition*, p. 256; *CSP Col.* 1710–11, nos. 380–81. The fact that Lord Treasurer Sidney Godolphin and other British leaders including the Duke of Marlborough continued to give low priority to the American theater of operations is manifest in the Godolphin-Marlborough correspondence from April to July 1710. See Snyder, *Marlborough-Godolphin Correspondence*, 3:1471–1578, passim.

12. Graham, *Walker Expedition*, pp. 268–89, 300–301; Morgan, "Queen Anne's Canadian Expedition of 1711," pp. 6–21.

13. Graham, *Walker Expedition*, pp. 303, 305–6.

14. Ibid., pp. 25, 146, 240, 249, 296, 332, 340, 358, 379; Waller, *Samuel Vetch*, p. 218.

15. Graham, *Walker Expedition*, pp. 126–27, 176–79.

16. *CSP Col.* 1689–92, no. 2283. See also *CSP Col.* 1693–96, nos. 42, 225.

17. BL, Add. Mss. 32694, ff. 106–7; Graham, *Walker Expedition*, pp. 279–86, 347.

18. Graham, *Walker Expedition*, p. 188.

19. *CSP Col.* 1702, no. 768; CO 5/751, ff. 87–88; CO 5/862, ff. 345–60; CO 5/910, ff. 260–72; Adm. 1/1979; Mass. HS *Coll.*, 6th ser., 3:336; Pencak, "Massachusetts Politics," pp. 114–15.

20. CO 5/751, ff. 32–39, 57–60; *CSP Col.* 1693–96, nos. 3, 28, 79, 88, 214, 224–25, 239, 247, 293, 728, 826–27, 879; Pencak, "Massachusetts Politics," pp. 52–53.

21. *CSP Col.* 1693–96, nos. 410, 423, 441, 452, 475, 545, 578; Pencak, "Massachusetts Politics," pp. 55–56.

22. Sewall, *Diary*, 2:662, 665.

23. See Graham, *Walker Expedition*, which is indispensable for anyone exploring this subject.

24. SP 42/98, ff. 96–97.

25. Graham, *Walker Expedition*, pp. 104, 106, 139, 344–45; Nash, *Urban Crucible*, pp. 59–65, 76–80.

26. Sewall, *Diary*, 2:665; BL, Add. Mss. 32694, f. 102; McCusker, *Money and Exchange in Europe and America*, p. 140.

27. CO 5/10, ff. 255–60; Graham, *Walker Expedition*, pp. 121, 322, 347, 379.

28. Graham, *Walker Expedition*, p. 82.

29. CO 5/10, ff. 255–60.

30. Ibid.; Graham, *Walker Expedition*, pp. 110–11, 192–93, 337, 342–43.

31. Graham, *Walker Expedition*, pp. 118, 344.

32. Ibid., pp. 121, 317; *CSP Col.* 1711–12, no. 46. See also Graham, *Walker Expedition*, pp. 121–22, 124, 130–31, 203–8, 225–28, 230–31, 338, 346, 348, 356–57.

33. Graham, *Walker Expedition*, p. 325.

34. Ibid., pp. 151, 315.

35. As recently as the preceding February the secretary of state himself had been pondering the advantages of "putting the whole Empire of North America on one uniform plan of government." Ibid., p. 278.

36. Ibid., p. 117. See also ibid., pp. 116–18, 196–200, 214, 236–37, 362, 372–74, 378; *CSP Col.* 1711–12, no. 1641. As late as 26 July, only a few days before the expedition was to sail, Southack remained unwilling to assume the responsibility assigned him. Then, when he eventually did acquiesce, Walker sent him on a different mission, which prevented him from carrying out his original assignment. Graham, *Walker Expedition*, pp. 129, 131, 374.

37. Graham, *Walker Expedition*, pp. 30, 324, 346; General Hill to Colonel Hunter, Boston, 23 July 1711, HS Pa., Gratz Collection, case 4, box 7.

38. Graham, *Walker Expedition*, pp. 333–34, 350–53.

39. Ibid., pp. 235–38, 330–33, 350–55, 365–66, 373–74.

40. Dummer, *Letter to a Noble Lord.*

41. While conceding that "the bitter recriminations which followed the disaster had a bad effect on British colonial relations," Professor Graham insists that "the effect was neither serious nor enduring." *Walker Expedition*, p. 40. My own assessment is less sanguine.

CHAPTER 3

1. Foote, "American Independent Companies of the British Army," pp. 301–10; Reese, "Britain's Military Support of Georgia in the War of 1739–1748," p. 3.

2. *S.C. CR*, 2:159–61; Leach, *Arms for Empire*, p. 213.

3. *S.C. CR*, 2:199.

4. CO 5/655, ff. 20–21; *S.C. CR*, 2:296–97; *South Carolina Gazette*, 1 April 1740.

5. *S.C. CR*, 3:98, 152–54, 189–90, 197.

6. Ibid., pp. 175, 190, 199.

7. Ibid., p. 217.

8. Ibid., p. 161. See also ibid., pp. 113, 192–93, 196–97; Ivers, *British Drums on the Southern Frontier*, pp. 114–18; Torres-Reyes, *British Siege of St. Augustine*, pp. 47–50.

9. *S.C. CR*, 3:123–24, 146–47, 163, 222–27, 242–43; Beatson, *Naval and Military Memoirs*, 1:72–73; Warren, *Papers*, p. 21; Ivers, *British Drums on the Southern Frontier*, pp. 126–27.

10. Warren, *Papers*, p. 24. See also *S.C. CR*, 3:146–47, 157–59, 242–43; Ga. HS *Coll.* 7, part 1, p. 59; Log of HMS *Hector*, 28 June 1740, Adm. 51/445.

11. *S.C. CR*, 3:137–38, 235–36, 245–46; CO 5/655, ff. 20–21; Ga. HS *Coll.* 7, part 1, pp. 59–60; Ivers, *British Drums on the Southern Frontier*, pp. 129–30.

12. Pringle, *Letterbook*, vol. 1. See especially Pringle's letter of 14 July 1740, pp. 231–32, and subsequently his letter of 10 November 1740, p. 266, in which he placed the entire blame at Oglethorpe's door.

13. BL, Add. Mss. 32695, ff. 190–91. See also Byrd, *Correspondence*, 2:568–69.

14. The report was reprinted in London in 1743. More recent versions may be found in *S.C. CR*, 3:78–247, and an edition published by the South Carolina Archives Department in 1954.

15. CO 5/655, f. 95. "You know," concluded this partisan advocate, "I have the honour to bear a Commission in the Army, not inconsiderable, therefore ought not, nor dare not tell an Untruth. You may publish the whole of this Letter as an absolute fact." After reading Heron's profession of truth, one is

tempted to render the old army song, "Old soldiers never *lie*; they just fade away." See also CO 5/655, ff. 20–21.

16. Cadogan, *Spanish Hireling Detected*, p. 4.

17. *S.C. CR*, 5:350–51.

18. [Kimber], *Relation*, p. 34. This pamphlet is mainly concerned with events of 1743, but the quotation given refers to the siege of 1740.

19. CO 5/655, ff. 289–90.

20. The ensuing section on the Cartagena expedition, in slightly different form, has been published as a chapter in Maarten Ultee, ed., *Adapting to Conditions: War and Society in the Eighteenth Century*, copyrighted in 1986 by the University of Alabama Press. It is published here by permission.

21. CO 318/3. Minutes of a meeting on 15 March 1740. See also BL, Add. Mss. 32695, ff. 186–89.

22. BL, Add. Mss. 32694, ff. 3–8.

23. Various documents, January to April 1740, in CO 318/3. See also CO 5/752, ff. 217–20, 250–52, 353–54; BL, Add. Mss. 32698, ff. 177–78.

24. BL, Add. Mss. 32693, ff. 161–68; Copy of royal instructions, 2 April 1740, CO 318/3.

25. BL, Add. Mss. 32693, ff. 161–68; CO 5/752, ff. 355–63; Bladen to Newcastle, 24 January 1740, Copy of royal instructions, 2 April 1740, CO 318/3.

26. CO 318/3, Draft of instructions to Cathcart (in Bladen's letter of 7 July 1740); BL, Add. Mss. 32694, ff. 251–53, 258–63, 270–73.

27. For details of that earlier experience see CO 5/751, ff. 91, 146–49; *CSP Col.* 1702, no. 1131; *CSP Col.* 1702–3, nos. 30, 315, 319, 764, 1071, 1399; Foote, "American Independent Companies," pp. 237–43.

28. CO 5/41, ff. 215–16; *N.Y. CD*, 6:164. See also ibid., pp. 167, 171; CO 5/41, ff. 223–26.

29. Franks Family, *Correspondence*, pp. 72, 76.

30. CO 5/41, ff. 227–28.

31. Franklin, *Papers*, 2:288. But see also CO 5/41, ff. 250–52 in which Blakeney mentions difficulties.

32. Franklin, *Papers*, 2:288–89; *Pa. CR*, 4:435–43, 448–69.

33. Pencak, *War, Politics, & Revolution in Provincial Massachusetts*, p. 121.

34. *Boston Weekly News-Letter*, 12–19 March 1741.

35. Vernon, *Papers*, p. 421.

36. *Boston Weekly News-Letter*, 12–19 March 1741; *Boston Evening-Post*, 29 June 1741. See also CO 5/41, ff. 253–55, 262–63; Vernon, *Papers*, p. 154; Foote, "Pennsylvania Men of the American Regiment," p. 36.

37. CO 5/41, ff. 253–57, 262–63; BL, Add. Mss. 32696, ff. 139–48, 172–73. Colebrooke's interesting letter to Charles Hanbury Williams, who was a member of Parliament and paymaster general of the marines, is found in Adm. 96/512, f. 7.

38. CO 5/42, ff. 26–27. See also ibid., ff. 28–29. Lack of military discipline,

which meant both precision in drill and unquestioning obedience, was, according to the regulars, the common failing of just about all militia and newly raised provincial troops.

39. CO 5/41, ff. 289, 294. See also [Knowles], *Account of the Expedition to Carthagena*, pp. 38n., 56.

40. CO 5/41, ff. 264–65; CO 5/42, ff. 54–55.

41. BL, Add. Mss. 33028, ff. 386–95. These instructions are found also in CO 318/3. For comparison with very similar instructions of 1710 see *CSP Col. 1710–11*, no. 302.

42. CO 5/42, ff. 21–22, 30–34, 84–85; *Boston Weekly News-Letter*, 12–19 March 1741; Vernon, *Papers*, pp. 13–14.

43. CO 5/41, f. 310; *Boston Evening-Post*, 1 June 1741; Beatson, *Naval and Military Memoirs*, 1:103.

44. BL, Add. Mss. 19332, f. 117; CO 5/42, ff. 30–31. See also CL, Admiral Douglas Papers, slipcase B. Logbook kept aboard HMS *Tilbury*, entry for 6 April 1741; Douglas, Journal (DOU/1), 6 April 1741; CO 5/41, ff. 302, 308, 311.

45. CO 5/42, ff. 35–38; CO 5/41, 313–14; Beatson, *Naval and Military Memoirs*, 1:105–6.

46. BL, Add. Mss. 35407, f. 33; CO 5/41, f. 315; CO 5/42, ff. 35–38.

47. BL, Add. Mss. 34207, ff. 9–11.

48. CO 5/1337, ff. 254–55 (Colonial Williamsburg Foundation).

49. *Boston Weekly News-Letter*, 25 June–2 July 1741, 2–9 July 1741, 30 July–6 August 1741.

50. BL, Add. Mss. 32698, ff. 175–76. See also ibid., ff. 177–78; CO 5/42, ff. 54–55.

51. CO 5/42, ff. 97–98, 104–7.

52. Ibid., ff. 190–91. The memorial contains allegations, not proofs, but there is little likelihood that such officers would have endorsed the complaints without being convinced that the abuse was serious.

53. Ibid., ff. 164–65.

54. Ibid., ff. 190–91.

55. Ibid.

56. CO 5/42, ff. 164–65. At a council of war on 22 July 1742 Wentworth engaged in a heated argument with Vernon as to whether soldiers on temporary duty on board ship were subject to army discipline or navy discipline. This was an issue that remained long in dispute between the two services. Ibid., ff. 242–46.

57. During the summer of 1741, soldiers belonging to Gooch's American Foot participated in a futile invasion of Cuba. The following year a group of volunteers from the same regiment, lured no doubt by some lingering hope of material gain, was involved in a British project for colonizing the island of Roatán off the coast of Honduras.

58. BL, Add. Mss. 32699, ff. 350–54, 359–64.

59. CO 5/1338, ff. 6–7, 11–12 (Colonial Williamsburg Foundation). I am grateful to Dr. John Hemphill of the Colonial Williamsburg Foundation for bringing this document to my attention.

60. Periodic muster returns for the American regiment, giving some idea of losses, may be found in CO 5/42.

61. Harkness, "Americanism and Jenkins' Ear," pp. 61–90.

62. *Ga. CR*, 6:241–42, and 24:246–69, 283–88, 385–92, 397–411; Ivers, *British Drums on the Southern Frontier*, pp. 185, 204–7.

63. *Ga. CR*, 24:249.

64. Ibid., p. 283.

65. Ibid., p. 269.

66. Ibid., 6:241–42; Ivers, *British Drums on the Southern Frontier*, pp. 205–7.

CHAPTER 4

1. An earlier version of this chapter was first published in Mass. HS *Proc.* 89 (1978): 36–54. The revised version appears here by permission.

2. Shirley, *Correspondence*, 1:205; Schutz, *William Shirley*, pp. 96–97; Rawlyk, *Yankees at Louisbourg.*

3. The evidence is scattered through official correspondence deposited in the Public Record Office in London, numerous private journals kept by persons engaged in the operation, the Peter Warren Papers and a collection of Louisbourg letters in the William L. Clements Library at the University of Michigan, contemporary newspapers, and the Pepperrell Papers and Louisbourg Papers in the library of the Massachusetts Historical Society. Although the evidence is widely dispersed and somewhat sparse, when assembled it does enable us to form a reasonably clear picture of Anglo-American tensions at Louisbourg in 1745–46.

4. Mass. HS *Coll.*, 6th ser., 10:330. See also ibid., 1st ser., 1:29.

5. Ibid., 6th ser., 10:169. See also ibid., pp. 162, 164, 172 and also William Pepperrell to Peter Warren, 13 and 16 May 1745, Mass. HS, Louisbourg Papers, vol. 3 (Warren, *Papers*, pp. 91–92).

6. Douglas, Journal (DOU/1), 4 and 16 June 1745 (similar to the log kept aboard HMS *Vigilant* by Thomas Shortland, CL, Admiral Douglas Papers, slipcase C); Pepperrell to Warren, 19 June 1745, Mass. HS, Louisbourg Papers, vol. 3 (Warren, *Papers*, p. 129); Conn. HS *Coll.*, 1:135; AAS *Proc.*, 20:164; Mass. HS *Coll.*, 1st ser., 1:44, and 6th ser., 10:301.

7. Wrong, *Louisbourg in 1745*, pp. 57–58; Rawlyk, "New England and Louisbourg, 1744–1745," p. 295.

8. Mass. HS *Coll.*, 1st ser., 1:46; Wrong, *Louisbourg in 1745*, p. 58.

9. Thomas Waldron to [Richard Waldron], 9 July 1745, CL, Louisbourg Let-

ters. See also Durell, *Particular Account*, pp. 3–5; Mass. HS *Coll.*, 1st ser., 1:50–51, and 6th ser., 10:330; W. Clarke's letter of 13 December 1745, Mass. HS, Davis Papers, vol. 2.

10. Mass. HS *Coll.*, 1st ser., 1:50–54, and 6th ser., 10:341–42.

11. CO 5/44, ff. 53–56 (Warren, *Papers*, pp. 125–26).

12. CO 5/44, ff. 61–62 (Mass. HS *Coll.*, 6th ser., 10:300); De Forest, *Louisbourg Journals*, p. 94.

13. Craft, "Journal," p. 194. See also Stearns, "Diary," pp. 325–26; Conn. HS *Coll.*, 1:149, 153–54; Mass. HS *Coll.*, 6th ser., 10:32–33, 36–37, 40–41; Mass. HS *Proc.*, 2d ser., 11:437–38.

14. Warren to Clinton, 28 August 1745, N.Y. HS, George Clinton Papers, vol. 2 (Warren, *Papers*, pp. 156–57). See also Warren's letter of 21 August in the same collection. Gwyn, *Enterprising Admiral*, explores this subject in detail. See also Judd, Journal, 29 July and 2 August 1745; "Extracts From Letters Written by Capt. Geo. Curwen of Salem, Mass.," EI *Hist. Coll.*, 3:188; Thomas Waldron to Richard Waldron, 24–26 July 1745, CL, Louisbourg Letters; Joseph Clement to James West, [Virginia, 1745], BL, Add. Mss. 34728, ff. 10–11; [Shirley], *Memoirs*, pp. 60–61; Mass. HS *Coll.*, 6th ser., 10:375; *Boston Weekly News-Letter*, 15 August 1745; *Boston Gazette*, 20 August 1745.

15. AAS *Proc.*, 20:172–73; Judd, Journal, 29 July 1745; EI *Hist. Coll.*, 6:190.

16. So far as I am aware, the brawl is mentioned in only two of the many Louisbourg journals, which seems rather strange. Benjamin Stearns called it "Sumtheing of a Crumuge [scrimmage] Between Sum of the Land: armey and the Seafarreing men." "Diary," p. 329. Dudley Bradstreet of Groton, Massachusetts, an officer in the same regiment as Stearns, wrote of "a Great Disturbance betweene the men of wars men and our men which was Exceeding hot." Mass. HS *Proc.*, 2d ser., 11:440.

17. Warren to Clinton, 21 August 1745, N.Y. HS, George Clinton Papers, vol. 2 (Warren, *Papers*, pp. 154–55). See also the *Boston Gazette*, 30 July 1745; Mass. HS *Coll.*, 6th ser., 10:322–24, 335–36, 341–42.

18. [Shirley], *Memoirs*, pp. 66–71; Warren to Thomas Corbett, 23 November 1745, Adm. 1/480, ff. 19–23; *Boston Gazette*, 10 September 1745; *Boston Weekly News-Letter*, 12 September 1745; Judd, Journal, 19 October and 27 November 1745.

19. Newcastle to Shirley, 11 September 1745, BL, Add. Mss. 32705, ff. 169–70; Mass. HS *Coll.*, 6th ser., 10:419–20.

20. Warren to Thomas Corbett, January or February 1746, Adm. 1/480, ff. 24–27; Shirley to Newcastle, 10 May 1746, CO 5/901, ff. 8–11; Knowles to the Admiralty, 5 July 1746, Adm. 1/2007; Mass. HS *Coll.*, 6th ser., 10:437–45. Pepperrell estimated in May 1746 that the sickness of the past winter had caused about 1,200 deaths. Letter to Newcastle, 21 May 1746, CO 5/44, ff. 57–58, 89–91 (Mass. HS *Coll.*, 6th ser., 10:477–79); CO 5/45, ff. 38–43.

21. Mass. HS *Coll.*, 6th ser., 10:79.

22. Knowles to the Admiralty, 5 July 1746, Adm. 1/2007; Knowles to [Newcastle], 9 July 1746, CO 5/44, ff. 136–41.

23. Knowles to Newcastle, 20 January 1747, CO 5/44, ff. 188–91. See also Knowles to Newcastle, 8 July 1746, CO 5/44, ff. 116–19; Knowles to [Newcastle], 9 July 1746, CO 5/44, ff. 136–41; Knowles to [Newcastle], 8 November 1746, CO 5/44, ff. 178–81.

CHAPTER 5

1. [Livingston], *Review of the Military Operations in North America*, p. 187.

2. Bouquet, *Papers*, 2:397. See also CO 5/49, ff. 63–64; Johnson, *Papers*, 1:515; Laurens, *Papers*, 1:322; Pargellis, *Military Affairs*, pp. 170–71; Beer, *British Colonial Policy*, pp. 70–71.

3. Yates, Copy Book & Journal; Pargellis, *Military Affairs*, p. 225.

4. BL, Add. Mss. 21631, ff. 71–80 (CO 5/48, ff. 338–44). See also BL, Add. Mss. 21632, f. 1.

5. Loudoun to Pownall, 15 November 1757, CO 5/49, ff. 100–104 (HL, Loudoun Papers 4838).

6. Forbes, *Writings*, pp. 224–25. See also BL, Add. Mss. 21644, ff. 207–8, 300–301.

7. Keppel, Order Book A (KEP/1), pp. 278, 379–80. For yet other examples of profiteering at the expense of the military see Massey to [Gage], 21 April 1760, CL, Thomas Gage Papers, American Series, vol. 6; Amherst, *Journal*, p. 210.

8. Loudoun to Pitt, 3 May 1757, CO 5/48, ff. 208–13. See also Loudoun to Pitt, 14 February 1758, CO 5/49, ff. 1–13 (HL, Loudoun Papers 5598); Pitt, *Correspondence*, 1:187.

9. Forbes, *Writings*, p. 68 (HL, James Abercromby Papers 175).

10. [Abercromby] to [Forbes], 24 April 1758, HL, Abercromby Papers 189.

11. Pencak, "Massachusetts Politics in War and Peace, 1676–1776," p. 284n. See also Beer, *British Colonial Policy*, pp. 53–69.

12. Shirley, *Correspondence*, 2:97–101; *N.Y. CD*, 6:915–16; *Pa. Arch.*, 1st ser., 2:203–7.

13. BL, Add. Mss. 32853, ff. 346–55 (CO 5/46, ff. 2–6; HL, Loudoun Papers 560). Braddock's difficulty in the matter of the common fund later caused him to recommend to the ministry, in a letter dated, ironically, exactly twenty years prior to Lexington and Concord, a system of general taxation for the British colonies. "I can't help taking the liberty of mentioning," he wrote, "the Necessity there appears to me to be of some Tax being laid throughout His Majesty's Dominions in North America . . . for repaying the large Sums which must be advanced, for His Service, and the Interest of His Colonies, at this important

Crisis." CO 5/46, ff. 11–16 (HL, Loudoun Papers 572). Governor Dinwiddie of Virginia also advocated a general tax to be levied by Parliament. Dinwiddie, *Records*, 2:16–18.

14. *Pa. CR*, 6:415.

15. Pargellis, *Military Affairs*, p. 93; *Pa. CR*, 6:368–69. See also Dinwiddie, *Records*, 2:49.

16. Isaac Norris to Charles [Norris], 28 April 1755, HS Pa., Isaac Norris Letterbook.

17. Braddock to Newcastle, 19 April 1755, BL, Add. Mss. 32854, ff. 184–91; Braddock to Robinson, 19 April 1755, CO 5/46, ff. 11–16; Braddock to Napier, 19 April 1755, Pargellis, *Military Affairs*, pp. 81–84; Keppel to Secretary of the Admiralty, 30 April 1755, Adm. 1/480, ff. 548–53.

18. Dinwiddie, *Records*, 2:52, 72; Braddock to Newcastle, 5 June 1755, BL, Add. Mss. 32855, ff. 336–39. See also Dinwiddie, *Records*, 2:34, 46; Braddock to Robinson, 5 June 1755, CO 5/46, ff. 21–26 (HL, Loudoun Papers 581). For a revealing comment on the behavior of the Pennsylvania assembly by the governor of that province see *Pa. Arch.*, 1st ser., 2:396.

19. Washington, *Papers*, 1:277. See also Pargellis, *Military Affairs*, pp. 82–83.

20. Braddock to Robinson, 5 June 1755, CO 5/46, ff. 21–26 (HL, Loudoun Papers 581). See also *Pennsylvania Gazette*, 22 May 1755; Dinwiddie, *Records*, 2:41; Franklin, *Papers*, 6:19–22, 59; *Pa. CR*, 6:415–16; Pargellis, *Military Affairs*, pp. 84–85; Zimmerman, "Benjamin Franklin and the Quaker Party," p. 301. Earlier, Franklin had been largely responsible for a good-will gift of delicacies sent to Braddock's junior officers by the Pennsylvania legislature. Nichols, "Braddock Expedition," pp. 226–27; Franklin, *Papers*, 6:208–9.

21. Mass. HS *Coll.*, 4th ser., 4:367–70.

22. *Pennsylvania Gazette*, 11 September and 16 October 1755; Nichols, "Braddock Expedition," p. 452n.

23. Note the case of one John Smith (an alias?) in Philadelphia. Having been assessed a heavy fine for a criminal offense, Smith pleaded inability to pay, whereupon the authorities remitted the penalty "upon Condition that he inlist himself a Soldier with Capt. David Allen, now raising Recruits for Colonel Lasscelles Regiment of Foot at Hallifax, but not otherwise." Apparently the thought of John Smith in distant Nova Scotia was more appealing to the town fathers than either the fine or John Smith languishing in the local lockup. Philadelphia Municipal Archives, Common Council Minutes, 16 August 1755.

24. For evidence of resentment at the recruiting of apprentices in England see WO 1/975, ff. 391–92; WO 4/53, f. 457.

25. *Pennsylvania Gazette*, 16 October 1755; *Pa. CR*, 7:39 (*Pa. Arch.*, 1st ser., 2:417–18).

26. Sharpe to Shirley, 2 February 1756, CO 5/46, ff. 205–6.

27. Ibid.; Pitcher to Fox, 23 February 1756, CO 5/46, ff. 428–29; *Pennsylvania Gazette*, 19 February 1756; *Pa. Arch.*, 1st ser., 2:572–74; *Pa. CR*, 6:777–

78, and 7:37–40 (CO 5/46, ff. 197–98; WO 1/4, f. 53); Franklin, *Papers*, 6:397–400n.; Shirley, *Correspondence*, 2:391–92, 399n. For cases of recruiting officers actually arrested at the behest of aggrieved masters see Captain Robert Ross to [Governor Sharpe], 11 April 1756, HS Pa., Dreer Collection, Officers Serving in America Before the Revolution, vol. 2; *Pa. Arch.*, 1st ser., 2:640–42 (HS Pa., Gratz Collection, Colonial Wars, case 4, box 7); *Pa. CR*, 7:103.

28. John Smyth to [William Alexander], 29 March 1756, N.Y. HS, William Alexander Papers (film). Quoted by courtesy of the New-York Historical Society, New York City.

29. Webb to Loudoun, 10 April 1756, HL, Loudoun Papers 1034.

30. BL, Egerton Mss. 3490, ff. 219–21; Fox to Lyttelton, 13 March 1756, CL, Lyttelton Papers; *Pa. Arch.*, 8th ser., 5:4251; Franklin, *Papers*, 6:397–400n.; *Pennsylvania Gazette*, 2 September 1756; *N.Y. CD*, 7:76; Pargellis, *Lord Loudoun*, pp. 116–21. A lucid explanation of why, even with compensation, the enlisting of servants was a harmful practice is found in Franklin, *Papers*, 6:474–75. Parliament's new instructions on recruiting were first carried to the American colonies by Lord Loudoun in July 1756. Working instructions issued to a recruiting party by Colonel Henry Bouquet reveal much about the procedure under parliamentary regulation. See BL, Add. Mss. 21631, ff. 49–50. The Act of Parliament requiring proportional compensation for deprived masters unfortunately did not spell out exactly how this was to be given, which caused no little perplexity for all involved—except possibly the irresponsible servant. Pertinent to the continuing problem is a notice published in the 11 November 1756 issue of the *Pennsylvania Gazette*, inviting all aggrieved masters to submit the relevant details to the assembly's committee of grievances, including the original cost of the servant and the time remaining to be served under the terms of indenture. As late as December of that same year, it seems, many masters in Pennsylvania still had not received satisfactory compensation. See Stanwix to Haldimand, 20 September 1756, BL, Add. Mss. 21666, ff. 6–10; [Loudoun] to Stanwix, 23 September 1756, HL, Loudoun Papers 1885; Loudoun to Fox, 8 October 1756, CO 5/47, ff. 393–96; *Pennsylvania Gazette*, 23 December 1756. The complications of the recruiting process as well as the policy for compensating masters may be appreciated by consulting Loudoun to Pitt, 25 April 1757, CO 5/48, ff. 137–55.

31. Corbin Lee to Horatio Sharpe, 30 April 1757, HL, Loudoun Papers 3506.

32. Jeremiah Gridley to Loudoun, 6 June 1757, HL, Loudoun Papers 3797. See also a writ dated 9 March 1758, HL, Loudoun Papers 5738.

33. Cottnam to Forbes, 12 December 1757, HL, Loudoun Papers 5003; Mackay to Forbes, 16 December 1757, HL, Loudoun Papers 5023. For an especially intriguing case of conflict over the behavior of a recruiting party in New London, Connecticut, see Pargellis, *Lord Loudoun*, pp. 126–28.

34. Pownall to Loudoun, 6 February 1758, HL, Loudoun Papers 5547. An angry mob was what the recruiters feared the most. In 1758 a captain of the

Forty-third Regiment reported from Boston that after the enlistment of one man a mob had assembled to display its resentment. Skey to [Loudoun], 5 March 1758, HL, Loudoun Papers 5703.

35. BL, Add. Mss. 21631, ff. 58–59, 71–80. For a South Carolina farmer's complaint about the recruiting of servants see his petition of 24 June 1757 in S.C. Arch., Journals of the Commons House, no. 31, part 2.

36. *CSP Col.* 1726–27, no. 524.

37. *Pa. Arch.*, 8th ser., 5:3950–52, 3968 (*Pa. CR*, 6:535); Yates, Copy Book & Journal, 21 October and 22 November 1755; Bailyn, *Pamphlets of the American Revolution*, 1:702; Zimmerman, "Governor Denny and the Quartering Act of 1756."

38. Franklin, *Papers*, 7:39–41n.

39. Abercromby to Loudoun, 30 June 1756, HL, Loudoun Papers 1263. For a less favorable report see Yates, Copy Book & Journal, April–June 1756.

40. Yates, Copy Book & Journal, 29 July 1756.

41. Loudoun to Fox, 19 August 1756, CO 5/47, ff. 15–26 (HL, Loudoun Papers 1522); Pitt to Loudoun, 4 February 1757, NMM, Holburne Papers (RUSI/NM/90); Pargellis, *Military Affairs*, p. 233 (HL, Loudoun Papers 1626). See also Pargellis, *Military Affairs*, pp. 239–43, 272–74.

42. Cornelius Cuyler to Philip Cuyler, 7 September 1756, Cuyler, Letter Book. See also Yates, Copy Book & Journal, April–August 1756.

43. Loudoun to Hardy, 21 November 1756, BL, Add. Mss. 21687, ff. 1–4 (CO 5/48, ff. 33–37).

44. CO 5/48, ff. 109–16 (WO 1/1, ff. 257–58); PRO 30 8/95, ff. 223–24; List of the inhabitants of Albany, November 1756, HL, Loudoun Papers 3515; [Loudoun] to Denny, 22 December 1756, HL, Loudoun Papers 2382. From a source strongly biased against Loudoun comes the story of one curious episode during that winter of discontent. Some of Albany's young blades engaged a fiddler to play for a dance. A group of army officers also planned a dance for the same evening and sought the services of the same musician. Being already engaged, he of course declined. Shortly before the first affair was to begin, an officer of the Thirty-fifth Regiment stalked into the room where the fiddler was preparing to play and forced him to go instead to the officers' ball, where he was compelled to scrape away for the greater part of the night—without pay. Yates, Copy Book & Journal, Winter 1756–57.

45. Loudoun to Denny, 22 September 1756, HS Pa., Penn Mss., Official Correspondence 1756–57, 8:163 (*Pa. CR*, 7:269–71); Richard Peters to [Thomas Penn], 26 December 1756, HS Pa., Penn Mss., Official Correspondence 1756–57, 8:211–13; Loudoun to Fox, 8 October 1756, CO 5/47, ff. 393–96; [Loudoun] to Denny, 28 October 1756, HL, Loudoun Papers 2104 (*Pa. CR*, 7:340); *Pa. Arch.*, 1st ser., 3:85–86, and 8th ser., 6:4440, 4442, 4447–48; *Pa. CR*, 7:349–50; Richard Peters letter of 11 December 1756, HS Pa., Peters, Letters to Proprietaries; *Pennsylvania Gazette*, 23 December 1756; Philadelphia Munici-

pal Archives, Common Council Minutes, 1745–1776, 9 December 1756; Zimmerman, "Governor Denny and the Quartering Act of 1756," pp. 271–81.

46. *Pa. Arch.*, 1st ser., 3:82.

47. Franklin, *Papers*, 7:49.

48. *Pa. Arch.*, 1st ser., 3:112.

49. [Loudoun] to Denny, 22 December 1756, HL, Loudoun Papers 2382.

50. Richard Peters to [Thomas Penn], 26 December 1756, HS Pa., Penn Mss., Official Correspondence 1756–57, 8:211–13; *Pa. Arch.*, 1st. ser., 3:110–12. Later, when it became known in Philadelphia that Loudoun himself was coming to town for a conference with some of the provincial governors, the municipal council showed remarkable zeal in trying to make him feel welcome. They made available to him a comfortable house with ample provision for fuel, wine, and other amenities, and arranged for a dinner in his honor. After his arrival, the council greeted him with a glowing address to which the gratified commander in chief responded in kind. Both statements are recorded in Philadelphia Municipal Archives, Common Council Minutes, 1745–1776, February 1757.

51. S.C. Arch., Journals of the Commons House, no. 31, part 2, May–July 1757; S.C. HS, Journals of the Commissioners of the Fortifications, 28 July and 1 August 1757; Memorandum of conference at Charleston, 2 December 1757, BL, Add. Mss. 21643, ff. 47–48 (Bouquet, *Papers*, 1:248–50).

52. Bouquet to Ellis, 17 September 1757, BL, Add. Mss. 21632, f. 5. See also S.C. Arch., Journals of the Commons House, no. 32, October and December 1757; S.C. HS, Journals of the Commissioners of the Fortifications, October and November 1757; CL, Lyttelton Papers, 10–21 October and 6 December 1757; Bouquet to Loudoun, 16 October 1757, BL, Add. Mss. 21632, ff. 10–16; Memorandum of conference at Charleston, 2 December 1757, BL, Add. Mss. 21643, ff. 47–48; Lyttelton to Board of Trade, 2 December 1758, S.C. Arch., film of CO 5/376, ff. 71–73. For a thorough discussion of this subject see Greene, "South Carolina Quartering Dispute, 1757–1758."

53. Letters of 16 and 18 October and 10 December 1757, BL, Add. Mss. 21632, ff. 10–17, 21–24. See also S.C. Arch., Journals of the Commons House, no. 32, 6 and 8 December 1757; Lyttelton to Board of Trade, 22 December 1757, S.C. Arch., film of CO 5/376, ff. 39–40.

54. Loudoun to Bouquet, 25 December 1757, BL, Add. Mss. 21640, f. 22 (Bouquet, *Papers*, 1:267).

55. Remonstrance of 19 January 1758, BL, Add. Mss. 21632, f. 26; Petition of 27 January 1758, S.C. Arch., Journals of the Commons House, no. 32.

56. S.C. Arch., Journals of the Commons House, no. 32, 24 January, 9 February, 9 March, 12 May 1758; S.C. HS, Journals of the Commissioners of the Fortifications, 11 and 20 February, 3 March, 20 April 1758; S.C. Arch., Council Journals, no. 26, 1 March 1758; Bouquet letters of 1, 16, 21, 28 February 1758, BL, Add. Mss. 21632, ff. 26–33; Commons House of Assembly to Lyttelton, 10 February 1758, CL, Lyttelton Papers (S.C. Arch., Journals of the Com-

mons House, no. 32); Loudoun to Lyttelton, 13 February 1758, Lyttelton Papers; HL, Abercromby Papers, 1674–1787, 42, 54, 60 (S.C. Arch., Journals of the Commons House, no. 32).

57. Loudoun to Pownall, 15 November 1757, CO 5/49, ff. 100–104 (HL, Loudoun Papers 4838). Helpful accounts of the controversy in Massachusetts are found in Hutchinson, *History of Massachusetts-Bay*, 3:46–48, and Schutz, *Thomas Pownall*, pp. 110–18.

58. Mackinen to [Forbes], 4 November 1757, HL, Loudoun Papers 4763. See also *Mass. JHR* 34, part 1, pp. 111, 129 (HL, Loudoun Papers 4346, 4366); Pownall to Loudoun, 2 September 1757, HL, Loudoun Papers 4389; Cox to [Forbes], 4 November 1757, HL, Loudoun Papers 4760; Mackay to Forbes, 4 November 1757, HL, Loudoun Papers 4755; Mackinen to [Forbes], 4 November 1757, HL, Loudoun Papers 4763; Pownall to Loudoun, 1 November 1757, CO 5/49, ff. 86–87; Pownall to Loudoun, 4 November 1757, CO 5/49, ff. 94–97 (HL, Loudoun Papers 4757); Pownall to Loudoun, 7 November 1757, CO 5/49, ff. 98–99; Pownall to General Court, 26 November 1757, CO 5/49, ff. 107–8 (HL, Loudoun Papers 4905); Precis of Loudoun's letter of 14 February 1758, PRO 30 8/96, ff. 27–29; Pitt, *Correspondence*, 1:183–96 (CO 5/49, ff. 1–13; HL, Loudoun Papers 5598).

59. PRO 30 8/95, ff. 337–42. See also Loudoun to Pownall, 15 November 1757, CO 5/49, ff. 100–104 (HL, Loudoun Papers 4838); Loudoun to Pownall, and Pownall to Loudoun, 9 January 1758, CO 5/49, ff. 128–34; Loudoun to Pownall, 6 December 1757, PRO 30 8/95, ff. 351–55 (HL, Loudoun Papers 4955); Loudoun to Pownall, 6 December 1757, CO 5/49, ff. 114–15 (HL, Loudoun Papers 4958); Loudoun to Pownall, 26 December 1757, ff. 122–23 (HS Pa., Etting Collection, Revolutionary Papers, Colonial Wars); Loudoun to the Duke of Argyle, 14 February 1758, PRO 30 8/96, ff. 30–39.

60. Pownall to Loudoun, 28 November 1757, PRO 30 8/95, ff. 343–50.

61. *Mass. A and R*, 4:47–48 (CO 5/49, ff. 111–13; HL, Loudoun Papers 4928).

62. General Court to Pownall, 16 December 1757, CO 5/49, ff. 118–21 (HL, Loudoun Papers 5021). See also *Mass. JHR* 34, part 2, pp. 255–56 (CO 5/49, ff. 135–37; HL, Loudoun Papers 5338); Pownall to Loudoun, 15 December 1757, PRO 30 8/95, ff. 362–65 (HL, Loudoun Papers 5014); Pownall to Loudoun, 16 December 1757, CO 5/49, ff. 116–17; Extract of Robertson to Bouquet, 27 December 1758 [1757?], BL, Add. Mss. 21632, f. 34; Pownall to Secretary at War, 1 April 1758, WO 1/1, ff. 322–23; Pencak, "Massachusetts Politics in War and Peace," pp. 303–5; Pencak, *War, Politics, & Revolution in Provincial Massachusetts*, pp. 156–57.

63. Yates, Copy Book & Journal, 7 December 1757. See also ibid., October 1757–May 1758; Christie to Gage, 11 December 1759, CL, Gage Papers, American Series, vol. 4. A later high sheriff, who also was a thorn in the side of the British army at Albany, was forced to accept into his home nine soldiers plus

a number of army wives and children. See N.Y. HS *Coll.* 54 (1921): 380–86, 388, 391–93.

64. N.Y. HS *Coll.* 14 (1881): 122.

65. *Conn. CR*, 11:176–78. For a good example of the army's expectations with regard to quartering see Deputy Quartermaster General John Bradstreet's order of 13 October 1758 in Conn. HS *Coll.*, 17:356. Cases of quartering problems are recorded in HL, Abercromby Papers 99, 117, 118, 137, 142; Philadelphia Municipal Archives, Common Council Minutes, 1745–1776, 6 April 1758; *Pa. CR*, 8:282–84, 330–31; Bouquet to Stanwix, 29 December 1759, BL, Add. Mss. 21652; Franklin, *Papers*, 9:10–12. As John Woolman revealed, quartering could even become an issue for the tender Quaker conscience. See *Works*, pp. 89–90.

66. Moneypenny, "Moneypenny Orderly Book," *Bulletin of the Fort Ticonderoga Museum* 13 (1970):160. A later entry (p. 162) reveals a shifting of military personnel "for the Ease of the Inhabitants."

67. WO 34/16, ff. 196–97. See also ibid., ff. 198–99, 210.

68. Conn. HS *Coll.*, 17:256–59 (CO 5/47, ff. 291–94). At a more trivial level, the Massachusetts assembly once had the temerity to inform General Amherst that provincial troops should be fed peas instead of rice. *Mass. JHR* 35:275.

69. Fitch to Loudoun, 8 October 1756, HL, Loudoun Papers 1990. See also Pownall to Loudoun, 28 November 1757, PRO 30 8/95, ff. 343–50.

70. N.Y. HS *Coll.* 54 (1921): 123–24. See also Massachusetts Committee of War to Loudoun, 21 September 1756, CO 5/47, ff. 300–302; Spencer Phips to Loudoun, 13 October 1756, HL, Loudoun Papers 2019; *Mass. JHR* 34, part 2, pp. 303, 305–6; Gridley to Kilby, 28 January 1758, PRO 30 8/96, ff. 21–22 (HL, Loudoun Papers 5485).

71. Pitt, *Correspondence*, 1:216.

72. PRO 30 8/96, ff. 272–73. One of the most prolonged and thorny attempts by a provincial legislature to dictate the employment of troops occurred in Maryland starting in 1757. A contingent of Maryland soldiers under the command of Captain John Dagworthy was stationed at Fort Cumberland, an important frontier supply base on the Maryland side of the Potomac River. About thirty miles east of that place was Fort Frederick. Lord Loudoun, knowing the importance of Fort Cumberland, wanted Dagworthy and his men to remain there; the popular house of the Maryland legislature, believing that Fort Cumberland was more important for the defense of Virginia than Maryland, wanted those troops withdrawn eastward to Fort Frederick where they could more effectively protect Maryland's interior settlements. Whose command would prevail—that of the British commander, who was responsible for the overall war effort, or that of the Maryland assembly, which had raised the troops in the first place? This controversy may be traced through the following

sources: *Md. Arch.*, 55:666–73; CO 5/48, ff. 225–31; CO 5/49, ff. 1–13, 21–30, 35–67, 70–75, 78–80; CO 5/50, ff. 30–32, 405–11, 416–17; PRO 30 8/95, ff. 252–53; HL, Abercromby Papers 162, 294; HL, Loudoun Papers 5598; Bouquet, *Papers*, 1:340; Pitt, *Correspondence*, 1:185, 235–38; Forbes, *Writings*, pp. 76, 103. For a somewhat similar case involving Connecticut, Massachusetts, and New Hampshire see [Abercromby] to Fitch, 14 May 1758, HL, Abercromby Papers 252.

73. [Abercromby] to De Lancey, 22 May 1758, HL, Abercromby Papers 278; De Lancey to Abercromby, 28 May 1758, HL, Abercromby Papers 279. The role of Albany County's high sheriffs Abraham Yates and Jacobus Van Schaick, as adversaries of the British army, deserves further investigation. See, for example, Yates, Copy Book & Journal, 11 October 1757; N.Y. HS *Coll.* 54 (1921): 322–26, 380–88, 391–93. Both men, diligent in serving writs against British officers, were quick to claim that they were merely doing their civic duty and upholding the civil law. It is worth noting that during the period of the American Revolution Yates was a radical patriot.

74. [Abercromby] to De Lancey, 10 October 1758, HL, Abercromby Papers 739; Yates, Copy Book & Journal, 12 September 1758.

75. Gage to Amherst, 9 March 1759, CL, Gage Papers, Letter Books, 1759–1760. See also Amherst to Gage, 20 February 1759, CL, Amherst Papers, vol. 4.

76. Forbes, *Writings*, p. 93; Thayer, *Pennsylvania Politics*, pp. 67–68. The *Pennsylvania Gazette* of 11 May 1758 carried Forbes's advertisement for the required transport. In one area where transport was being solicited, the people repeatedly referred to a certain horse that had been sent off to the army in 1757, never again to be seen by its owner. Wrote Bouquet to Forbes, "I cannot avoid recommending a trifle, which is to find some way of paying . . . the cost of that cursed horse which was drowned last year in the service of the second battalion of the R. A. That will have a very good effect, and will smooth over many difficulties." Bouquet, *Papers*, 2:50. Referring earlier to the same problem Bouquet wrote, "I hope that for a Dead Horse, the People of York County, will not Distress the Service in such urging Circumstances, and Load themselves with the Consequences of such undutiful Behaviour towards their King and Country." Ibid., p. 28. Such appeals to the colonists' supposed sense of duty and patriotism were not uncommonly heard from exasperated British officers.

77. Bouquet, *Papers*, 1:378–79, 382–91, 399–400, 405, and 2:18.

78. Ibid., 2:180. See also ibid., pp. 73, 105–6.

79. Forbes, *Writings*, p. 191.

80. Ibid., pp. 213–14. See also ibid., p. 207 (*Pa. Arch.*, 8th ser., 6:4829–32; *Pa. CR*, 8:167–69); Forbes to Pitt, 20 October 1758, CO 5/50, ff. 424–25.

81. *Pa. CR*, 8:282–84.

82. Bouquet to Stanwix, 26 April 1759, BL, Add. Mss. 21638, ff. 5–6; Mercer to Bouquet, 28 September 1759, BL, Add. Mss. 21644, ff. 417–20; Bouquet

to Stanwix, 26 April 1759, BL, Add. Mss. 21652; Bouquet to Shippen, 2 June 1759, BL, Add. Mss. 21652. See also the notices published in the *Pennsylvania Gazette* of 26 April 1759.

83. *Pa. CR*, 8:373.

84. Graydon to Bouquet, 30 August 1759, BL, Add. Mss. 21644, ff. 351–52. For a more favorable report see Hambright to Bouquet, 31 August 1759, BL, Add. Mss. 21654.

85. *Pa. Arch.*, 1st ser., 3:670–71. The worst form of impressment is depicted in the following deposition, dated 27 August 1759: "Personaly Appeared Before Me one of his Majestys Justices for the County of Cumberland John Sanderson and being Solemnly Sworn saith that as he was Carrying A Load of Pork from Carlisle to Bedford for the use of the Army that on his way at fort Loudon Major Armstrong Impressed his wagon and ordered out the Load Imediatly and took his wagon and Gave him no receipt for the same and this deponant was Left there with his Load and horses and no way provided Either to take it in to a store or Carried further and this deponant hath neither Gott his wagon nor no value for her." BL, Add. Mss. 21644, f. 339.

86. Bouquet to Gates, 1 September 1759, N.Y. HS, Gates Papers (Film, Reel 1). See also Sinclair to Bouquet, 9 August 1759, BL, Add. Mss. 21639, ff. 82–83; Record of a meeting of magistrates at Lancaster, 9 August 1759, BL, Add. Mss. 21644, f. 295; Shippen to Bouquet, 11 August 1759, BL, Add. Mss. 21644, ff. 300–301; Sinclair to Bouquet, 19 August 1759, BL, Add. Mss. 21639, ff. 90–91; Sinclair to the magistrates of Lancaster County, BL, Add. Mss. 21639, ff. 94–95. In New York, General Gage demonstrated how thorough he could be in obtaining required transport by ordering his troops to seize all wagons. When winter snows arrived, he also threatened to commandeer the people's sleighs if they refused to feed the troops quartered among them. See Gage to Amherst, 25 April 1759, CL, Gage Papers, Letter Books, 1759–1760; Gage to Grant, 6 January 1760, ibid.; Gage to Campbell, 8 January 1760, ibid.; Gage to Grant, 8 January 1760, ibid.; Gage to Mackenzie, 8 January 1760, ibid.; Gage to Campbell, 20 April 1760, ibid.; Gage to Amherst, 27 April 1760, ibid.; Gage to Campbell, 28 April 1760, ibid.; N.Y. HS *Coll.* 54 (1921):383.

CHAPTER 6

1. Anderson, *People's Army.*

2. Johnson, *Papers*, 9:206.

3. Anderson, "Why Did Colonial New Englanders Make Bad Soldiers?" pp. 395–417.

4. Orders to Captain Wrightson, 24 July 1758, HL, James Abercromby Papers 941; Quoted in Barton, "Thomas Barton and the Forbes Expedition," p. 483.

5. Winslow's order of 19 July 1756, Mass. HS, Winslow Papers; Grubb, Orderly Book, 19 June 1759.

6. Simmons and Thomas, *Proceedings and Debates*, 1:28; Report to Robinson, 3 December 1754, SP 41/21 (HL, Loudoun Papers 522).

7. Simmons and Thomas, *Proceedings and Debates*, 1:28–40; Robinson to Braddock, 23 January 1755, HL, Loudoun Papers 546; Lowdermilk, *History of Cumberland*, appendix, p. iv; Nichols, "Braddock Expedition," pp. 149–50. On 17 June 1757 one provincial soldier noted in his diary, "We ware all mustered and Vewed By A Regular major and had the marshall Law Red to us." Metcalf, *Diary and Journal*. By coincidence, on that same day a British commander in chief was commenting sourly on a New Jersey act that seemed to exempt troops of that colony from being disciplined by regular officers. If those troops were to join him and thought themselves exempt, he averred, "I believe they would find, they were mistaken." Loudoun to Pitt, 17 June 1757, CO 5/48, ff. 225–31. See also Gage to [Haldimand], 4 April 1759, BL, Add. Mss. 21662, ff. 28–29.

8. S.C. Arch., Journals of the Commons House, no. 31, part 2, 2 July 1757; Dinwiddie to Lyttelton, 27 August 1757, CL, Lyttelton Papers. Governor Shirley of Massachusetts informed Secretary of State Henry Fox on 6 May 1756 that he had succeeded in persuading his assembly to adopt the British Articles of War for the government of the colony's own troops, but examination of the assembly's enactment reveals no such provision. See Shirley, *Correspondence*, 2:433–38 (CO 5/46, ff. 247–52); *Mass. A and R*, 3:962–63; *Mass. JHR* 32, part 1, pp. 488, 491.

9. Not only the provincial troops but also "All Waggoners Horse Drivers Sutlers Servants and others following the Army" were made subject to the military laws. Forbes's order of 5 July 1758, Shippen, Orderly Book. See also Bouquet, *Papers*, 2:676; Hervey, *Journals*, p. 116. Early in 1757, to allay provincial dissatisfaction with the system of military justice, Lord Loudoun promised that all but the most heinous offenses committed by provincial soldiers would be tried by courts consisting entirely of provincial officers. N.Y. HS *Coll.* 54 (1921): 124–26 (Mass. HS, Israel Williams Papers; Conn. HS *Coll.*, 17:286–87). It is doubtful that this leniency survived for long, unless Loudoun defined "heinous" very broadly. For examples of mixed courts martial see Hervey, *Journals*, pp. 67, 70, 101, 105; Spaulding, Diary, 13 and 17 July 1757; *Bulletin of the Fort Ticonderoga Museum*, 12:449–51, and 13:105, 107; Henderson, Diary, 23 July 1758; Joseph Williams, Orderly Book, 31 August 1758; Shippen, Orderly Book, 12–13 July 1758; Extract of a court martial held on 24 May 1759, CL, Amherst Papers, vol. 4.

10. Comstock, Journal, 16 September 1759. See also Lowdermilk, *History of Cumberland*, appendix, pp. xxxiv, xlvi; Procter, "Diary," p. 40. For other examples of severe corporal punishment, some involving provincials, see Shippen, Orderly Book, 13 July 1758; LC, Manuscript Division, Massachusetts Miscellaneous, 17 July 1758; Proceedings of a court martial at Raystown, 11 August

1758, BL, Add. Mss. 21682, f. 8; LC, Forbes Orderly Book (transcript), pp. 9–15; Gallup, Orderly Book, June 1759; Knox, *Historical Journal*, 1:488–89; Hervey, *Journals*, pp. 70, 105, 116; Court martial held at Fort Pitt, 3 November 1760, BL, Add. Mss. 21682, f. 25; Monckton to Bouquet, 12 February 1761, BL, Add. Mss. 21638. At Lake George on 24 August 1758 the provincial troops were treated to a remarkable spectacle, the punishment of two redcoats by a method known as "picketing." Probably at one time or another most colonial soldiers had watched a comrade undergo the humiliating and intensely uncomfortable experience of "riding the wooden horse," but what they now witnessed was a long step beyond that in the saga of calculated sadism. Each of the two offenders was suspended from either the limb of a tree or a gallows by one arm, the other arm and a leg being tied together. Planted in the ground directly below each victim was a pointed stake. Whenever the agonized soldier felt compelled to ease the terrible strain on his arm, his only recourse was to plant his bare foot on the point of the stake. This punishment lasted a full hour. Champion, Journal, 24 August 1758. On "picketing" see Grose, *Military Antiquities*, 1:200.

11. Amherst to Gage, 29 May 1759, CL, Amherst Papers, vol. 4.

12. Clough, "Journal," p. 104.

13. The Nova Scotia campaign was simultaneous with the Braddock expedition, which, as is well known, also produced considerable Anglo-American friction.

14. Even before leaving home territory the men from New England felt some apprehension at the prospect of serving with the king's men. Noted one provincial officer in his journal, "This Day I went a Board with Ensign Willard and 45 of my Company Captain Probeys Ship the Syrene man of war. . . . The Sould-[iers] Loockt very soober being with Strangers and in a man of war." Willard, "Journal," 14–15 May 1755.

15. N.S. HS *Coll.*, 4:181.

16. Willard, "Journal," 5 July 1755; N.S. HS *Coll.*, 4:197–98.

17. N.S. HS *Coll.*, 4:228.

18. Ibid., p. 238.

19. Ibid., p. 240. See also Willard, "Journal," 14 August 1755.

20. N.S. HS *Coll.*, 3:151–52.

21. Extracts from Lawrence to Cunningham, 7 July 1756, CO 5/47, ff. 175–79. See also Willard, "Journal," 7–8 October 1755; N.S. HS *Coll.*, 3: 187–88, 190–91, 196; *Mass. JHR* 32, part 2, pp. 317–19, 331; Shirley, *Correspondence*, 2:464–65 (CO 5/46, ff. 261–64); Shirley to Halifax, [14?] June 1756, HL, Loudoun Papers 1246.

22. BL, Add. Mss. 4164, f. 37. See also Williams to Dwight, 7 July 1756, Mass. HS, Israel Williams Papers.

23. Letter of 6 June 1759, CO 5/51, ff. 62–63.

24. Mass. HS *Proc.*, 2d ser., 4:404.

25. Extract of Alexander to Morris, HS Pa., Penn Mss., Official Correspondence, 1756–57, 8:119.

26. Winslow to Hardy, 5 July 1756, Mass. HS, Winslow Papers. See also Abercromby to Loudoun, 30 June 1756, HL, Loudoun Papers 1263; Copy of a paper delivered by Abercromby to Winslow, July 1756, Mass. HS, Winslow Papers; *Pennsylvania Gazette*, 5 August 1756; Shirley, *Correspondence*, 2:492–98 (Mass. HS, Winslow Papers; CO 5/46, ff. 356–57; CO 5/47, ff. 127–28).

27. Williams to Dwight, 7 July 1756, Mass. HS, Israel Williams Papers; Flint to his wife, 14 July 1756, Mass. HS, Hutchinson Papers, Misc. Bound (CS Mass. *Pub.*, 24:441). See also Franklin, *Papers*, 6:473.

28. Waldo's letter of 14 January 1757, PRO 30 8/95, ff. 227–29; Rogers, *Empire and Liberty*, pp. 156–57.

29. Fox to Demere, 25 August 1754, SP 41/21 (CO 324/38, f. 428). Colonel George Washington suffered under this policy in 1754. See Leach, *Arms for Empire*, p. 337.

30. CO 324/38, ff. 429A–D. See also SP 44/189, ff. 38–40, 493–97; *Pa. Arch.*, 1st ser., 2:203–7; Pargellis, *Military Affairs*, pp. 34–36, 43–44.

31. Shirley, *Correspondence*, 2:497–98. See also Dinwiddie, *Records*, 2:324; Flint to his wife, 14 July 1756, Mass. HS, Hutchinson Papers, Misc. Bound (CS Mass. *Pub.*, 24:440–41); Mass. HS, Winslow Papers, July–August 1756; Dwight to Williams, 26 July 1756, Mass. HS, Israel Williams Papers; CO 5/47, ff. 38–39, 92–94 (HL, Loudoun Papers 1368, 1377); PRO 30 8/95, ff. 66–76, 188–91; BL, Egerton Mss. 3490; Loudoun to Hardy, 21 November 1756, BL, Add. Mss. 21631, ff. 2–8 (BL, Add. Mss. 21687, ff. 1–4; HL, Loudoun Papers 2250); *Historical Magazine*, 2d ser., 7:215. The kind of mischief that could be caused by the official policy on rank is well illustrated by a dispute involving Colonel George Washington and Captain John Dagworthy. The former, as commander of the Virginia Regiment, was in charge of frontier defense; the latter, also a provincial officer, commanded at Fort Cumberland in Maryland. Dagworthy refused to take orders from Washington on the grounds that he once had held a commission in the regular army. It took the intervention of the commander in chief to bring the Maryland captain down to his proper level. See Extract from Dinwiddie to Shirley, 23 January 1756, WO 1/4, ff. 58–59; Extract from Shirley to Sharpe, 5 March 1756, WO 1/4, ff. 54–55; *Md. Arch.*, 6:347–50; Dinwiddie, *Records*, 2:261.

32. Even so knowledgeable an officer as Captain John Bradstreet thought that if Shirley were still commander in chief the New Englanders could be persuaded to participate in a joint operation. See Extract from Bradstreet to Shirley, 24 July 1756, WO 1/4, ff. 188–89 (CO 5/46, ff. 341–42). See also Loudoun's letter of 24 July 1756, Adm. 1/481, ff. 234–35; Johnson, *Papers*, 9:484–85 (CO 5/47, ff. 33–37; HL, Loudoun Papers 1314); Johnson's memorandum, 17 July 1756, CO 5/47, ff. 203–4; Abercromby to Loudoun, 3 August 1756, CO 5/47, ff. 27–30. See also CO 5/47, ff. 142–43.

33. Royal command, 12 May 1756, BL, Add. Mss. 21631, f. 9 (CO 324/38, f. 458; HL, Loudoun Papers 1143).

34. Loudoun to Winslow, 31 July 1756, CO 5/47, ff. 92–94 (HL, Loudoun Papers 1377; Mass. HS, Winslow Papers). For an attempt at mediation by Connecticut's Governor Fitch see Fitch to Winslow, 4 August 1756, Mass. HS, Winslow Papers.

35. Loudoun to Winslow, 5 August 1756, CO 5/47, ff. 95–96; Winslow to Shirley, 21 August 1756, Mass. HS, Winslow Papers.

36. Loudoun to Winslow, 9 August 1756, CO 5/47, ff. 97–98 (HL, Loudoun Papers 1450; Mass. HS, Winslow Papers).

37. Winslow to Loudoun, 12 August 1756, CO 5/47, ff. 105–8; Winslow to Shirley, 21 August 1756, Mass. HS, Winslow Papers. See also Loudoun to Fox, 19 August 1756, CO 5/47, ff. 15–16 (HL, Loudoun Papers 1522); Pargellis, *Military Affairs*, p. 226 (HL, Loudoun Papers 1525); Hardy's letters of 27 August and 12 September 1756, Adm. 1/481, ff. 238–39, 242–43.

38. Thomas Williams to Colonel Williams, 28 August 1756, Mass. HS, Israel Williams Papers.

39. In the wake of the unsuccessful 1756 campaign there was an ongoing and mostly cordial exchange of letters between Loudoun and Winslow. See, for example, Mass. HS, Winslow Papers, 27 August–5 September 1756. But note also Loudoun's frank comment to Fox concerning the provincial officers: "I have nothing Pleasant at present to say of them, but their agreeing to be under directions, in spite of all the Pains that has been taken to prevent it." CO 5/47, ff. 205–7. See also Winslow's own report to Fox. CO 5/46, ff. 455–58. For an excellent summary of Loudoun's view of the problem of colonial as opposed to royal control of provincial forces see his statement to the intercolonial conference at Boston on 29 January 1757. N.Y. HS *Coll.* 54 (1921): 121–24 (HL, Loudoun Papers 2728; Mass. HS, Israel Williams Papers; Conn. HS *Coll.*, 17:276–80).

40. SP 44/189, ff. 501–3 (HL, Abercromby Papers 8). See also George II to Abercromby, 30 December 1757, HL, Abercromby Papers 7; Pitt's letter to the governors, 30 December 1757, CL, Lyttelton Papers. An American soldier serving at Fort Edward heard news of this concession on 9 March 1758. Fitch, *Diary*, p. 52.

41. Loudoun to Pownall, 6 February 1758, CO 5/49, ff. 149–52. See also Pencak, *War, Politics, & Revolution in Provincial Massachusetts*, p. 156.

42. Bouquet, *Papers*, 2:430–37, 631–32; Burd's letters of 28 August 1758, HS Pa., Shippen Family Papers, Letter-Books of Col. James Burd, 1756–1758; Barton, "Thomas Barton and the Forbes Expedition," p. 467.

43. Gage to Haldimand, 20 February 1759, BL, Add. Mss. 21662, ff. 15–16 (CL, Thomas Gage Papers, Gage Letter Book). See also Partridge to Williams, 30 September 1758, Mass. HS, Israel Williams Papers; Haldimand correspon-

dence, 17 February–2 April 1759, CL, Gage Papers, American Series, vols. 1–2; Gage to Amherst, 5 March 1759, CL, Gage Papers, Gage Letter Book.

44. Colonel John Bradstreet encountered the problem in August 1758. See Bradstreet to Abercromby, 15 August 1758, HL, Abercromby Papers 542; Stanwix to Abercromby, 20 August 1758, HL, Abercromby Papers 547; Godfrey, *Pursuit of Profit and Preferment*, pp. 127–28. Sometimes provincial officers from different colonies disputed with each other about relative rank. In August 1758, for example, as one observer with General Forbes's expedition reported, "The Field Officers in pitching their Tents, contend for Rank with some Warmth; Some claiming it from the Seniority of their Troops; and Others from the Age of the Charters of their respective Provinces." Barton, "Thomas Barton and the Forbes Expedition," p. 458.

45. Bouquet, *Papers*, 2:152 (BL, Add. Mss. 21639, f. 32).

46. Harris, Regimental Journal, 1 July 1758. General Abercromby once remarked, perhaps without intending a social slur, that some of the provincial officers could readily assume the responsibility of supervising the work of the army's carpenters, as they themselves were of that craft. [Abercromby] to Stanwix, 18 July 1758, HL, Abercromby Papers 446.

47. Barnard, Diary, 23 September 1756; Wells, Diary, 23 September 1756. See also Winslow to Hardy, 28 July 1756, Mass. HS, Winslow Papers; Pargellis, *Military Affairs*, pp. 170, 175–76.

48. The nine ringleaders, most of them noncommissioned officers, were smartly whipped for the desertion. See Barnard, Diary, 23 October 1756; Wells, Diary, 23 October 1756; Abercromby to Loudoun, 27 September 1756, HL, Loudoun Papers 1901; Extract from Morris's letter, 8 October 1756, HS Pa., Penn Mss., Official Correspondence, 1756–57, vol. 8; Pargellis, *Military Affairs*, p. 239.

49. N.Y. HS *Coll.* 14 (1881): 29–30.

50. Ibid., 54 (1921): 179; Montrésor's report to Marlborough, 1 October 1757, WO 55/283, ff. 4–13.

51. Putnam, *Journal*, pp. 51–58. Although New Englanders generally seemed the most recalcitrant of the provincials, troops from other areas also were inclined to abscond when disillusioned by their experiences. A court martial under General Forbes in 1758, for example, convicted a number of deserters, including one from Pennsylvania, one from Maryland, and one from North Carolina. Forbes, Orderly Book, pp. 9–15. The following winter the Maryland troops in garrison at Fort Cumberland, angry because the legislature of their own colony had neglected to provide for continuation of their pay, began deserting, and for a time it looked as though the post might have to be abandoned by the British. Bouquet, *Papers*, 2:648–49 (BL, Add. Mss. 21640, f. 203); Bouquet to the Maryland troops, 22 January 1759, BL, Add. Mss. 21652.

52. Appy to Wood, 2 July 1758, CO 5/50, ff. 188–97.

53. Nichols, Diary, 31 October 1758.

54. Stanwix to Abercromby, 6 August 1758, HL, Abercromby Papers 948. See also [Abercromby] to Stanwix, 23 July 1758, ibid. 468; Abercromby's orders of 23 July 1758, ibid. 939; [Abercromby] to Forbes, 2 August 1758, ibid. 500; Examinations of three deserters, 2 August 1758, ibid. 497; Bradstreet to Abercromby, 6 August 1758, ibid. 511; [Williams] to [Hutchinson], 7 August 1758, Mass. HS, Israel Williams Papers.

55. Cruickshank to Christie, 19 July 1758, HL, Abercromby Papers 455.

56. [Abercromby] to Stanwix, 12 August 1758, ibid. 531. See also ibid. 482, 483, 495, 498, 503, 516, 517, 525, 531, 536, 556; Hutchinson to Williams, 31 July 1758, Mass. HS, Israel Williams Papers; Pitt, *Correspondence*, 1:316–27 (CO 5/50, ff. 256–78).

57. Amherst, *Journal*, pp. 186–89; Comstock, Journal, 3 November 1759; Dibble, Diary, 1 and 3 November 1759 (Society of Colonial Wars in the State of Connecticut *Proceedings*, 1:319).

58. Gage to Browning, 2 November 1759, CL, Gage Papers, Letter Books.

59. Clough, "Journal," p. 105; Procter, "Diary," p. 32; Whitmore to Amherst, 12 November 1759, WO 34/17, ff. 44–45.

60. Amherst to Gage, 29 May 1759, CL, Amherst Papers, vol. 4; Knox, *Journal*, 3:25–26.

61. Henderson, Diary, 15 June 1759.

62. N.Y. HS *Coll.* 14 (1881): 93.

63. Dunbar to Gage, 7 April 1760, CL, Gage Papers, American Series, vol. 6.

64. Nichols, Diary, 3 July, 20 August, 10 September 1758.

65. Mass. HS *Proc.* 25 (1890): 361.

66. Graham, "Journal," p. 212.

67. For some examples of good personal relations and respect see Loudoun to Fox, 22 November and 26 December 1756, CO 5/48, ff. 1–26 (HL, Loudoun Papers 2263); Forbes to Lords of the Treasury, PRO, Treasury 1/389; Bouquet, *Papers*, 2:10–20, 143 (BL, Add. Mss. 21652, ff. 25, 49); Loring's letter of 19 August 1758, PRO 30 8/96, ff. 96–101; Amherst to Stanwix, 18 December 1759, BL, Add. Mss. 21634, ff. 27–28; Mass. HS *Proc.* 25 (1890): 363; Moneypenny, "Diary," p. 323; French, "Journal," p. 294.

68. Mass. HS *Proc.* 25 (1890): 389.

69. Moneypenny, "Diary," p. 331n; Laurens, *Papers*, 3:86n; Gadsden, *Writings*, pp. 14–15; Franklin, *Letters to the Press*, pp. 279–82; Rogers, "Papers of James Grant," pp. 146–48.

70. Fitch, *Diary*, 27 and 29 May, 8 June, 17 July, 26 August, 12 and 17 December 1757.

71. Mass. HS *Proc.* 25 (1890): 361. See also ibid., 24 (1889): 394. Two days after this affray, a regular soldier was flogged "for Striking one of the Proventials at the Spring and Braking Two of his Ribs." Ibid., pp. 394–95. For an ear-

lier, less violent argument between regulars and provincials see EI *Hist. Coll.* 93 (1957): 53.

72. McKenzie to Bouquet, 6 January 1759, BL, Add. Mss. 21644, ff. 7–8. See also Forbes, *Writings*, p. 274.

73. Braddock to Robinson, 5 June 1755, CO 5/46, ff. 21–26 (HL, Loudoun Papers 581).

74. Pargellis, *Military Affairs*, p. 64.

75. Montrésor to Napier, 12 January 1756, Houghton Library, Siege and Fall of Quebec, Letters and Manuscripts.

76. Extracts from Abercromby's letters, 30 August 1756, PRO 30 8/95, ff. 188–91.

77. Loudoun to Holderness, 16 August 1757, CO 5/48, ff. 277–95 (HL, Loudoun Papers 4239; Houghton Library, Loudoun Correspondence).

78. Johnson to Loudoun, 20 December 1756, HL, Loudoun Papers 2371.

79. Montrésor to Marlborough, 1 October 1757, WO 55/283, ff. 4–13.

80. Wolfe, *Life and Letters*, p. 392.

81. Forbes, *Writings*, pp. 113, 205; Bouquet, *Papers*, 2:477–78 (BL, Add. Mss. 21640, f. 161).

82. Bouquet, *Papers*, 2:215.

83. Cruickshank to Christie, 19 July 1758, HL, Abercromby Papers 456.

84. Bouquet, *Papers*, 2:153.

85. Extract from Robertson to Calcraft, 22 June 1760, HL, Loudoun Papers 6251.

86. Amherst to Duncan, 6 December 1761, WO 34/20, f. 84.

87. For yet more examples of derogation see Pargellis, *Military Affairs*, pp. 84–85; PRO 30 8/95, ff. 188–91; Burton to Loudoun, 27 August 1756, CO 5/47, ff. 323–26; Wolfe, *Life and Letters*, pp. 365, 394; Bouquet, *Papers*, 2:72; [Abercromby] to Stanwix, 2 August 1758, HL, Abercromby Papers 495; Extract from Napier's letter of 19 August 1758, WO 1/1, f. 237; General Abercromby to James Abercromby, 19 August 1758, BL, Add. Mss. 32884, ff. 362–65 (PRO 30 8/98, ff. 27–30); Bouquet to Forbes, 13 January 1759, BL, Add. Mss. 21640. For some favorable comments see St. Clair to Bouquet, 27 May 1758, BL, Add. Mss. 21639, f. 1 (Bouquet, *Papers*, vol. 1); Forbes to Pitt, 20 October 1758, CO 5/50, ff. 424–25; Knox, *Journal*, 1:481, 486. One of the most commended of the American officers was Robert Rogers, the commander of the Rangers. See, for example, Abercromby to Stanwix, 12 August 1758, HL, Abercromby Papers 531; Pitt, *Correspondence*, 1:322 (CO 5/50, ff. 256–78).

CHAPTER 7

1. Portions of this chapter were presented as a paper at the meeting of the Southern Historical Association at Charleston, S.C., in November 1983.

2. See, for example, Glen to Ward, 18 September 1746, Adm. 1/3818; *S.C. CR*, 8:44–45; Message of the House to the Governor, 27 June 1757, S.C. Arch., Journals of the Commons House, no. 31, part 2; Instructions to Wright, 8 July 1757, CL, Lyttelton Papers.

3. *South Carolina Gazette*, 13–20 November 1740.

4. Ibid., 18 March 1745.

5. *N.Y. CD*, 4:1055–56. See also ibid., p. 1062. As a matter of fact, after 1702 a colonial governor's authority over navy captains in his colony was greatly diminished. Stout, *Royal Navy in America*, p. 7.

6. Baugh, *British Naval Administration*, p. 7.

7. Byrd, *Correspondence*, pp. 327, 569. See also Petition of New York merchants, 17 February 1712, Bodleian Library, Rawlinson Mss. A, f. 266; Petition of Silbey and deposition of the Harveys, 28 November 1693, Mass. Arch., 61:414–15; *Mass. JHR* 20:98–99; *N.Y. CD*, 4:1183–84, 1189–91.

8. *N.Y. CD*, 4:1056; *South Carolina Gazette*, 9–16 August 1742; Pringle, *Letterbook*, 1:380; Stock, *Proceedings and Debates*, 5:127; Warren, *Papers*, p. 5. See also *N.Y. CD*, 5:60; Pringle, *Letterbook*, 1:260, 322–23; *Boston Evening-Post*, 1 June 1741; *South Carolina Gazette*, 4 and 11 April 1743.

9. *S.C. CR*, 9:200.

10. Glen to Reynolds, 16 September 1749, Reynolds to the Admiralty, 24 September 1749, Adm. 1/2382.

11. *Va. EJ*, 1:177–82. See also ibid., pp. 163, 165; *Va. LJ*, 1:141–51; *Va. JHB*, 1659/60–1693, pp. 355–56, 361, 365–68; *CSP Col.* 1689–92, nos. 1452–53, 1476–77, 1505, 1510, 1520, 1934, 1947.

12. Complaint of Tomson, 2 July 1692, CO 5/751, ff. 15–20. See also ibid., ff. 9–14; Deposition of March and Hatch, 4 January 1693, CO 5/751, ff. 35, 39 (*CSP Col.* 1693–96, no. 3); Phips to Nottingham, 15 February 1693, CO 5/751, ff. 32–33, 36–37 (*CSP Col.* 1693–96, no. 88); Letter from officers and crew of HMS *Nonesuch*, 20 February 1693, CO 5/751, ff. 34, 38 (*CSP Col.* 1693–96, no. 88I); Phips to Nottingham, 6 April 1693, CO 5/751, ff. 57–60 (*CSP Col.* 1693–96, no. 247); Stoughton to Trenchard, 17 September 1694, CO 5/751, ff. 77–78; *CSP Col.* 1693–96, nos. 28, 79, 99, 130–31, 192, 205, 214, 224–25, 239, 258, 293, 423, 728, 826–27, 879; Pencak, "Massachusetts Politics in War and Peace," pp. 52–53.

13. *N.Y. CD*, 4:1056. See also *CSP Col.* 1702–1703, nos. 103, 127, 140, 174, 191, 214, 364, 876; *WMQ*, 2d ser., 15 (July 1935): 255. I am grateful to Robert Pace for bringing this case to my attention.

14. *Boston Gazette*, 6 and 20 June 1749; Adm. 1/2466; Adm. 1/3676, ff. 231, 234.

15. For a Bermuda case involving a vessel flying the union flag see Popple to the Admiralty, 7 March 1750, Adm. 1/3818.

16. Adm. 1/3676, ff. 235–45. See also Roddam, Log of HMS *Greyhound*; Log of HMS *Hector*, Adm. 51/425; Roddam to Maisterson, How to Maisterson, 15 June 1750, Adm. 1/2106; Maisterson to Corbett, 18 July 1750, Adm. 1/2106; Maisterson to Corbett, 20 July 1750, Adm. 1/2106; Maisterson to Clevland, 24 July 1750, Adm. 1/2106; Maisterson's letter of 2 August 1750, Adm. 1/2106; Maisterson to Clevland, 8 August 1750, Adm. 1/2106; Adm. 1/3676, ff. 235–45, 248–49, 276–77, 306–7; Catherwood to Clevland, 31 July 1750, Adm. 1/3818; Roddam to [Admiralty], 29 October, 6 and 27 November 1751, Adm. 1/2383; *N.Y. CD*, 6:571–76, 583–86; *N.Y. HS Coll.* 53 (1920): 210–18, 222–25, 242; *New-York Gazette Revived in the Weekly Post-Boy*, 11 June 1750; *New-York Evening Post*, 11 June 1750; *New-York Weekly Journal*, 11 June 1750; Stokes, *Iconography of Manhattan Island*, 4:620; Goebel and Naughton, *Law Enforcement in Colonial New York*, pp. 303–6.

17. In a similar case in the West Indies in 1744, involving the lieutenant of HMS *Otter*, Captains Charles Knowles and Peter Warren agreed that the admiralty had exclusive jurisdiction, despite a contrary claim by civil authority. See Knowles to the Admiralty, 22 June 1744, Adm. 1/2007.

18. Seddon's report, 25 February 1752, Adm. 1/3676, ff. 306–7. It is quite erroneous to say, as one historian has done, that "How and Parks were committed to jail, but escaped New York on board the H.M.S. *Hector* on June 8. There is no evidence to indicate that either man was ever recaptured or punished for the crime." Greenberg, *Crime and Law Enforcement in the Colony of New York*, p. 123.

19. Baugh, *British Naval Administration*, p. 500.

20. Ibid., p. 216; Trelawny to the Admiralty, 21 December 1743, Adm. 1/3817; Pares, *Historian's Business*, p. 183. For some early examples of impressment in the colonies see *CSP Col.* 1689–92, nos. 1370, 1398, 2283; New York State Library, *Calendar of Council Minutes 1668–1783*, pp. 63–71; *Va. EJ*, 3:190.

21. Teate to [Admiralty], 10 March 1709, Adm. 1/2573. See also Royal order to Wager, 22 April 1708, Adm. 2/37; Teate to [Admiralty], 4 August 1709, Adm. 1/2573; Teate to [Admiralty], 10 December 1709, Adm. 1/2573; *CSP Col.* 1710–11, no. 81; Graham, *Walker Expedition*, p. 357.

22. Instructions to Balchen, 9 March 1715, Adm. 2/48, f. 178; *South Carolina Gazette*, 10 January 1743; *Pa. Arch.*, 1st ser., 1:637–41 (N.Y. HS, George Clinton Papers, vol. 1); Maier, "Popular Uprisings and Civil Authority," p. 22. The question was not definitively settled until 1775 when Parliament actually repealed the Sixth of Anne.

23. *Pa. Arch.*, 1st ser., 1:637–41 (N.Y. HS, George Clinton Papers, vol. 1); Warren, *Papers*, pp. 279–80 (N.Y. HS, George Clinton Papers, vol. 3).

24. Hardy to the Admiralty, 3 January 1743, Adm. 1/1883; *South Carolina*

Gazette, 17 and 31 January 1743. See also Hardy to the Admiralty, 29 June 1743, Adm. 1/1883; Pringle, *Letterbook*, 2:491–93, 497, 569–70, 580–83. Later Hardy became governor of New York, where he learned still more about the whimsical ways of determined American colonists. There is some evidence to suggest that on the South Carolina station, and perhaps in other parts of coastal North America as well, some unscrupulous navy captains used impressment for personal monetary gain, a charge which, even if exaggerated or ill founded, heightened the resentment felt by those Americans who considered themselves victimized. See Stock, *Proceedings and Debates*, 5:127–28.

25. Knowles to the Admiralty, 18 January 1748, Adm. 1/234, ff. 74–77. Since the Americans also continued to insist that the Sixth of Anne remained in force, their objection to the act of 1746 seems superfluous if not inconsistent. Practically speaking, however, the cessation of impressment in the West Indies could intensify it farther north.

26. Jackson to Burchett, 28 July 1702, Adm. 1/1979; Povey to Nottingham, 20 July 1702, CO 5/751, ff. 87–88. Various documents concerning the Jackson case are to be found in Adm. 1/1979; CO 5/862, ff. 345–60; CO 5/910, ff. 260–72. See also Mass. HS *Coll.*, 6th ser., 3:336; *CSP Col.* 1702, no. 768; Pencak, "Massachusetts Politics in War and Peace," pp. 114–15, 355–56.

27. Deposition of John Gullison, CO 5/862, f. 350.

28. Deposition of Nathaniel Holmes, CO 5/862, ff. 355–56.

29. Affidavit of Sewall and Belcher, 18 July 1702, CO 5/862, f. 359. Oddly, Sewall failed to mention the episode in his diary.

30. Jackson's letter of 17 July 1702, Adm. 1/1979.

31. Stock, *Proceedings and Debates*, 5:129–30. See also *South Carolina Gazette*, 17–24 May 1740; Pringle, *Letterbook*, 1:206–7.

32. *Boston Weekly News-Letter*, 25 June–2 July 1741. See also Mass. Arch., 8:270–71, and 64:93–98, 163, 166–76, 200; *Boston Evening-Post*, 8 and 15 June, 6 July 1741; *New England Weekly Journal*, 16 and 23 June 1741; *Mass. JHR* 19:32, 197–99; Shirley to Townsend, 12 September 1746, Adm. 1/480, ff. 291–94. For an amusing story about how three mariners were successfully hidden from a press gang by being crammed into a pair of concealed "press beds" consult Bowen, *Journals*, pp. 9–10.

33. *Mass. JHR* 19:196. See also Mass. Arch., 64:175–76.

34. Vernon himself, at Jamaica, was having difficulties with the issue of impressment. See chapter 3 above, and also Vernon, *Papers*, pp. 238–39; CO 5/42, ff. 218–19, 228–30, 242–46, 270–71, 280–81.

35. Warren, *Papers*, pp. 85–86; Shirley to the Admiralty, 1 June 1745, Adm. 1/3817; Warren to Knowles, 2 June 1746, CO 5/44, ff. 33–38 (Warren, *Papers*, pp. 254–59); Shirley, *Correspondence*, 1:227–28; *Mass. JHR* 22:75–77, 87–88; *Boston Weekly News-Letter*, 25 July 1745; *Boston Evening-Post*, 9 September 1745 (supplement). In May, HMS *Winchester* lost seventeen men at Boston by desertion. Local merchants informed Governor Shirley that a certain Roger

Passmore "made it his business to entice Seamen to desert his Majesty's Service, and kept Houses in the Country . . . , where he harboured them till he had an Opportunity of Disposing of them to Masters of Merchant Ships." Seddon to the Admiralty, 18 October 1750, Adm. 1/3676, f. 251. Why the merchants chose to inform on Passmore is not known. The governor now saw a good opportunity to strike at a practice that long had been a source of great annoyance to the Royal Navy and clearly fostered impressment. He had the sheriff arrest Passmore and deposit him as a free contribution on board the *Winchester*! As a result, Passmore gained a working passage to England, where he deserted and then sued the captain for having brought him there.

36. General Court to Warren, 2 November 1745, CL, Peter Warren Papers, vol. 5 (Warren, *Papers*, pp. 185–86). See also NMM, Lieutenant's Log, HMS *Wager*; Communications from Captain Arthur Forrest, Adm. 1/1782; SP 42/30, ff. 110–27; *Boston Gazette*, 17 September 1745; *Boston Evening-Post*, 30 September and 14 October 1745; *Boston Weekly News-Letter*, 29 August, 10 and 15 October 1745.

37. Warren to Corbett, 2 June 1746, Adm. 1/480, ff. 45–48, 60–63. See also Log of HMS *Shirley*, Adm. 51/4341; Warren, *Papers*, pp. 211–12; Townsend to Shirley, 17 August 1746, Adm. 1/480, ff. 256–57; Shirley to Townsend, 12 September 1746, Adm. 1/480, ff. 291–94; Rouse to the Admiralty, 7 April 1746, Adm. 1/2381; Shirley to Newcastle, 20 April (July?) 1746, CO 5/45, ff. 44–47; Admiralty to Granville, 11 February 1746, SP 42/30, ff. 108–9; *Mass. JHR* 22: 204–5, 210–12, 219–22; Lynde, *Diaries*, p. 166; *Boston Gazette*, 25 March, 27 May, 3 June, 1 July 1746.

38. SP 42/30; Adm. 1/1782. For Boston's emotional view of the episode see the *Boston Evening-Post*, 25 November 1745 (supplement).

39. SP 42/30.

40. Admiralty to Granville, 11 February 1746, SP 42/30, ff. 108–9. The two men from the *Wager* were convicted, as anyone could have foretold, and subsequently received sentence of death. Lynde, *Diaries*, p. 166; Warren to Corbett, 2 June 1746, Adm. 1/480, ff. 45–48, 60–63 (Warren, *Papers*, pp. 259–62); *Boston Gazette*, 25 March 1746. One of the convicted men expired in jail; his youthful companion, reprieved by royal command, still languished in confinement as late as November 1747.

41. [Samuel P. Savage] to Rev. Sir, Letter of 21 November 1747, Mass. HS, Samuel P. Savage Papers, vol. 2. See also Knowles to [Admiralty], 18 January 1748, Adm. 1/234, ff. 74–77; Shirley to the Admiralty, 1 December 1747, Adm. 1/3818; Hopson to [Newcastle], 30 November 1747, CO 5/44, ff. 236–41; CO 5/45, ff. 83–96; Shirley, *Correspondence*, 1:406–23; *Mass. JHR* 24:208, 212–13, 215–16; AAS *Proc.*, 73:113, 118; *Boston Evening-Post*, 30 November 1747; *Boston Weekly News-Letter*, 17 and 31 December 1747; Hutchinson, *History of Massachusetts-Bay*, 2:330–33; Pencak, "Massachusetts Politics in War and Peace," pp. 250–54.

42. The so-called Knowles Riot has been thoroughly described in Lax and Pencak, "Knowles Riot and the Crisis of the 1740's in Massachusetts."

43. *Boston Evening-Post*, 7 December 1747. In the aftermath, Governor Shirley agreed to write to the ministry and the admiralty, expressing his colony's deep sense of the damage it was suffering because of impressment. See Draft of address from the general court to the king, 11 December 1747, Mass. Arch., 20:490; Shirley to Newcastle, 1 and 31 December 1747, CO 5/901, ff. 236, 318–24, 331–32 (SP 44/226, ff. 202–5); *Mass. JHR* 24:235.

44. Pencak, "Massachusetts Politics in War and Peace," pp. 250–54. Ten years after the Knowles Riot HMS *Enterprise* and HMS *Mermaid* were at Portsmouth, New Hampshire, when a press gang from the *Mermaid* aroused local fury by seizing one of the inhabitants. On the evening of 22 December 1757 a mob of several hundred, eager for revenge, assembled at the waterfront. Finding there a longboat from the *Enterprise*, the crowd hauled it ashore and dragged it inland for a distance of two miles, the centerpiece of a jubilant procession. The longboat's crew seems to have disappeared, perhaps seizing the opportunity to desert the service. Captain Donkley, believing that his men had been murdered by the mob, appealed to the provincial governor for justice. See MacKay to Forbes, 23 December 1757, HL, Loudoun Papers 5073.

45. *Mass. JHR* 33, part 2, p. 434. It is worth noting, however, that in 1759 the government of Massachusetts apparently had no compunction about impressing seamen from arriving vessels for service on board the province's own warship *King George*. See ibid., 35, p. 317.

46. Adams, Log of HMS *Hunter*.

47. Loudoun to Pitt, 30 May 1757, CO 5/48, ff. 220–24; N.Y. HS *Coll.* 14 (1881): 150; Gaine, *Journals*, 2:8–9; Pargellis, *Military Affairs*, p. 376. For similar impressment at Philadelphia see Griffiths to Gates, 20 April 1757, N.Y. HS, Gates Papers (film, reel 1).

48. Warrant, 16 January 1760, Adm. 1/2588; Deposition of Church, 16 January 1760, Adm. 1/2588; Tonyn to [Admiralty], 1 March 1760, Adm. 1/2588.

49. Tonyn to [Admiralty], 1 March 1760, Adm. 1/2588. Perhaps worth noting is the fact that of the four New York officials who signed the warrant for Tonyn's arrest, Cruger later was to serve as a delegate to the Stamp Act Congress, Scott was to become a radical political leader and eventually a brigadier general in the War for Independence, and Livingston was to sign the Declaration of Independence. For a more violent episode at New York later that same year see the documents concerning an occurrence on 18 August 1760, Adm. 1/1895; *New York Gazette*, 25 August 1760; N.Y. CD, 7:444–46, 454–55; Goebel and Naughton, *Law Enforcement in Colonial New York*, pp. 306–11.

50. Pargellis, *Military Affairs*, p. 52; Keppel to Rouse and Kinsey, 28 February 1755, Keppel, Order Book A (KEP/1). See also *Pa. CR*, 6:323.

51. The fact of the matter was that the health of the British colonial economy, as well as that of the French colonies in Canada and the Caribbean, virtually re-

quired such intercourse. George Louis Beer has pointed out, however, that special wartime conditions did reduce to an appreciable degree the normal American reliance on trade with the French West Indies. *British Colonial Policy*, pp. 129–30. As producers of large quantities of fish, grain, meat, and lumber for export, far beyond what British North America alone could consume, many Americans could see no compelling reason why they should not take advantage of French need for their products, even though the trade obviously contributed to the enemy's own ability to continue battling the British. Obviously, too, French colonial merchants felt much the same way.

52. Ibid., pp. 87–88, 127–28.

53. Forrest to Clevland, 14 September 1756, Adm. 1/1784.

54. Documents concerning illicit trade ca. 1759, PRO, Treasury 1/389; Johnson, *History of Domestic and Foreign Commerce*, 1:96–99; Beer, *British Colonial Policy*, chap. 6; Pares, *War and Trade in the West Indies*, chap. 9; Johnson, "Fair Traders and Smugglers in Philadelphia"; Wainwright, "Governor William Denny in Pennsylvania," p. 194. For Rear Admiral Charles Knowles's acerbic comments about the flag-of-truce trade as early as 1747–48 see Knowles to [Newcastle], 20 November 1747, BL, Add. Mss. 32713, ff. 472–73; Knowles to [Admiralty], 6 April 1748, Adm. 1/234, ff. 94–98; Knowles's letter of 23 January 1748, ibid., ff. 106–7.

55. The list may be found in PRO 30 8/78, f. 149.

56. N.Y. HS *Coll.* 61 (1928): 27. See also Cotes to Long, 28 February 1759, PRO 30 8/98, ff. 226–27; Extract from Vassall to Drake and Long, 3 March 1759, PRO 30 8/96, ff. 172–73; Moore's letter of 29 March 1759, PRO 30 8/78, ff. 147–48; Beer, *British Colonial Policy*, pp. 96–99; Johnson, *History of Domestic and Foreign Commerce*, 1:98–99; Pares, *War and Trade in the West Indies*, pp. 456–67.

57. N.Y. *CD*, 7:163. See also ibid., 76; Abstract of instructions to Loudoun, BL, Egerton Mss. 3490, f. 220; Fox to the Admiralty, 5 May 1756, Adm. 1/4121 (SP 44/226, ff. 421–22); Royal instructions to the governors, 5 July 1756, CO 324/38, ff. 461–62 (*Pa. CR*, 7:269); *Pa. Arch.*, 8th ser., 5:4251.

58. Fox to the Board of Trade, 27 September 1756, CO 324/38, ff. 467–68; Savelle, *Origins of American Diplomacy*, pp. 223–24, 302–5, 436–38; Stout, *Royal Navy in America*, pp. 15–23.

59. Beatson, *Naval and Military Memoirs*, 2:49; Clowes, *Royal Navy*, 3:166–67; Bezanson, *Prices in Colonial Pennsylvania*, pp. 37–38, 304–5; Rogers, *Empire and Liberty*, pp. 91–97, 162.

60. Journal of a Voyage to Halifax, 4 March 1757, PRO 30 8/78, ff. 276–93; [Loudoun] to governors, 2 March 1757, HL, Loudoun Papers 2959 (*Pa. CR*, 7:429–30); Hutchinson to Loudoun, 23 April 1757, HL, Loudoun Papers 3437; Mante, *History of the Late War*, pp. 85–86.

61. *Pa. Arch.*, 8th ser., 6:4573 (HL, Loudoun Papers 3836; *Pa. CR*, 7:567). See also *Pa. Arch.*, 8th ser., 6:4571–76; Petitions to Denny, April 1757, HL,

Loudoun Papers 3420 and 3488; Pargellis, *Military Affairs*, p. 352; Loudoun to Denny, 30 April 1757, CL, Misc. Mss., 1746–1764 (*Pa. Arch.*, 1st ser., 3:145–46); Loudoun to Pitt, 17 June 1757, CO 5/48, ff. 225–31.

62. In 1758 General James Abercromby imposed a general embargo involving all the colonies. The eventual lifting of that embargo provides a revealing illustration of the state of communication at the time. Abercromby's letter ordering Governor Lyttelton of South Carolina to end the restriction in that colony was dated 8 May but did not come to the governor's hand until 2 August! Commented Lyttelton to William Pitt, "Some new regulations in the Post throughout the Provinces, I humbly conceive Sir, are highly Necessary for the King's Service." Pitt, *Correspondence*, 1:312. See also ibid., pp. 159–60, 204, 217; Pitt to Abercromby, 11 January 1758, HL, Abercromby Papers 13; [Abercromby] to Durell, 15 March 1758, ibid. 43; Circular letter, 15 March 1758, ibid. 44–45; [Abercromby] to Pitt, 16 March 1758, ibid. 47; [Abercromby] to Lyttelton and Dobbs, 16 March 1758, ibid. 49; Montgomery to Abercromby, 27 April 1758, ibid. 206.

63. Johnson, "Fair Traders and Smugglers in Philadelphia," p. 148.

64. Amherst to Hale, 8 May 1762, Adm. 1/3819.

CONCLUSION

1. *Colonies in Transition*, p. 147.

BIBLIOGRAPHY

Citations accompanying the text indicate my frequent reliance upon various collections of government records and other contemporary documents, published and unpublished. It is recommended that the serious student who wishes to explore these for himself consult first the always useful *Harvard Guide to American History*, together with the available published guides to archives, libraries, and other repositories. The following selective bibliography also may prove helpful.

GENERAL REFERENCE

The American Historical Association's Guide to Historical Literature. New York, 1961.

Hamer, Philip M., ed. *A Guide to Archives and Manuscripts in the United States*. New Haven, 1961.

Higham, Robin, ed. *A Guide to the Sources of British Military History*. Berkeley and Los Angeles, 1971.

Higham, Robin, ed. *A Guide to the Sources of United States Military History*. Hamden, Conn., 1975.

Higham, Robin, and Mrozek, Donald J., eds. *A Guide to the Sources of United States Military History: Supplement I*. Hamden, Conn., 1981.

Roach, John, ed. *A Bibliography of Modern History*. Cambridge, 1968.

Social Science Research Council. *The Social Sciences in Historical Study: A Report of the Committee on Historiography* (Bulletin 64). New York, 1954.

Spiller, Roger J. *Dictionary of American Military Biography*. 3 vols. Westport, Conn., 1984.

DIARIES, JOURNALS, LOGS, AND ORDERLY BOOKS

Adams, William. Log of HMS *Hunter*. Public Record Office, Admiralty Papers 51/465.

Amherst, Gen. Jeffery. *The Journal of Jeffery Amherst, Recording the Military Career of General Amherst in America from 1758 to 1763*. Edited by J. Clarence Webster. Chicago, 1931.

Baldwin, Jeduthan. "Extracts from the Diary of a Revolutionary Patriot." *Journal of the Military Service Institution of the United States* 39 (1906): 123–30.

Barber, John. Journal. *New England Historical and Genealogical Register* 27 (1873): 281–85.

Barnard, John, Jr. Diary. Connecticut Historical Society.

Barton, Thomas. "Thomas Barton and the Forbes Expedition." Edited by William A. Hunter. *Pennsylvania Magazine of History and Biography* 95 (1971): 431–83.

Bass, Benjamin. "Account of the Capture of Fort Frontenac by the Detachment under the Command of Col. Bradstreet." *New York History* 16 (1935): 449–51.

Bidwell, Rev. Adonijah. Journal. *New England Historical and Genealogical Register* 27 (1873): 153–60.

Booth, Joseph. Journal. Connecticut Historical Society.

Bowen, Ashley. *The Journals of Ashley Bowen (1728–1813) of Marblehead.* Edited by Philip Chadwick Foster Smith. 2 vols. Salem, 1973. Colonial Society of Massachusetts *Publications* 44–45 (1973).

Braddock, Gen. Edward. Orderly Books. In *History of Cumberland (Maryland)*, by Will H. Lowdermilk, appendix. Washington, 1878.

Bradstreet, Dudley. Diary. Massachusetts Historical Society *Proceedings*, 2d ser., 11 (1897): 423–46.

Bremner, John. Journal, 1756–1764. New-York Historical Society. Typed copy.

Browne, Charlotte. "With Braddock's Army: Mrs. Browne's Diary in Virginia and Maryland." Edited by Fairfax Harrison. *Virginia Magazine of History and Biography* 32 (1924): 305–20.

Buckingham, Rev. Thomas. *The Private Journals Kept by Rev. John [i.e., Thomas] Buckingham, of the Expedition Against Canada, in the Years 1710 & 1711.* New York, 1825.

Bull, Lt. Joseph. Orderly Book, 25 May–1 Nov. 1759. Henry E. Huntington Library.

Burd, Col. James. Journal, 1756–57. Historical Society of Pennsylvania. Microfilm.

Burrell, John. Diary. *New England Historical and Genealogical Register* 59 (1905): 352–54.

Champion, Henry. Accounts and Journal, 1758. Connecticut State Library.

Chandler, Rev. Samuel. Extracts from the Diary of Rev. Samuel Chandler. *New England Historical and Genealogical Register* 17 (1863): 346–54.

Cleaves, Benjamin. Journal. *New England Historical and Genealogical Register* 66 (1912): 113–24.

Clough, Gibson. "Extracts from Gibson Clough's Journal." Edited by B. F. Browne. Essex Institute *Historical Collections* 3 (1861): 99–106, 195–201.

Comstock, Christopher. Journal. Connecticut Historical Society.

Craft, Benjamin. "Craft's Journal of the Siege of Louisburg." Edited by W. P. Upham. Essex Institute *Historical Collections* 6 (1864): 181–94.

De Forest, Louis Effingham, ed. *Louisbourg Journals, 1745.* New York, 1932. A collection of ten journals.

Dibble, Ebenezer. Diary. Society of Colonial Wars in the State of Connecticut

Proceedings 1 (n.d.): 311–29. A photostatic copy of the diary is in the Connecticut State Library.

Dorr, Moses. "A Journel of an Expedition Against Canaday." *New York History* 16 (1935): 452–64.

Douglas, James. Journal (DOU/1). National Maritime Museum.

"Extracts from A Journal of the Proceedings of the Detachment of Seamen, order'd by Commodore Kepple, to assist on the late Expedition to the Ohio." Edited by M. E. S. Laws. *Journal of the Society for Army Historical Research* 57 (1979): 193–205.

Fisher, Samuel. Diary of operations around Lake George, 1758. Library of Congress.

Fitch, Jabez, Jr. *The Diary of Jabez Fitch, Jr. in the French and Indian War, 1757.* N.p., n.d.

Forbes, Gen. John. Orderly Book. Library of Congress. Transcript.

Foster, Capt. Asa. Diary. *New England Historical and Genealogical Register* 54 (1900): 183–88.

French, Capt. Christopher. "Journal of an Expedition to South Carolina." *Journal of Cherokee Studies* 2 (1977): 275–301.

French, Jonathan. Journal. William L. Clements Library.

Fuller, Archelaus. Journal. Essex Institute *Historical Collections* 46 (1910): 209–20.

G., L. *A Brief Journal Of the Taking of Cape-Breton, Put in Metre, by L. G. one of the Soldiers in the Expedition.* Massachusetts Broadsides. Massachusetts Historical Society.

Gaine, Hugh. *The Journals of Hugh Gaine, Printer.* Edited by Paul L. Ford. 2 vols. New York, 1902.

Gallup, Benadam. Orderly Book. Connecticut Historical Society.

Gibson, James. *A Journal Of the Late Siege by the Troops from North America, against The French at Cape Breton. . . .* London, 1745.

Giddings, Lt. Daniel. "Journal Kept by Lieut. Daniel Giddings of Ipswich During the Expedition Against Cape Breton in 1744–5." Essex Institute *Historical Collections* 48 (1912): 293–304.

Graham, Rev. John. "The Journal of the Rev. John Graham, Chaplain to Connecticut Troops in the Expedition Toward Crown Point, 1756." *Magazine of American History* 8 (1882): 206–13.

Grant, John. Orderly Book, June–October 1761. Henry E. Huntington Library.

Griswold, Shubael. Journal. Connecticut State Library.

Grubb, Capt. Samuel. Orderly Book, June–July 1759. Henry E. Huntington Library.

Hale, Robert. Chronicle. American Antiquarian Society.

Hamilton, Charles, ed. *Braddock's Defeat: The Journal of Captain Robert Cholmley's Batman, The Journal of a British Officer, Halkett's Orderly Book.* Norman, 1959.

Hammond, Lawrence. Diary. Massachusetts Historical Society *Proceedings*, 2d ser., 7 (1892): 145–71.

Hardy, Constantine. Extracts from the Journal of Constantine Hardy. *New England Historical and Genealogical Register* 60 (1906): 236–38.

Harris, Obadiah. Regimental Journal, May–October 1758. Henry E. Huntington Library.

Hawks, John. Orderly Books. Henry E. Huntington Library and Library of Congress. Photocopy in Massachusetts Historical Society. (The portion for 1759–60 has been published in *Orderly Book and Journal of Major John Hawks on the Ticonderoga-Crown Point Campaign*, edited by Hugh Hastings. New York, 1911.)

Hayward, Benjamin. Journal. Connecticut Historical Society.

Henderson, James [or William]. Diary, 1758–59. New England Historic Genealogical Society. Photocopy in New York Public Library.

Hervey, William. *Journals of the Hon. William Hervey, In North America and Europe, From 1755 to 1814; with Order Books at Montreal, 1760–1763.* Edited by S. H. A. Hervey. London, 1906.

Hill, James. "The Diary of a Private on the First Expedition to Crown Point." Edited by Edna V. Moffett. *New England Quarterly* 5 (1932): 602–18.

Hitchcock, Aaron. Diary, 1745–46. Connecticut Historical Society.

Holden, David. "Journal of Sergeant Holden." Massachusetts Historical Society *Proceedings*, 2d ser., 4 (1889): 387–409.

Holt, Joseph. Journals. *New England Historical and Genealogical Register* 10 (1856): 307–10.

Huse, Carr. Diary, April–July 1758. New-York Historical Society.

Jenks, Capt. Samuel. Diary. Massachusetts Historical Society *Proceedings*, 2d ser., 5 (1890): 352–91.

Judd, Philip. Journal. Connecticut Historical Society.

Keppel, Adm. Augustus. Order Book A (KEP/1). National Maritime Museum.

King, Duane H., and Evans, E. Raymond, eds. *Journal of Cherokee Studies* 2 (Summer 1977). Special Issue: Memoirs of the Grant Expedition against the Cherokees in 1761.

Knap, Jonathan. Journal. Connecticut State Library.

Knox, John. *An Historical Journal of the Campaigns in North America, For the Years 1757, 1758, 1759, and 1760.* Edited by Arthur G. Doughty. 3 vols. Champlain Society *Publications* (1914–16).

Kopperman, Paul E., and Freiling, Michael J., eds. "A British Officer's Journal of the Braddock Expedition—Et Cetera." *Western Pennsylvania Historical Magazine* 64 (1981): 269–87.

Lynde, Benjamin, and Lynde, Benjamin, Jr. *The Diaries of Benjamin Lynde and of Benjamin Lynde, Jr.* Boston, 1880.

Marshall, John. Diary, 1689–1711. Massachusetts Historical Society.

Metcalf, Seth. *Diary and Journal (1755–1807) of Seth Metcalf*. Edited by William S. Piper. Boston, 1939.

Moneypenny, Alexander. Orderly Books. *Bulletin of the Fort Ticonderoga Museum* 12 (1969) and subsequent issues.

———. "Diary of Alexander Monypenny, March 20–May 31, 1761." *Journal of Cherokee Studies* 2 (Summer 1977): 302–31.

Montrésor, Col. James. Journals of Col. James Montrésor, 1757–1759. New-York Historical Society *Collections* 14 (1881).

Murray, James. *Governor Murray's Journal of the Siege of Quebec, from 18th September, 1759, to 25th May, 1760*. Toronto, 1939.

Mygate, George. Journal. In *Louisbourg Journals, 1745*, edited by L. E. De Forest, 97–108.

Nichols, Joseph. Diary. Henry E. Huntington Library.

Nicholson, Col. Francis. "Journal of Colonel Nicholson at the Capture of Annapolis, 1710." Nova Scotia Historical Society *Collections* 1 (1878): 59–104.

Noyes, John. Journal. Essex Institute *Historical Collections* 45 (1909): 73–77.

Orderly Book, Expedition of Gen. John Forbes to Fort Pitt. Toner Mss. Collection, Library of Congress. Transcript.

Pepperrell, William. *The Journal of Sir William Pepperrell During the Expedition Against Louisbourg, Mar. 24–Aug. 22, 1745*. Edited by C. H. Lincoln. American Antiquarian Society *Proceedings* 20 (1909–10): 133–83.

Perry [or Peary], Josiah. Orderly Book. *New England Historical and Genealogical Register* 54 (1900): 70–76, 164–67.

Pomeroy, Seth. *The Journals and Papers of Seth Pomeroy*. Edited by L. E. De Forest. [New York], 1926.

Procter, Jonathan. "Diary Kept at Louisburg, 1759–1760, by Jonathan Procter of Danvers." Essex Institute *Historical Collections* 70 (1934): 31–57.

Putnam, Rufus. *Journal of Gen. Rufus Putnam Kept in Northern New York During Four Campaigns of . . . 1757–1760*. Edited by E. C. Dawes. Albany, 1886.

Roddam, Capt. Robert. Log of HMS *Greyhound*. National Maritime Museum.

Rogers, Robert. *Journals of Major Robert Rogers*. Introduction by Howard H. Peckham. New York, 1961.

Sewall, Samuel. *The Diary of Samuel Sewall, 1674–1729*. Edited by M. Halsey Thomas. 2 vols. New York, 1973.

Sherburne, Capt. Joseph. Journal. In *Louisbourg Journals, 1745*, edited by L. E. De Forest, 56–60.

Shippen, Joseph. Journals and Orderly Book, 1756–58. Shippen Family Papers. Historical Society of Pennsylvania.

Shute, Rev. Daniel. Journal, 1758. Essex Institute *Historical Collections* 12 (1874): 132–51.

Smith, Joseph. "Journal of Joseph Smith, of Groton." Society of Colonial Wars in the State of Connecticut *Proceedings* 1 (n.d.): 303–10.

Spaulding, Leonard. Diary. New-York Historical Society.

Spaulding, Lt. Diary, 1758. Library of Congress. Photocopy.

Stearns, Benjamin. "Benjamin Stearns's Diary, 11 March–2 August, 1745."
Edited by J. C. L. Clark. *Acadiensis* 8 (1908): 317–29.

Stephens, William. "A Journal of the Proceedings in Georgia Beginning October
20, 1737." In *Colonial Records of the State of Georgia*, edited by A. D. Can-
dler, vol. 4 and supplement. Atlanta, 1906–1908.

————. *The Journal of William Stephens, 1741–1743*. Edited by E. Merton
Coulter. Athens, 1958. *The Journal of William Stephens, 1743–1745*. Athens,
1959.

Sweat, William. Diary, 1758. Edited by Paul O. Blanchette. Essex Institute *Historical Collections* 93 (1957): 36–57.

Thomas, John. Diary, 1755. Nova Scotia Historical Society *Collections* 1
(1878): 119–40.

Thomas, John, Jr. Diary, 1747. New England Historic Genealogical Society.

True, Capt. Henry. Memorandum and Account Book, 1696–1719. New York
Public Library.

Upton, Daniel. Diary, 1758. New York Public Library.

Washington, George. *The Diaries of George Washington*. Vol. 1, *1748–65*.
Edited by Donald Jackson and Dorothy Twohig. Charlottesville, 1976.

Waterman, Asa. Diary, 1760. Connecticut State Library.

Wells, Capt. Edmund. Diary, 1756–57. Connecticut State Library.

Willard, Abijah. Orderly Book and Journal, 1755–56. Henry E. Huntington Library. (The "Journal," edited by John Clarence Webster, has been published in
New Brunswick Historical Society *Collections* 13: 1–75.)

Williams, Joseph. Orderly Book, 1758. Houghton Library, Harvard University.

Williams, Joshua. Orderly Book. New York Public Library.

Williams, Stephen. Journal. In *Louisbourg Journals, 1745*, edited by L. E. De
Forest, 122–69.

Winslow, Col. John. Journal, 1755. Nova Scotia Historical Society *Collections* 3
(1882–83): 71–196; 4 (1884): 113–246.

Wolcott, Roger. "Journal of Roger Wolcott at the Siege of Louisbourg." Connecticut Historical Society *Collections* 1 (1860): 131–61.

Wood, Lemuel. Diaries. Essex Institute *Historical Collections* 19 (1882): 61–74,
143–52, 183–92; 20 (1883): 156–60, 198–208, 289–96; 21 (1884): 63–68.

Wood, William, ed. *The Logs of the Conquest of Canada*. Champlain Society
Publications 4. Toronto, 1909.

Woodhull, Col. Nathaniel. "A Journal Kept by General Nathaniel Woodhull,
When Colonel of the 3d Regiment New York Provincials, in the Expedition to
Montreal, in 1760." *The Historical Magazine* 5 (1861): 257–60.

EARLY NARRATIVES AND COMMENTARIES

An Accurate Journal and Account of the Proceedings of the New-England Land-Forces, During the late Expedition Against the French Settlements on Cape Breton, To the Time of the Surrender of Louisbourg. Exeter, 1746. See also *A letter from William Shirley, Esq; Governor of Massachusetts-Bay, To his Grace the Duke of Newcastle: With a Journal of the Siege of Louisbourg.* . . . London, 1746.

[Alexander, William.] *The Conduct of Major Gen. Shirley, Late General and Commander in Chief of His Majesty's Forces in North America. Briefly Stated.* London, 1758.

Bartman, George. "The Siege of Fort William Henry: Letters of George Bartman." Edited by John A. Schutz. *Huntington Library Quarterly* 12 (1948–49): 415–25.

Beatson, Robert. *Naval and Military Memoirs of Great Britain, from 1727 to 1783.* Introduction by George Athan Billias. Vol. 1 and 2. Boston, 1972.

Bolling, John. "A Private Report of General Braddock's Defeat." Edited by John A. Schutz. *Pennsylvania Magazine of History and Biography* 79 (1955): 374–77.

Bradstreet, John. In *Louisbourg Journals, 1745,* edited by L. E. De Forest, 171–78.

Breslaw, Elaine G. "A Dismal Tragedy: Drs. Alexander and John Hamilton Comment on Braddock's Defeat." *Maryland Historical Magazine* 75 (1980): 118–44.

Cadogan, George. *The Spanish Hireling Detected: Being a Refutation of the Several Calumnies and Falshoods in a late Pamphlet, Entitul'd An Impartial Account of the Late Expedition against St. Augustine under General Oglethorpe.* London, 1743.

[Chauncy, Charles.] *A Letter to a Friend; Giving a concise, but just, Account . . . of the Ohio-Defeat.* Boston, 1755.

———. *A Second Letter to a Friend; Giving a more particular Narrative of the Defeat of the French Army at Lake-George, By the New-England Troops, than has yet been published.* Boston, 1755.

The Conduct of a Noble Commander in America, Impartially reviewed. London, 1758. A defense of Lord Loudoun.

Dummer, Jeremiah. *A Letter to a Noble Lord, Concerning the late Expedition to Canada.* London, 1712.

Durell, Philip. *A Particular Account Of the Taking Cape Breton From the French, by Admiral Warren, and Sir William Pepperrell, The 17th of June, 1745.* London, 1745.

Entick, Rev. John. *The General History of the Late War: Containing It's Rise, Progress, and Event, in Europe, Asia, Africa, and America.* 3d ed. 5 vols. London, 1766–72.

Gordon, Harry. "A Letter from Will's Creek: Harry Gordon's Account of Braddock's Defeat." Edited by Charles M. Stotz. *Western Pennsylvania Historical Magazine* 44 (1961): 129–36. (Also in *Military Affairs in North America, 1748–1765: Selected Documents from the Cumberland Papers in Windsor Castle*, edited by Stanley Pargellis, 104–9. London and New York, 1936.)

Grose, Francis. *Military Antiquities Respecting a History of the English Army, from the Conquest to the Present Time.* 2 vols. London, 1786–88.

Harrington, James. *The Commonwealth of Oceana.* London, 1656.

Hutchinson, Thomas. *The History of the Colony and Province of Massachusetts-Bay.* Edited by Lawrence Shaw Mayo. 3 vols. Cambridge, Mass., 1936.

An Impartial Account of Lieut. Col. Bradstreet's Expedition to Fort Frontenac. . . . London, 1759.

Johnson, William. "Battle Report, General William Johnson's Letter to the Governors, Lake George, September 9–10, 1755." Edited by Milton W. Hamilton. *American Antiquarian Society Proceedings* 74 (1964): 21–24.

Kennedy, Archibald. *Serious Advice to the Inhabitants of the Northern-Colonies, on the Present Situation of Affairs.* New York, 1755.

————. *Serious Considerations on the Present State of the Affairs of the Northern Colonies.* New York, 1754.

[Kilpatrick, James.] *A Full Reply to Lieut. Cadogan's Spanish Hireling, &c. and Lieut. Mackay's Letter, Concerning the Action at Moosa.* London, 1743.

————. *An Impartial Account Of the Late Expediton Against St. Augustine Under General Oglethorpe.* London, 1742.

[Kimber, Edward.] *A Relation or Journal, Of a Late Expedition to the Gates of St. Augustine, on Florida.* London, 1744. Reprint ed. Boston, 1935.

[Knowles, Charles.] *An Account of the Expedition to Carthagena, with Explanatory Notes and Observations.* 2d ed. London, 1743.

[Livingston, William.] *A Review of the Military Operations in North-America: from the commencement of the French hostilities on the frontiers of Virginia, in 1753, to the surrender of Oswego, on the 14th of August, 1756.* Dublin and London, 1757.

Mante, Thomas. *The History of the Late War in North-America, and the islands of the West-Indies, including the campaigns of MDCCLXIII and MDCCLXIV against His Majesty's Indian enemies.* London, 1772.

[Mitchell, John.] *The Contest in America between Great Britain and France, with Its Consequences and Importance.* London, 1757.

Narrative of the Military Opperations in America in 1755–56. New-York Historical Society. Rufus King Papers 84, no. 58.

Neville, Henry. *Plato Redivivus.* London, 1681.

Perry, David. *Recollections of an Old Soldier.* Windsor, Vt., 1822. Reprint ed. Cottonport, La., 1971.

"A Ranger's Report of Travels with General Oglethorpe, 1739–1742." In *Travels in the American Colonies,* edited by N. D. Mereness, 218–36. New York, 1916.

Russell, Peter. Letters. Ontario Historical Society *Papers and Records* 29 (1933): 121–40. Russell, an officer in the British army, defends Braddock.

The St. Augustine Expedition of 1740: A Report to the South Carolina General Assembly Reprinted from the Colonial Records of South Carolina with an Introduction by John Tate Lanning. Columbia, 1954. The "Report" was published in the *Journal of the Commons House of Assembly, 1741–1742,* 78–247.

[Shirley, William.] *Memoirs of the Principal Transactions of the Last War Between the English and French in North America. From the Commencement of it in 1744, to the Conclusion of the Treaty at Aix la Chapelle.* London, 1757.

[Smith, William.] *A Brief State of the Province of Pennsylvania, in which The Conduct of their Assemblies for several Years past is impartially examined.* London, 1755.

―――. *A Brief View Of the Conduct of Pennsylvania, For the Year 1755.* London, 1756.

[Trenchard, John.] *An Argument, Shewing, That a Standing Army is Inconsistent with a Free Government.* London, 1697.

―――. *A Short History of Standing Armies in England.* London, 1698.

[Trenchard, John, and Gordon, Thomas.] *Cato's Letters; or, Essays on Liberty, Civil and Religious, and Other Important Subjects.* 3d ed. London, 1730.

"A True Narrative of the Rise, Progresse, and Cessation of the Late Rebellion in Virginia, Most Humbly and Impartially Reported by his Majestyes Commissioners Appointed to Enquire into the Affaires of the Said Colony." In *Narratives of the Insurrections, 1675–1690,* edited by C. M. Andrews, 105–41. New York, 1915.

Vinal, William. *A Sermon on the Accursed Thing That hinders Success and Victory in War, Occasioned by the Defeat of the Hon. Edward Braddock, Esq.* Newport, 1755.

Webb, Thomas. *A Military Treatise on the Appointments of the Army . . . Proposing some New Regulations in the Army, which will be particularly useful in carrying on the War in North-America.* Philadelphia, 1759.

Woolman, John. *The Works of John Woolman.* New York, 1970.

Wrong, George M., ed. *Louisbourg in 1745: The Anonymous Lettre d'un Habitant de Louisbourg.* University of Toronto Studies. History, 2d ser., 1. Toronto, 1897.

COLLECTIONS OF DOCUMENTS AND OTHER SOURCES

Andrews, Charles M., ed. *Narratives of the Insurrections, 1675–1690.* New York, 1915.

The Andros Tracts. Edited by William Henry Whitmore. Prince Society *Publications* 5–7. Boston, 1868–74.

Bailyn, Bernard, ed. *Pamphlets of the American Revolution, 1750–1776.* Vol. 1., *1750–1765.* Cambridge, 1965.

Beers, H. P., comp. "The Papers of the British Commanders in Chief in North America, 1754–1783." *Military Affairs* 13 (1949): 79–94. Gives the location of various collections.

Doughty, Sir Arthur G. *The Siege of Quebec and the Battle of the Plains of Abraham.* 6 vols. Quebec, 1901.

Graham, Gerald S., ed. *The Walker Expedition to Quebec, 1711.* Champlain Society *Publications* 32. Toronto, 1953.

Hall, Michael G.; Leder, L. H.; and Kammen, M. G., eds. *The Glorious Revolution in America: Documents on the Colonial Crisis of 1689.* Chapel Hill, 1964.

Leder, Lawrence H., ed. "Records of the Trials of Jacob Leisler and His Associates." New-York Historical Society *Quarterly* 36 (1952): 431–57.

Lowdermilk, Will H. *History of Cumberland, (Maryland).* Washington, 1878. Includes General Braddock's Orderly Books.

Munsell, Joel, ed. *The Annals of Albany.* 10 vols. Albany, 1850–59.

Neville, John Davenport, comp. *Bacon's Rebellion: Abstracts of Materials in the Colonial Records Project.* Jamestown, Va., 1976.

O'Callaghan, Edmund B., ed. *The Documentary History of the State of New-York.* 4 vols. Albany, 1849–51.

Pargellis, Stanley, ed. *Military Affairs in North America, 1748–1765: Selected Documents from the Cumberland Papers in Windsor Castle.* London and New York, 1936.

Samuel, Sigmund, comp. *The Seven Years War in Canada, 1756–1763.* Toronto, 1934.

Sargent, Winthrop, ed. *The History of an Expedition Against Fort Duquesne in 1755.* Philadelphia, 1856.

Simmons, R. C., and Thomas, P. D. G., eds. *Proceedings and Debates of the British Parliaments Respecting North America, 1754–1783.* Vol. 1, *1754–1764.* Millwood, N.Y., 1982.

Stock, Leo F., ed. *Proceedings and Debates of the British Parliaments Respecting North America.* 5 vols. Washington, 1924–41.

Tanner, J. R., ed. *A Descriptive Catalogue of the Naval Manuscripts in the Pepysian Library at Magdalene College, Cambridge,* vol. 3. Navy Records Society *Publications* 36 (1909).

LETTERS AND OTHER PERSONAL DOCUMENTS

Bouquet, Henry. *The Papers of Henry Bouquet.* Edited by S. K. Stevens et al. 2 vols. Harrisburg, Pa., 1951–72.

Byrd, William. *The Correspondence of the Three William Byrds of Westover, Virginia, 1684–1776.* Edited by Marion Tinling. 2 vols. Charlottesville, 1977.

Colden, Cadwallader. "Letters and Papers, 1711–1775." New-York Historical Society *Collections* 50–56, 67–68 (1918–37).

Curwen, George. "Extracts From Letters Written by Capt. Geo. Curwen of Salem, Mass., to His Wife, While on the Expedition Against Louisbourgh." Essex Institute *Historical Collections* 3 (1861): 186–88.

Cuyler, Cornelius. Letter Book. American Antiquarian Society.

Dinwiddie, Robert. *The Official Records of Robert Dinwiddie, lieutenant-governor of the colony of Virginia, 1751–1758.* . . . Edited by Robert A. Brock. Virginia Historical Society *Collections* 3–4 (1883–84).

Forbes, John. *Writings of General John Forbes Relating to His Service in North America.* Edited by Alfred P. James. Menasha, Wis., and Pittsburgh, Pa., 1938.

Franklin, Benjamin. *Benjamin Franklin's Letters to the Press, 1758–1775.* Edited by Verner W. Crane. Chapel Hill, 1950.

――――. *The Papers of Benjamin Franklin.* Edited by Leonard W. Labaree. Vols. 1–9. New Haven, 1959–66.

Franks Family. *The Lee Max Friedman Collection of American Jewish Colonial Correspondence: Letters of the Franks Family (1733–1748).* Edited by Leo Hershkowitz and Isidore S. Meyer. Waltham, Mass., 1968.

[Gadsden, Christopher.] Philopatrios [pseud.] *Some Observations on the Two Campaigns against the Cherokee Indians, in 1760 and 1761.* Charles-Town, 1762.

――――. *The Writings of Christopher Gadsden, 1746–1805.* Edited by Richard Walsh. Columbia, 1966.

Johnson, William. *The Papers of Sir William Johnson.* Edited by James Sullivan and Alexander C. Flick. 13 vols. Albany, 1921–62.

Knox, Howard V. *Report on Manuscripts . . . of . . . Captain H. V. Knox.* Historical Manuscripts Commission. Dublin, 1909. Reprinted with an introduction and preface by George Athan Billias. Boston, 1972.

Laurens, Henry. *The Papers of Henry Laurens.* Edited by Philip M. Hamer. Vols. 1–3. Columbia, 1968–72.

Lee, Charles. The Lee Papers. New-York Historical Society *Collections* 4–7 (1871–74).

Mason, George. *The Papers of George Mason, 1725–1792.* Edited by Robert A. Rutland. 3 vols. Chapel Hill, 1970.

Maury, Rev. James. Letters. In *Memoirs of a Huguenot Family,* edited by Ann Maury. New York, 1853.

Montiano, Don Manuel de. *Letters of Montiano, Siege of St. Augustine.* Georgia Historical Society *Collections* 7 (1909): part 1.

Norris, Isaac. Norris Letterbook. Historical Society of Pennsylvania.

Oglethorpe, James. "Letters from General Oglethorpe." Georgia Historical Society *Collections* 3 (1873): 1–156.

Pendleton, Edmund. *The Letters and Papers of Edmund Pendleton, 1734–1803.* Edited by David J. Mays. 2 vols. Charlottesville, 1967.

Pitt, William. *Correspondence of William Pitt, when secretary of state, with colonial governors and military and naval commissioners in America.* Edited by G. S. Kimball. 2 vols. New York, 1906.

Pringle, Robert. *The Letterbook of Robert Pringle.* Edited by Walter B. Edgar. 2 vols. Columbia, 1972.

Randolph, Edward. *Edward Randolph: including his letters and official papers from the New England, middle, and southern colonies. . . .* Prince Society *Publications* 24–28, 30–31. Boston, 1898–1909.

Saltonstall Family. *The Saltonstall Papers, 1607–1815. Selected and Edited and with Biographies of Ten Members of the Saltonstall Family in Six Generations.* Edited by Robert E. Moody. Vol. 1. Massachusetts Historical Society *Collections* 80. Boston, 1972.

Shippen, Joseph. "Military Letters of Captain Joseph Shippen of the Provincial Service, 1756–1758." *Pennsylvania Magazine of History and Biography* 36 (1912): 357–78, 385–463.

Shirley, William. *Correspondence of William Shirley, Governor of Massachusetts and Military Commander in America, 1731–1760.* Edited by Charles H. Lincoln. 2 vols. New York, 1912.

Snyder, Henry L., ed. *The Marlborough-Godolphin Correspondence.* 3 vols. New York, 1975.

Spotswood, Alexander. *The Official Letters of Alexander Spotswood, Lieutenant-Governor of the Colony of Virginia, 1710–1722.* Edited by Robert A. Brock. Virginia Historical Society *Collections*, n.s., 1–2 (1882–85).

Vernon, Edward. *The Vernon Papers.* Edited by B. McL. Ranft. Navy Records Society *Publications* 99 (1958).

Warren, Peter. *The Royal Navy and North America: The Warren Papers, 1736–1752.* Edited by Julian Gwyn. Navy Records Society *Publications* 118 (1973).

Washington, George. *The Papers of George Washington.* Colonial Series. Edited by W. W. Abbot et al. 4 vols. to date. Charlottesville, 1983–84.

———. *The Writings of George Washington from the Original Manuscript Sources, 1745–1799.* Edited by John C. Fitzpatrick. Vols. 1–2. Washington, 1931.

Watts, John. *Letter Book of John Watts, Merchant and Councillor of New York.* New-York Historical Society *Collections* 61 (1928).

Williams, Thomas. "Correspondence of Doctor Thomas Williams, of Deerfield,

Mass., a Surgeon in the Army." *Historical Magazine*, 2d ser., 7 (1870): 209–16.

Wolfe, James. *The Life and Letters of James Wolfe*. Edited by Beckles Willson. London, 1909.

Yates, Abraham, Jr. Copy Book & Journal, June 1754–Sept. 1758. Yates Papers. New York Public Library.

DISSERTATIONS AND THESES

Cole, David William. "The Organization and Administration of the South Carolina Militia System, 1670–1783." Ph.D. dissertation, University of South Carolina, 1953.

Foote, William A. "The American Independent Companies of the British Army, 1664–1764." Ph.D. dissertation, University of California at Los Angeles, 1966.

Hayes, James W. "The Social and Professional Background of the Officers of the British Army, 1714–1763." M.A. thesis, University of London, 1956.

McCormick, Charles Howard. "Leisler's Rebellion." Ph.D. dissertation, The American University, 1971.

Nichols, Franklin Thayer. "The Braddock Expedition." Ph.D. dissertation, Harvard University, 1946.

Parker, King Lawrence. "Anglo-American Wilderness Campaigning 1754–1764: Logistical and Tactical Developments." Ph.D. dissertation, Columbia University, 1970.

Pencak, William Andrew. "Massachusetts Politics in War and Peace, 1676–1776." Ph.D. dissertation, Columbia University, 1978.

Rawlyk, George A. "New England and Louisbourg, 1744–1745." Ph.D. dissertation, University of Rochester, 1966.

Sharp, Morrison. "The New England Trainbands." Ph.D. dissertation, Harvard University, 1938.

Washburn, Wilcomb E. "Bacon's Rebellion." Ph.D. disssertation, Harvard University, 1955.

Webb, Stephen S. "Officers and Governors: The Role of the British Army in Imperial Politics and the Administration of the American Colonies, 1689–1722." Ph.D. dissertation, University of Wisconsin, 1965.

Young, Chester Raymond. "The Effects of the French and Indian War on Civilian Life in the Frontier Counties of Virginia, 1754–1763." Ph.D. dissertation, Vanderbilt University, 1969.

BOOKS

Albion, Robert G. *Forests and Sea Power: The Timber Problem of the Royal Navy, 1652–1862.* Cambridge, Mass., 1926.

Alden, John Richard. *Robert Dinwiddie: Servant of the Crown.* Williamsburg, 1973.

Anderson, Fred. *A People's Army: Massachusetts Soldiers and Society in the Seven Years' War.* Chapel Hill, 1984.

Archdeacon, Thomas F. *New York City, 1664–1710: Conquest and Change.* Ithaca, 1976.

Barnes, Viola F. *The Dominion of New England: A Study in British Colonial Policy.* New Haven, 1923.

Baugh, Daniel A. *British Naval Administration in the Age of Walpole.* Princeton, 1965.

Beer, George Louis. *British Colonial Policy, 1754–1765.* New York, 1907.

Bezanson, Anne; Gray, R. D.; and Hussey, M. *Prices in Colonial Pennsylvania.* Philadelphia, 1935.

Bruce, Anthony. *The Purchase System in the British Army, 1660–1871.* London, 1980.

Bruce, Philip A. *Institutional History of Virginia in the Seventeenth Century.* 2 vols. New York and London, 1910.

Burns, John F. *Controversies between Royal Governors and Their Assemblies in the Northern American Colonies.* Boston, 1923.

Chapin, Howard Millar. *Privateer Ships and Sailors: The First Century of American Colonial Privateering, 1625–1725.* Toulon, 1926.

Childs, John. *The Army of Charles II.* Buffalo, 1976.

Cleland, Hugh. *George Washington in the Ohio Valley.* Pittsburgh, 1955.

Clowes, Sir William Laird. *The Royal Navy: A History from the Earliest Times to the Present.* 7 vols. London, 1897–1903.

Cognets, Louis de, Jr. *Amherst and Canada.* Princeton, 1962.

Corbett, Sir Julian S. *England in the Seven Years' War: A Study in Combined Strategy.* 2d ed. 2 vols. London, 1918.

Corvisier, André. *Armies and Societies in Europe, 1494–1789.* Translated by A. T. Siddall. Bloomington, 1979.

Craven, Wesley F. *The Colonies in Transition, 1660–1713.* New York, 1968.

Cress, Lawrence Delbert. *Citizens in Arms: The Army and the Militia in American Society to the War of 1812.* Chapel Hill, 1982.

Cuneo, John R. *Robert Rogers of the Rangers.* New York, 1959.

De Watteville, Herman G. *The British Soldier: His Daily Life from Tudor to Modern Times.* London, 1954.

Ehrman, John. *The Navy in the War of William III, 1689–1697: Its State and Direction.* Cambridge, Eng., 1953.

Ekirch, Arthur A., Jr. *The Civilian and the Military.* New York, 1956.

Ettinger, Amos Aschbach. *James Edward Oglethorpe, Imperial Idealist*. Oxford and New York, 1936.

Ferling, John E. *A Wilderness of Miseries: War and Warriors in Early America*. Westport, Conn., 1980.

Firth, Sir Charles Harding. *Cromwell's Army: A History of the English Soldier during the Civil Wars, the Commonwealth and the Protectorate*. Reprint of 3d ed. London and New York, 1962.

Flexner, James Thomas. *Mohawk Baronet: Sir William Johnson of New York*. New York, 1959.

Fortescue, Sir John W. *A History of the British Army*. 13 vols. in 14. London, 1910–35.

Freeman, Douglas Southall. *George Washington, a Biography*. 7 vols. New York, 1948–57.

Frey, Sylvia R. *The British Soldier in America: A Social History of Military Life in the Revolutionary Period*. Austin, 1981.

Gipson, Lawrence Henry. *The British Empire before the American Revolution*. 15 vols. New York, 1936–70.

Godfrey, William G. *Pursuit of Profit and Preferment in Colonial North America: John Bradstreet's Quest*. Waterloo, Ont., 1982.

Goebel, Julius, Jr., and Naughton, T. R. *Law Enforcement in Colonial New York: A Study in Criminal Procedure (1664–1776)*. New York, 1944.

Gradish, Stephen F. *The Manning of the British Navy during the Seven Years' War*. London, 1980.

Graham, Gerald S. *Empire of the North Atlantic: The Maritime Struggle for North America*. Toronto, 1950.

Greenberg, Douglas. *Crime and Law Enforcement in the Colony of New York, 1691–1776*. Ithaca, 1976.

Greene, Jack P. *The Quest for Power: The Lower Houses of Assembly in the Southern Royal Colonies, 1689–1776*. Chapel Hill, 1963.

Gwyn, Julian. *The Enterprising Admiral: The Personal Fortune of Admiral Sir Peter Warren*. Montreal, 1974.

Haffenden, Philip S. *New England in the English Nation, 1689–1713*. London, 1974.

Hamilton, Edward P. *The French and Indian Wars: The Story of Battles and Forts in the Wilderness*. Garden City, N.Y., 1962.

Hassler, Warren W. *With Shield and Sword: American Military Affairs, Colonial Times to the Present*. Ames, Iowa, 1982.

Houlding, J. A. *Fit for Service: The Training of the British Army, 1715–1795*. New York, 1981.

Ivers, Larry E. *British Drums on the Southern Frontier: The Military Colonization of Georgia, 1733–1749*. Chapel Hill, 1974.

Johnson, Emory R. et al. *History of Domestic and Foreign Commerce of the United States*. 2 vols. Washington, 1915.

Johnson, Richard R. *Adjustment to Empire: The New England Colonies, 1675–1715.* New Brunswick, N.J., 1981.

Kopperman, Paul E. *Braddock at the Monongahela.* Pittsburgh, 1977.

Lanning, John Tate. *The Diplomatic History of Georgia: A Study of the Epoch of Jenkins' Ear.* Chapel Hill, 1936.

Leach, Douglas Edward. *Arms for Empire: A Military History of the British Colonies in North America, 1607–1763.* New York, 1973.

————. *Flintlock and Tomahawk: New England in King Philip's War.* New York, 1958.

————. *The Northern Colonial Frontier, 1607–1763.* New York, 1966.

Lewis, Michael. *The Navy of Britain, a Historical Portrait.* London, 1948.

Lloyd, Christopher. *The Capture of Quebec.* New York, 1959.

Long, John Cuthbert. *Lord Jeffery Amherst, a Soldier of the King.* New York, 1933.

Lovejoy, David S. *The Glorious Revolution in America.* New York, 1972.

McCardell, Lee. *Ill-Starred General: Braddock of the Coldstream Guards.* Pittsburgh, 1958.

McCusker, John J. *Money and Exchange in Europe and America, 1600–1775: A Handbook.* Chapel Hill, 1978.

McLennan, John S. *Louisbourg, from Its Foundation to Its Fall, 1713–1758.* London, 1918.

Millett, Allan R., and Maslowski, Peter. *For the Common Defense: A Military History of the United States.* New York, 1984.

Nash, Gary B. *The Urban Crucible: Social Change, Political Consciousness, and the Origins of the American Revolution.* Cambridge, Mass., 1979.

Nixon, Lily L. *James Burd, Frontier Defender, 1726–1793.* Philadelphia, 1941.

Olson, Alison Gilbert, and Brown, Richard Maxwell, eds. *Anglo-American Political Relations, 1675–1775.* New Brunswick, N.J., 1970.

Omond, John S. *Parliament and the Army, 1642–1904.* Cambridge, Eng., 1933.

Palfrey, John G. *History of New England.* Vol. 3. Boston, 1864.

Pares, Richard. *Colonial Blockade and Neutral Rights, 1739–1763.* Oxford, 1938.

————. *The Historian's Business, and Other Essays.* Edited by R. A. and Elisabeth Humphreys. Oxford, 1961.

————. *War and Trade in the West Indies, 1739–1763.* New York, 1936.

Pargellis, Stanley McCrory. *Lord Loudoun in North America, 1756–1758.* New Haven, 1933.

Peckham, Howard H. *The Colonial Wars, 1689–1762.* Chicago, 1964.

Pencak, William. *War, Politics, & Revolution in Provincial Massachusetts.* Boston, 1981.

Pound, Arthur, in collaboration with Day, R. E. *Johnson of the Mohawks: A Biography of Sir William Johnson, Irish Immigrant, Mohawk War Chief, American Soldier, Empire Builder.* New York, 1930.

Rawlyk, G. A. *Yankees at Louisbourg*. Orono, Me., 1967.

Reich, Jerome R. *Leisler's Rebellion: A Study of Democracy in New York, 1664–1720*. Chicago, 1953.

Richmond, Sir Herbert William. *The Navy as an Instrument of Policy, 1558–1727*. Edited by E. A. Hughes. Cambridge, Eng., 1953.

Ritchie, Robert C. *The Duke's Province: A Study of New York Politics and Society, 1664–1691*. Chapel Hill, 1977.

Robbins, Caroline. *The Eighteenth-Century Commonwealthman: Studies in the Transmission, Development and Circumstance of English Liberal Thought From the Restoration of Charles II Until the War With the Thirteen Colonies*. Cambridge, Mass., 1959.

Robinson, W. Stitt. *The Southern Colonial Frontier, 1607–1763*. Albuquerque, 1979.

Rogers, Alan. *Empire and Liberty: American Resistance to British Authority, 1755–1763*. Berkeley and London, 1974.

Savelle, Max. *The Origins of American Diplomacy: The International History of Angloamerica, 1492–1763*. New York, 1967.

Schutz, John A. *Thomas Pownall, British Defender of American Liberty: A Study of Anglo-American Relations in the Eighteenth Century*. Glendale, Calif., 1951.

_____. *William Shirley: King's Governor of Massachusetts*. Chapel Hill, 1961.

Schwoerer, Lois G. *"No Standing Armies!" The Antiarmy Ideology in Seventeenth-Century England*. Baltimore, 1974.

Scouller, R. E. *The Armies of Queen Anne*. Oxford, 1966.

Shea, William L. *The Virginia Militia in the Seventeenth Century*. Baton Rouge, 1983.

Sherrard, O. A. *Lord Chatham: Pitt and the Seven Years' War*. London, 1955.

Shy, John. *Toward Lexington: The Role of the British Army in the Coming of the American Revolution*. Princeton, 1965.

Sosin, J. M. *English America and the Restoration Monarchy of Charles II: Transatlantic Politics, Commerce, and Kinship*. Lincoln, Nebr., 1980.

Spalding, Phinizy. *Oglethorpe in America*. Chicago, 1977.

Stacey, C. P. *Quebec, 1759: The Siege and the Battle*. New York, 1959.

Steele, I. K. *Guerillas and Grenadiers: The Struggle for Canada, 1689–1760*. Toronto, 1969.

Stokes, I. N. P. *Iconography of Manhattan Island*. 6 vols. New York, 1895–1928.

Stout, Neil R. *The Royal Navy in America, 1760–1775: A Study of Enforcement of British Colonial Policy in the Era of the American Revolution*. Annapolis, 1973.

Teitler, G. *The Genesis of the Professional Officers' Corps*. Beverly Hills, Calif., 1977.

Thayer, Theodore G. *Israel Pemberton, King of the Quakers*. Philadelphia, 1943.

———. *Pennsylvania Politics and the Growth of Democracy, 1740–1776.* Harrisburg, Pa., 1953.

Torres-Reyes, Ricardo. *The British Siege of St. Augustine in 1740. . . .* Denver, 1972.

Waller, G. M. *Samuel Vetch: Colonial Enterpriser.* Chapel Hill, 1960.

Ward, Harry M. *"Unite or Die": Intercolony Relations, 1690–1763.* Port Washington, N. Y., 1971.

Warden, G. B. *Boston 1689–1776.* Boston, 1970.

Washburn, Wilcomb E. *The Governor and the Rebel: A History of Bacon's Rebellion in Virginia.* Chapel Hill, 1957.

Webb, Stephen Saunders. *The Governors-General: The English Army and the Definition of the Empire, 1569–1681.* Chapel Hill, 1979.

———. *1676: The End of American Independence.* New York, 1984.

Webster, J. Clarence. *The Forts of Chignecto: A Study of the Eighteenth-Century Conflict between France and Great Britain in Acadia.* Shediac, N.B., 1930.

Weigley, Russell F. *History of the United States Army.* New York, 1967.

Wertenbaker, Thomas J. *Torchbearer of the Revolution: The Story of Bacon's Rebellion and Its Leader.* Princeton, 1940.

Whitton, F. E. *Wolfe and North America.* Boston, 1929.

Wiener, Frederick B. *Civilians under Military Justice: The British Practice since 1689 Especially in North America.* Chicago, 1967.

ARTICLES

Anderson, F. W. "A People's Army: Provincial Military Service in Massachusetts during the Seven Years' War." *William and Mary Quarterly* 40 (1983): 499–527.

———. "Why Did Colonial New Englanders Make Bad Soldiers? Contractual Principles and Military Conduct during the Seven Years' War." *William and Mary Quarterly* 38 (1981): 395–417.

Anderson, Niles. "The General Chooses a Road: The Forbes Campaign of 1758 to Capture Fort Duquesne." *Western Pennsylvania Historical Magazine* 42 (1959): 109–38, 241–58, 383–401.

Bean, Walton E. "War and the British Colonial Farmer: A Reevaluation in the Light of New Statistical Records." *Pacific Historical Review* 11 (1942): 439–47.

Berkeley, Francis L., Jr. "The War of Jenkins' Ear." In *The Old Dominion: Essays for Thomas Perkins Abernethy,* edited by Darrett B. Rutman, 41–61. Charlottesville, 1964.

Branch, E. Douglas. "Henry Bouquet: Professional Soldier." *Pennsylvania Magazine of History and Biography* 62 (1938): 41–51.

Breen, Timothy H. "English Origins and New World Developments: The Case of the Covenanted Militia in Seventeenth-Century Massachusetts." *Past & Present* 57 (November 1972): 74–96.

Buffinton, Arthur H. "The Canadian Expedition of 1746: Its Relation to British Politics." *American Historical Review* 45 (1940): 552–80.

Bumsted, J. M. " 'Things in the Womb of Time': Ideas of American Independence, 1633 to 1763." *William and Mary Quarterly* 31 (1974): 533–64.

Calmes, Alan. "The Lyttelton Expedition of 1759: Military Failures and Financial Successes." *South Carolina Historical Magazine* 77 (1976): 10–33.

Cate, Margaret Davis. "Fort Frederica and the Battle of Bloody Marsh." *Georgia Historical Quarterly* 27 (1943): 111–74.

Charland, Thomas M. "The Lake Champlain Army and the Fall of Montreal." *Vermont History* 28 (1960): 293–301.

Clark, Dan E. "News and Opinion Concerning America in English Newspapers, 1754–1763." *Pacific Historical Review* 10 (1941): 75–82.

Clark, Dora Mae. "The Impressment of Seamen in the American Colonies." In *Essays in Colonial History Presented to Charles McLean Andrews by his Students*, 198–224. New Haven, 1931.

Cook, Roy Bird. "Virginia Frontier Defenses, 1719–1795." *West Virginia History* 1 (1940): 119–30.

Cowan, John P. "George Washington at Fort Necessity." *Western Pennsylvania Historical Magazine* 37 (1954–55): 153–80.

Cress, Lawrence Delbert. "Radical Whiggery on the Role of the Military: Ideological Roots of the American Revolutionary Militia." *Journal of the History of Ideas* 40 (1979): 43–60.

Dunn, Richard S. "Imperial Pressures on Massachusetts and Jamaica, 1675–1700." In *Anglo-American Political Relations, 1675–1775*, edited by Alison Gilbert Olson and Richard Maxwell Brown, 52–75. New Brunswick, N.J., 1970.

Fairchild, Byron. "Sir William Pepperrell: New England's Pre-Revolutionary Hero." *New England Historical and Genealogical Register* 130 (1976): 83–106.

Foote, William A. "The Pennsylvania Men of the American Regiment." *Pennsylvania Magazine of History and Biography* 87 (1963): 31–38.

———. "The South Carolina Independents." *South Carolina Historical Magazine* 62 (1961): 195–99.

Frey, Sylvia R. "Courts and Cats: British Military Justice in the Eighteenth Century." *Military Affairs* 43 (1979): 5–9.

Gilbert, Arthur N. "The Changing Face of British Military Justice, 1757–1783." *Military Affairs* 49 (1985): 80–84.

Graham, Dominick. "The Planning of the Beauséjour Operation and the Approaches to War in 1755." *New England Quarterly* 41 (1968): 551–66.

Graham, G. S. "The Naval Defence of British North America, 1739–1763."

Royal Historical Society *Transactions*, 4th ser., 30 (1948): 95–110.

Greene, Jack P. "The Seven Years' War and the American Revolution: The Causal Relationship Reconsidered." *Journal of Imperial and Commonwealth History* 8 (1980): 85–105.

———. "The South Carolina Quartering Dispute, 1757–1758." *South Carolina Historical Magazine* 60 (1959): 193–204.

Hall, Hubert. "Chatham's Colonial Policy." *American Historical Review* 5 (1900): 659–75.

Hamilton, Edward Pierce. "Colonial Warfare in North America." Massachusetts Historical Society *Proceedings* 80 (1968): 3–15.

Hamilton, Milton W. "Battle Report, General William Johnson's Letter to the Governors, Lake George, September 9–10, 1755." American Antiquarian Society *Proceedings* 74(1964): 19–36.

Hardaway, John A. "Colonial and Revolutionary War Origins of American Military Policy." *Military Review* 56 (1976): 77–89.

Harkness, Albert, Jr. "Americanism and Jenkins' Ear." *Mississippi Valley Historical Review* 37 (1950): 61–90.

Irvine, Dallas. "The First British Regulars in North America." *Military Affairs* 9 (1945): 337–54.

Ivers, Larry E. "The Battle of Fort Mosa." *Georgia Historical Quarterly* 51 (1967): 135–53.

Johnson, Victor L. "Fair Traders and Smugglers in Philadelphia, 1754–1763." *Pennsylvania Magazine of History and Biography* 83 (1959): 125–49.

Ketcham, Ralph L. "Conscience, War, and Politics in Pennsylvania, 1755–1757." *William and Mary Quarterly* 20 (1963): 416–39.

Kopperman, Paul E. "An Assessment of the Cholmley's Batman and British A Journals of Braddock's Campaign." *Western Pennsylvania Historical Magazine* 62 (1979): 197–218. See also 218–20.

Labaree, Leonard W. "Benjamin Franklin and the Defense of Pennsylvania, 1754–1757." *Pennsylvania History* 29 (1962): 7–23.

Lanning, John Tate. "American Participation in the War of Jenkins' Ear." *Georgia Historical Quarterly* 11 (1927): 191–215.

Lax, John, and Pencak, William. "The Knowles Riot and the Crisis of the 1740's in Massachusetts." *Perspectives in American History* 10 (1976): 161–214.

Leach, Douglas Edward. "Brothers in Arms?—Anglo-American Friction at Louisbourg, 1745–1746." Massachusetts Historical Society *Proceedings* 89 (1977): 36–54.

———. "The Cartagena Expedition, 1740–42." In *Adapting to Conditions: War and Society in the Eighteenth Century*, edited by Maarten Ultee, 43–55. University, Ala., 1986.

———. "Colonial Forces, 1607–1766." In *A Guide to the Sources of United States Military History*, edited by Robin Higham, 70–99. Hamden, Conn.,

1975. See also Supplement I, edited by Robin Higham and Donald J. Mrozek, 18–22. Hamden, Conn., 1981.

Leamon, James S. "Governor Fletcher's Recall." *William and Mary Quarterly* 20 (1963): 527–42.

Leder, Lawrence H. "Captain Kidd and the Leisler Rebellion." New-York Historical Society *Quarterly* 38 (1954): 48–53.

Lemisch, Jesse. "Jack Tar in the Streets: Merchant Seamen in the Politics of Revolutionary America." *William and Mary Quarterly* 25 (1968): 371–407.

Mahon, John K. "Anglo-American Methods of Indian Warfare, 1676–1794." *Mississippi Valley Historical Review* 45 (1958): 254–75.

Maier, Pauline. "Popular Uprisings and Civil Authority in Eighteenth-Century America." *William and Mary Quarterly* 27 (1970): 3–35.

Marietta, Jack D. "Conscience, the Quaker Community, and the French and Indian War." *Pennsylvania Magazine of History and Biography* 95 (1971): 3–27.

May, W. E. "Capt. Charles Hardy on the Carolina Station, 1742–1744." *South Carolina Historical Magazine* 70 (1969): 1–19.

———. "Captain Frankland's *Rose*." *American Neptune* 26 (1966): 37–62.

———. "His Majesty's Ships on the Carolina Station." *South Carolina Historical Magazine* 71 (1970): 162–69.

Morgan, Gwenda. "Virginia and the French and Indian War: A Case Study of the War's Effects on Imperial Relations." *Virginia Magazine of History and Biography* 81 (1973): 23–48.

Morgan, William Thomas. "Queen Anne's Canadian Expedition of 1711." Queen's University *Bulletin* 56 (1928).

———. "Some Attempts at Imperial Co-operation during the Reign of Queen Anne." Royal Historical Society *Transactions*. 4th ser., 10 (1927): 171–94.

Morton, Louis. "The Origins of American Military Policy." *Military Affairs* 22 (1958): 75–82.

Mullett, Charles F. "James Abercromby and French Encroachments in America." *Canadian Historical Review* 26 (1945): 48–59.

Murrin, John M. "The French and Indian War, the American Revolution, and the Counterfactual Hypothesis: Reflections on Lawrence Henry Gipson and John Shy." *Reviews in American History* 1 (1973): 307–18.

Nash, Gary B. "Governor Francis Nicholson and the New Castle Expedition of 1696." *Delaware History* 11 (1965): 229–39.

Nichols, Franklin Thayer. "The Organization of Braddock's Army." *William and Mary Quarterly* 4 (1947): 125–47.

Nixon, Lily Lee. "Colonel James Burd in the Campaign of 1759." *Western Pennsylvania Historical Magazine* 18 (1935): 109–24.

———. "Colonel James Burd in the Forbes Campaign." *Pennsylvania Magazine of History and Biography* 59 (1935): 106–33.

Norkus, Nellie. "Virginia's Role in the Capture of Fort Duquesne, 1758." *Western Pennsylvania Historical Magazine* 45 (1962): 291–308.

Pargellis, Stanley. "Braddock's Defeat." *American Historical Review* 41 (1936): 253–69.

———. "The Four Independent Companies of New York." In *Essays in Colonial History Presented to Charles McLean Andrews by his Students*, 96–123. New Haven, 1931.

Peckham, Howard H. "Speculations on the Colonial Wars." *William and Mary Quarterly* 17 (1960): 463–72.

Pencak, William. "Thomas Hutchinson's Fight against Naval Impressment." *New England Historical and Genealogical Register* 132 (1978): 25–36.

———. "Warfare and Political Change in Mid–Eighteenth-Century Massachusetts." *Journal of Imperial and Commonwealth History* 8 (1980): 51–73.

Reese, Trevor R. "Britain's Military Support of Georgia in the War of 1739–1748." *Georgia Historical Quarterly* 43 (1959): 1–10.

Rice, Otis. "The French and Indian War in West Virginia." *West Virginia History* 24 (1963): 134–46.

Riker, Thad W. "The Politics Behind Braddock's Expedition." *American Historical Review* 13 (1908): 742–52.

Robson, Eric. "British Light Infantry in the Mid–Eighteenth Century: The Effect of American Conditions." *Army Quarterly* 63 (1952): 209–22.

Rogers, George C., Jr. "The Papers of James Grant of Ballindalloch Castle, Scotland." *South Carolina Historical Magazine* 77 (1976): 145–60.

Rogers, J. Alan. "Colonial Opposition to the Quartering of Troops During the French and Indian War." *Military Affairs* 34 (1970): 7–11.

———. "Impressment in Western Pennsylvania, 1755–1759." *Western Pennsylvania Historical Magazine* 52 (1969): 255–62.

Russell, Peter E. "Redcoats in the Wilderness: British Officers and Irregular Warfare in Europe and America, 1740 to 1760." *William and Mary Quarterly* 35 (1978): 629–52.

Shy, John W. "A New Look at Colonial Militia." *William and Mary Quarterly* 20 (1963): 175–85.

———. "Quartering His Majesty's Forces in New Jersey." New Jersey Historical Society *Proceedings* 78 (1960): 82–94.

Stumpf, Stuart O. "Implications of King George's War for the Charleston Mercantile Community." *South Carolina Historical Magazine* 77 (1976): 161–88.

Swanson, Carl E. "American Privateering and Imperial Warfare, 1739–1748." *William and Mary Quarterly* 42 (1985): 357–82.

Thayer, Theodore. "The Army Contractors for the Niagara Campaign, 1755–1756." *William and Mary Quarterly* 14 (1957): 31–46.

Wainwright, Nicholas B. "Governor William Denny in Pennsylvania." *Pennsylvania Magazine of History and Biography* 81 (1957): 170–98.

Wall, Robert Emmet, Jr., "Louisbourg, 1745." *New England Quarterly* 37 (1964): 64–83.

Washburn, Wilcomb E. "The Effect of Bacon's Rebellion on Government in England and Virginia." *United States National Museum Bulletin* 225. Washington, 1962.

Webb, Stephen Saunders. "Army and Empire: English Garrison Government in Britain and America, 1569 to 1763." *William and Mary Quarterly* 34 (1977): 1–31.

Wellenreuther, Hermann. "The Political Dilemma of the Quakers in Pennsylvania, 1681–1748." *Pennsylvania Magazine of History and Biography* 94 (1970): 135–72.

Western, J. R. "Professionalism in Armies, Navies and Diplomacy." In *The Eighteenth Century: Europe in the Age of Enlightenment*, edited by Alfred Cobban, 181–216. New York, 1969.

Williams, W. R., comp. "British-American Officers, 1720 to 1763." *South Carolina Historical and Genealogical Magazine* 33 (1932): 183–96, 290–96.

Zimmerman, John J. "Benjamin Franklin and the Quaker Party, 1755–1756." *William and Mary Quarterly* 17 (1960): 291–313.

————. "Governor Denny and the Quartering Act of 1756." *Pennsylvania Magazine of History and Biography* 91 (1967): 266–81.

INDEX